Power and the Politics of Oil in the Soviet South Caucasus

Power and the Politics of Oil in the Soviet South Caucasus

Periphery Unbound, 1920–1929

Sara G. Brinegar

BLOOMSBURY ACADEMIC
LONDON • NEW YORK • OXFORD • NEW DELHI • SYDNEY

BLOOMSBURY ACADEMIC

Bloomsbury Publishing Plc, 50 Bedford Square, London, WC1B 3DP, UK
Bloomsbury Publishing Inc, 1385 Broadway, New York, NY 10018, USA
Bloomsbury Publishing Ireland, 29 Earlsfort Terrace, Dublin 2, D02 AY28, Ireland

BLOOMSBURY, BLOOMSBURY ACADEMIC and the Diana logo are trademarks of Bloomsbury Publishing Plc

First published in Great Britain 2024
This paperback edition published 2025

Copyright © Sara G. Brinegar 2024

Sara G. Brinegar has asserted her right under the Copyright, Designs and Patents Act, 1988, to be identified as author of this work.

For legal purposes the Acknowledgments on pp. ix–xi constitute an extension of this copyright page.

Cover image: Oil Well To Baku In The Caucasus © Marka/Getty Images

All rights reserved. No part of this publication may be: i) reproduced or transmitted in any form, electronic or mechanical, including photocopying, recording or by means of any information storage or retrieval system without prior permission in writing from the publishers; or ii) used or reproduced in any way for the training, development or operation of artificial intelligence (AI) technologies, including generative AI technologies. The rights holders expressly reserve this publication from the text and data mining exception as per Article 4(3) of the Digital Single Market Directive (EU) 2019/790.

Bloomsbury Publishing Plc does not have any control over, or responsibility for, any third-party websites referred to or in this book. All internet addresses given in this book were correct at the time of going to press. The author and publisher regret any inconvenience caused if addresses have changed or sites have ceased to exist, but can accept no responsibility for any such changes.

Every effort has been made to trace the copyright holders and obtain permission to reproduce the copyright material. Please do get in touch with any enquiries or any information relating to such material or the rights holder. We would be pleased to rectify any omissions in subsequent editions of this publication should they be drawn to our attention.

A catalogue record for this book is available from the British Library.

A catalog record for this book is available from the Library of Congress.

ISBN: HB: 978-1-3502-8668-9
PB: 978-1-3502-8667-2
ePDF: 978-1-3502-8669-6
eBook: 978-1-3502-8670-2

Typeset by Newgen KnowledgeWorks Pvt. Ltd., Chennai, India

For product safety related questions contact productsafety@bloomsbury.com.

To find out more about our authors and books visit www.bloomsbury.com and sign up for our newsletters.

To Marcus

Contents

List of Illustrations	viii
Acknowledgments	ix
Note on the Text	xii
List of Abbreviations	xiv
Introduction	1
Prelude: A Historical Sketch	11
1. The Soviet Invasion of Baku and the Reconstruction of the Oil Industry	21
2. Revolution in the Muslim East: The Bolsheviks and a Soviet Republic in Iran	47
3. Bolsheviks on the World Stage: Soviet Concessions Policy and the Oil Question	75
4. The Bolsheviks Go into the Oil Business, Kevir-Khurian, Ltd.	105
5. A Contribution to the History of the Revolution in the Periphery	127
Conclusion	153
Notes	157
Selected Bibliography	193
Index	201

Illustrations

Maps
0.1 Regional map of the South Caucasus in the late 1920s   xv
4.1 Map of Soviet oil expedition, 1925   113

Figures
1.1 Commanders of the 11th Red Army at the train station in Baku, May 1920   26
3.1 Georgii Chicherin and Nariman Narimanov, 1922   81
3.2 Narimanov, Mdivani, Bekzadian, 1922   82
3.3 Leonid Krasin   85

Acknowledgments

I have received a tremendous amount of support in researching and writing this book and the dissertation that came before it. Fellowships at various stages throughout the process gave me the opportunity to travel and visit archives in Azerbaijan and Russia, dedicate time to learning Azerbaijani, and the space to write. A Foreign Language and Area Studies (FLAS) for Azerbaijani at Indiana University as well as a Critical Language Scholarship to spend a summer in Baku at the Azerbaijan University of Languages were immensely valuable. An International Research & Exchanges Board (IREX) Embassy Policy Specialist Fellowship to Baku as well as a Fulbright-Hays Doctoral Dissertation Fellowship supported research in Azerbaijan and Russia over the course of eighteen months. Back home, the University of Wisconsin (UW)-Madison provided numerous grants, including support from the Alice D. Mortenson Fund and a Chancellor's Borderland Fellowship. The Social Science Research Council Eurasia Program Dissertation Completion Fellowship provided support over my final year of writing.

UW-Madison was a wonderful place to work and live and I owe tremendous thanks to the community there. Francine Hirsch is unfailing in her support and a wonderful mentor. I am continually thankful that she still reads my drafts and offers advice. David McDonald was a consistent source of insight, and it was only in the final stages of writing this manuscript that I realized the extent of his influence on my thinking. Rudy Koshar, Judd Kinsley, and Michael Reynolds provided thoughtful feedback. The kruzhok in Madison read various chapters over the years and was also a solid source of comradery. I especially owe thank yous to Maya Holzman, Roberto Carmack, Benjamin Raiklin, Tamara Polyakova, and Heather Sonntag as well as many others. Melissa Anderson was my constant companion through graduate school and my work was stronger because of her. I also owe thanks to Mark Steinberg and Diane Koenker for their encouragement on an earlier iteration of this project.

I would like to thank the European Studies Council of the MacMillan Center and the Rice Faculty Fellowship Fund at Yale University for supporting this project during the two years of my fellowship there. I benefited from the mentorship and intellectual community in New Haven, especially from Paul

Bushkovitch, Doug Rogers, Peter Rutland, Oksan Bayulgen, Sarah Silverstein, and Anna Graber. Julia Sinitsky was a wonderful graduate assistant and helped me locate and scan sources. As a result of the Rice Fellowship, I was able to substantially revise sections of my dissertation, which I published as an article: "The Oil Deal: Nariman Narimanov and the Sovietization of Azerbaijan." *Slavic Review* 76, 2 (2017): 372–94. Sections are reprinted here with permission from the University of Cambridge Press Copyright © Association for Slavic, East European, and Eurasian Studies 2017.

I owe a debt to the participants of the unofficial Mandel Center writing group at the US Holocaust Memorial Museum, especially Katharine White, Alexandra Lohse, and Dallas Michelbacher. They shared materials, read drafts, and offered invaluable feedback. They were a welcome presence on Zoom as we navigated 2020 and moved our lives online. Katharine read later drafts and offered incisive suggestions. For support and encouragement, I would also like to thank Jan Lambertz and Steve Feldman. The Virtual Open Research Laboratory (VORL) at the University of Illinois at Urbana-Champaign in Spring 2021 was irreplaceable. The program staff for VORL and librarians at the Slavic Reference Service were nothing short of incredible during the Covid-19 pandemic and because of them I was able to access sources and continue writing. I would like to thank Michael David-Fox and the Russian History Seminar in Washington, DC, for critical feedback on the manuscript, including Eric Lohr, Sarah Cameron, and Isabelle Kaplan and the other participants. My thanks also to the anonymous reviewers at Bloomsbury who offered valuable suggestions that made the manuscript stronger as well as to the editorial and production team for shepherding this project though publication.

Friends and colleagues helped in numerous ways. Sean Guillory has long been a mentor and friend and offered his time and perspective on many aspects of this project and read numerous drafts. Faith Wilson Stein helped me navigate the book-publishing process, providing inspiration and advice. I am lucky enough to benefit from Rebecca Liebing's long and sustaining friendship. Her dedication to serious endeavors, as well as utterly distracting ones, is a welcome benefit. Alex Hazanov continues to answer my questions, edit my Russian, and talk shop. Krista Goff read the entire manuscript and offered helpful comments. Jeanine Navarette helped with Chapter 5 and made valuable suggestions. Brigid O'Keeffe was generous enough to share materials and offer much-needed advice. Aimee Dobbs, Jeff Sahadeo, and Khaila xanım helped me navigate Baku when I first arrived, and Gulnara xanım opened her home. In Azerbaijan and Russia, Aleksei Lund, Krista Goff, Michelle Brady, Marcy McCullough, Leah Feldman,

Rachel Koroloff, Maya Holzman, Amy Petersen, and Sarah Hennessey offered friendship, wonderful distraction, and an intellectual community. Jeremy Johnson helped with the index. Alison Ollivierre created the wonderful maps for this book. I would be remiss not to thank the archivists who patiently pointed me in the right direction and offered critical suggestions.

Last, and most important, my family deserves special mention. My mother Teresa Peterson provided love, encouragement, and a home over the long course of the project. My father John Brinegar and Mary Murnane are always there for adventure, perspective, and good advice. Thanks to my brother John and nephews Christopher and Daniel. I want especially to thank my sister Stacy and brother-in-law Ross who have been key sources of support. My sister provided more than moral support, giving much-needed help with the maps and cover design. Julie, Bill, Oliver, Sarah, and Madeline provided love and support from California. Most of all, I want to thank my husband and partner, Marcus Bacher. He is a steady source of inspiration and love. He also read numerous drafts. His suggestions, at home and on the page, always make things better.

Note on the Text

Many of the places and people covered during the period in this book were renamed and borders were redrawn, making consistency in transliteration and usage a challenge. The sources for this book were drawn primarily from Russian-language state and party archives, including sources from the archives in Azerbaijan. For the most part, I tried to reflect the usage prevalent in the sources and included contemporary names in a parentheses for places, for example, Tiflis (Tbilisi), Enzeli (Bandar e-Anazali). I use Iran rather than Persia, unless in a direct quotation or referring to the empire. I used common English-language spellings for most place names such as Baku rather than Bakı. To make the text more accessible to a broader audience, I elected to use a simplified version of the Library of Congress transliteration system for Russian, with some changes, including writing "ц" as "ts" and "ий" as "ii" and removed the soft sign "ь" for most entries in the text. I translated Soviet governmental institutions into English, Commissariat of Foreign Affairs, instead of Narkomindel, except for Gosplan and Politburo. However, I maintained the Russian-language Soviet, rather than Council, for example, Soviet of Labor and Defense.

I made some exceptions for proper names. For names more familiar to English-language readers, I used conventional renderings: Mikoyan rather than Mikoian. But used Orjonikidze instead of Ordzhonikidze. Most of the people in the book inhabited multiple cultural-linguistic worlds and their names, including Mikoyan and Orjonikidze, are generally transliterated from Russian. I wanted to capture that multiplicity, and for the Azeri names I chose to use a simplified version of the contemporary Latin orthography rather than a transliteration from the Russian sources. For example, I used Mirza Davud Huseynov instead of Mirza Davud Bagir ogly Guseinov or the contemporary Azerbaijani Mirzə Davud Bağır oğlu Hüseynov. For political parties, Hummet rather than Hümmət, Musavat rather than Müsavat, and Adalat rather Ədalət.

I conducted archival work in Azerbaijan and while I was able to gather a rich base of documents on the oil industry and Soviet business interests in Iran from the state archive, which I draw on extensively here, I was not granted access to the former Communist Party Archive. These sources would have allowed me to paint a more textured picture of the Azerbaijan Communist Party and Azeri communists such as Mirza Davud Huseynov, Ruhulla Akhundov, and Aiub Khanbudagov, but it would not have changed the overall story I am telling here. Even when focusing on Azerbaijan, the actors are by no means only ethnically Azeri. Baku was a polyglot of nations and ethnicities, and the Soviet Party and state apparatus was as well.

Abbreviations

ADR	Azerbaijan Democratic Republic
AO	Autonomous Oblast
ASSR	Autonomous Soviet Socialist Republic
Azneft	Azerbaijan Oil Trust
Caucasus Bureau	Caucasian Bureau of the Central Committee of the Russian Communist Party (b)
CC	Central Committee
Gosplan	State Planning Committee
Politburo	Political Bureau of the Central Committee of the Russian Communist Party
RSDWP	Russian Social Democratic Workers Party
RSFSR	Russian Soviet Federated Socialist Republic
SSR	Soviet Socialist Republic
Transcaucasian Republic	Transcaucasian Socialist Federative Soviet Republic

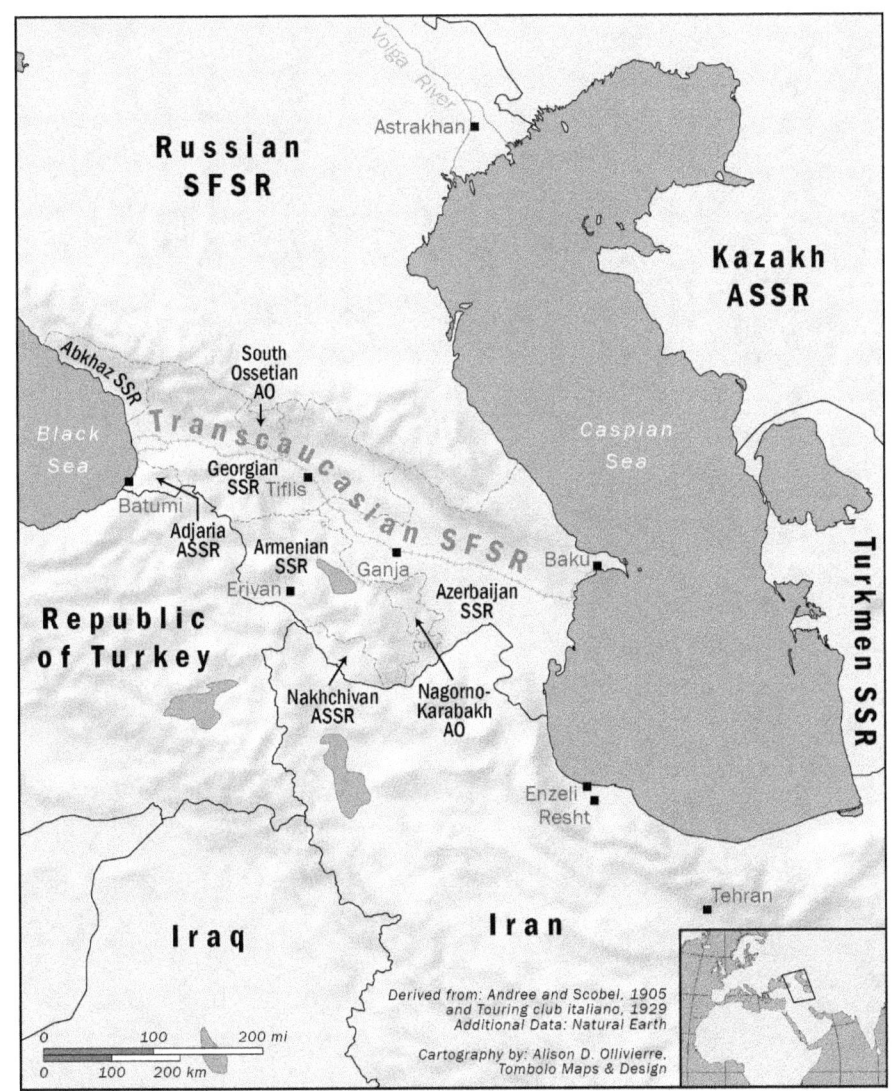

Map 0.1 Regional map of the South Caucasus in the late 1920s

Introduction

Under the cover of night on June 11, 1921, the steamship *Gorchakov* docked at the Black City quarter of Baku on the shore of the Caspian Sea in Soviet Azerbaijan. Black City was the heart of Baku's oil district and earned its name from the layers of grime and soot that seeped into every permeable surface. Factory workers secretly collected cannons, machine guns, a variety of firearms—as well as kitchen supplies—and loaded them onto the waiting steamer. The *Gorchakov* itself arrived in port courtesy of a rogue Iranian revolutionary who had duped the local Soviet command into signing orders for an unauthorized expedition to northern Iran, where Soviet troops were illegally occupying the province of Gilan.

Three days later the *Gorchakov*, now loaded with military supplies and unarmed Red Army soldiers, departed for the Iranian city of Enzeli (Bandar-e Anzali). It docked at a warehouse that had once belonged to the oil empire of the Noble Brothers Company. Its contents, including the passengers, were unloaded onto small boats and ferried onto a waiting barge. When they finally disembarked, the soldiers were instructed to be as quiet as possible and only when they arrived in the forest surrounding Enzeli were they told that they were joining the revolutionary leader, sometime friend and now foe of Soviet power, Mirza Kuchuk Khan.[1]

This was not the first time that the infrastructure of Baku's oil industry facilitated underground political activity. Revolutionaries, transients, and opportunists long ago had turned Black City and the surrounding districts into a notorious breeding ground for radicalism. In the early twentieth century, for example, Baku became a stronghold of the Bolshevik Party. Leonid Krasin, the future Soviet Commissar of Foreign Trade, who helped electrify the prerevolutionary oil industry, churned out radical literature on an illegal printing press hidden in Baku's Muslim quarter. These texts were then shipped throughout the Russian Empire.[2] Baku was an underground city for specific geopolitical reasons: it was an oil city, it was a port city on the Caspian Sea, and it was located on a permeable borderland at the nexus of three large states (Turkey, Iran, and the Soviet Union)—whose borders existed primarily on paper until the late 1920s.[3] The vignette mentioned earlier illustrates some of the key challenges the Bolsheviks faced in the early 1920s. As revolutionaries, the Bolsheviks had thrived in the South Caucasus and other frontier zones with lax authority, stealth arms shipments, and cross-border revolutionary alliances. But as leaders of a new state, the Bolsheviks faced dire material realities and came to see an unregulated borderland as a liability that needed to be secured.

This is a book about oil politics and foreign policy during a key period of Soviet state expansion. It looks at how the Soviet Union leveraged Baku's oil to consolidate power in the South Caucasus. The Soviet Union was a modernizing empire with a unique national-territorial structure, and most works about Soviet state-building have focused on questions of language, culture, and ideology.[4] But empire is also about material reality—natural resources, infrastructure, trade, and railroads. By focusing on Baku and its oil, this book sets out a new interpretation of the making of the Soviet Union. It shows that in the periphery, local Bolsheviks, including non-Russians, used these material connections to secure Soviet power.[5] In the South Caucasus, this took the form of oil politics. This book further demonstrates that local Baku-based Bolsheviks participated in state-building, and not just cultural production, from the early days of Soviet power. They used oil politics to pursue their own agendas, which sometimes aligned with that of Moscow's and sometimes sharply diverged. The Azeri statesman Nariman Narimanov, for example, used the promise of free-flowing oil from Baku to Moscow to achieve personal power. The invasion and exploitation of the South Caucasus was not just about an imposition of Russian power on non-Russians. Seizing Baku's oil and engaging in oil politics, whether that involved blocking Moscow's concessions policy in Baku or using the infrastructure of the oil industry—the warehouses, oil tankers, workers districts—to spread revolution in Iran depended on coalitions of local, regional, and Moscow-based Bolsheviks. The story of Baku and oil is not a Russian or Azerbaijani story but a Soviet story.[6]

Local politics and foreign policy overlapped in the borderlands, and Baku's oil industry is a perfect case study for understanding these dynamics. Baku was an international city with a vital resource, a previously robust economic and industrial base (in complete disrepair by 1920), a multiethnic and politically active population, and a prerevolutionary Bolshevik presence. The Bolshevik Party in the South Caucasus had a close relationship with Russians, Muslim social democrats, Armenian nationalists, and Persian migrants. The Soviet project needed all of these groups to participate in shoring up Soviet power and if it was going to survive.

Some of the most influential Bolsheviks in Soviet history—Iosif Stalin, Grigorii "Sergo" Orjonikidze, Sergei Kirov, Anastas Mikoyan—were based in or connected to Baku. This was not a coincidence. It is a reflection of how important securing Baku, and its oil, was to the Bolsheviks and how leveraging the economic potential of the industry as a tool of state-building could be translated into political power. Orjonikidze saw how advocating for the unification of the railroads in the South Caucasus, in no small part to transport Baku's oil to market, could be used to force the political unification of Transcaucasia. In doing so, he secured his own position and furthered the stability of the Soviet state.

Neither Orjonikidze nor Mikoyan were simply proxies for Moscow in this period—we see them as such because they later became completely intertwined with Stalin's power base. In fact, the Baku party organization helped Stalin to consolidate his power. Moscow's lack of resources meant that the Bolsheviks relied on political actors in the borderlands to help build Soviet power. Approaching the story from Baku also reveals the role of less familiar but no less important men like Nariman Narimanov, Leonid Krasin, and Aleksandr Serebrovskii in building the Soviet Union. These three men were committed revolutionaries who believed that the Soviet Union needed Baku's oil and the railroads of Transcaucasia to have a viable economy.

Disaggregating who represented Moscow and official policy, and who was a regional or even a local actor, is challenging because there were not static coalitions in this period. Orjonikidze, for example, viewed himself as a regional actor and was primarily interested in cementing Soviet power in the South Caucasus. Narimanov believed he represented Soviet power for Muslims in the South Caucasus as well as Iran; but he also claimed to speak with Vladimir Lenin's authority and blessing. Serebrovskii represented Moscow but fought to rebuild the oil industry with whatever means he could channel, at times defying central authorities. Kirov, on the other hand, was explicitly in Baku to report back to Moscow and more specifically to Stalin. It was only over the course of the 1920s that shifts in Soviet policy led to rifts among the Baku-based Bolsheviks; these rifts set them on different political trajectories and eventually ended with the names Orjonikidze and Mikoyan becoming synonymous with Moscow and Stalin. These shifting alliances were connected to the struggle for power in Moscow but also part of the regional dynamics of state-building.

Scholars interested in the early Soviet period have to contend with a series of contradictions when it comes to oil.[7] The oil industry was a center of the radical labor movement at the turn of the century—rocked by strikes and able to bring oil magnates to the bargaining table. Just a few years later it was burnt to the ground in the Revolution of 1905. Despite the ruin of 1905, Baku's oil was vital to Russia's effort in the First World War and the Bolsheviks were hellbent on occupying Azerbaijan for the oil fields in 1920. Several historians have argued that Soviet oil was insignificant in the 1920s and 1930s—and indeed economic and production data show paltry levels of production in these decades when compared to Baku's competitors abroad and to Baku's earlier output. But at precisely the time when Baku's oil lost significance for the global market it became critical to the survival of the Soviet state. Reconciling the irrelevance of Baku's oil industry to the world economy with its centrality to Bolshevik rule is one goal of this book.

In the 1920s, revenue from Baku's oil was one of the Soviet Union's few sources of hard currency and a critical resource on the international market, which it desperately needed.[8] But the Soviet government used Baku's oil for more than currency exchange, they used it to stake a claim for the Soviet Union in the global post-First World War order. The young Soviet Union was a weak state with a collapsed economy, and in the early 1920s it was isolated from global trade and diplomacy because the Allied powers (France, the UK, United States, Japan, Italy) withheld both trade agreements and diplomatic recognition. The Bolshevik leadership was keenly aware of the existing value—and even more of the *potential* value—of oil not just as a source of energy and hard currency but, just as importantly, as a tool of international politics. The Bolsheviks understood that if they could interest foreign investors in Baku, they could use the capital to reconstruct the industry and as a basis for further economic negotiations—which they hoped would pay off with diplomatic recognition.[9]

But Baku's oil had multiple claimants, from prerevolutionary oil magnates to local small-scale producers, and the promise of future oil proceeds was a double-edged sword. Baku's oil fields were relatively close to the porous border with Iran—and Moscow had a deep insecurity that they could be seized by a stronger state. It was here that spreading revolution, a key tenant of Bolshevik policy in 1920, came into direct confrontation with the necessity of securing Soviet borders. Leaders in Moscow wanted to use oil politics to secure Soviet power writ large. Looking from Baku, however, reveals that the expansionary aims of Orjonikidze, Narimanov, and other local Bolsheviks toward Iran threatened Moscow's larger ambitions. The party in Moscow realized it had to curb the foreign policy dreams of regional Bolsheviks if it was going to achieve stability. This interplay between regional agendas and high-level politics was a consistent feature of state-building in the South Caucasus.

Power and the Politics of Oil follows three intertwined threads. The first explores the political and economic struggle to rebuild the oil industry in Baku. The second looks at the conflict within the Bolshevik Party between advocates for local discretion and those who insisted on centralized control over the direction of the Revolution and the development of the oil industry in Azerbaijan. The third examines the Bolshevik effort to use oil politics to establish Soviet power on the world stage. The book focuses on the relationship between Moscow and Baku and situates the story of the South Caucasus in a wider discussion, both at the time and among historians today, about the formation of the Soviet Union and the consolidation of Soviet power. It demonstrates that the Azerbaijan Communist Party in Baku pursued its own objectives in the name of the Revolution even as those objectives threatened Moscow's ambitions. The result was that Moscow simultaneously relied on Baku to carry out its policies while seeking to contain Baku's agenda and to bind Azerbaijan and the Caucasus to Moscow.

The Red Army invaded the South Caucasus in April 1920 for imperial and geopolitical reasons—to control Baku's oil fields, the rail link between the Caspian and Black seas, and the Georgian ports in Batumi and Poti. To consolidate control over the South Caucasus the avowedly anti-imperialist Red Army overthrew newly independent states in an imperialist and expansionist power grab. Moreover, the policies that controlled Baku's oil industry were formulated in Moscow, which used the industry to prop up its power while the local population was divorced from its proceeds. Both of these elements—Soviet anti-imperialism and Soviet exploitation—must be incorporated into our understanding of the early Soviet Union.

This book foregrounds four men who shaped Soviet policy in Azerbaijan in the early-to-mid 1920s: Aleksander Serebrovskii, Nariman Narimanov, Sergo Orjonikidze, and Leonid Krasin. Each was tied to Baku in ways that illuminate the city's role as a prerevolutionary radical stronghold. Serebrovskii took refuge in Baku fleeing the Russian police, Krasin worked as an engineer for years in the oil fields, and Narimanov and Orjonikidze shuttled between the cultural capital Tiflis and industrial metropolis of Baku—and across the border into Iran. The focus on these actors demonstrates the importance of looking at oil, Soviet foreign policy, and geopolitics as the result of an ongoing negotiation between Moscow and regional and local interests.

Overview

Chapter 1 of *Power and the Politics of Oil* begins with the 11th Red Army's invasion of Baku in April 1920. The Red Army invaded Azerbaijan because the Bolsheviks wanted access to Baku's oil. The Bolshevik leadership believed that if it occupied Baku, the Red Army would have to secure the whole of Azerbaijan and that this military conquest would require the integration of Azerbaijan, and eventually the entire South Caucasus, into the Soviet system. The chapter follows the Soviet struggle to secure the fields, begin production, and start rebuilding the oil industry, a project led by Aleksandr Serebrovskii and the Moscow-run Azerbaijan Oil Trust (Azneft).

The necessity of reconstructing the Soviet oil industry forced the Bolsheviks to consider the significance of the infrastructure it inherited from the tsarist system. Geographical and physical realities—the pipelines and rail lines that began in Baku on the Caspian Sea and terminated in Batumi on the Black Sea—pushed them to construct policies around existing infrastructure networks. I argue that the needs of the oil industry strongly influenced the push for the unification of the South Caucasus into one republic, the Transcaucasian Federation, because members of the Bolshevik Party, both in Baku and in Moscow, saw the industry's infrastructure—the ports and railroads—as a non-negotiable part of the Soviet state and a precondition for the recovery of the Soviet economy.

In Chapter 2, I look at how the political effort to incorporate Azerbaijan into the Soviet family quickly became entangled with a separatist movement in northern Iran and the establishment of the short-lived Gilan Soviet Socialist Republic. The prospect of bringing revolution to the Muslim East, especially Iran, was one of the key reasons that Azeri Communists such as Nariman Narimanov, the head of the Azerbaijan Soviet government, supported Bolshevik power and helped enable the Red Army's initial entry into the city—and into the oil fields.[10] Local Bolsheviks in Baku largely ignored Moscow's orders to limit Soviet involvement in Iran. Instead, they seized the opportunity to expand their power, promptly plotting the spread of the Revolution across Iran by occupying sections of northern Iran, setting up political parties, and supplying weapons to guerrilla fighters. I look at how Soviet experiences in the ill-fated Gilan Republic and its greater context of revolution, trade politics, and economic recovery unequivocally showed the leadership in Moscow that the Baku comrades had their own agendas and that securing the South Caucasus, and its oil, would require bringing them to heel. In other words, the South Caucasus needed to be bound both tighter together and to Moscow.

Chapter 3 turns to one of the most significant challenges the Soviets faced in the immediate aftermath of the civil war. How were they going to obtain the resources, namely loans and capital, to rebuild? Public panic that the oil industry would collapse and dire predictions about flooded oil wells is part of what pushed the Soviet leadership to pursue foreign concessions. This became one of the main Bolshevik platforms at the 1922 Genoa Conference. Concessions and foreign investment had played a significant role in developing imperial Russia's economy as well as building infrastructure and industrializing the empire. Facing an economic catastrophe, desperate for an influx of capital and expertise, Vladimir Lenin took up the same strategy as his imperial predecessors.

I show that the Genoa Conference provoked a struggle within the party over who should make decisions about the industry—oil specialists, local communists, or diplomats in Moscow. One group, composed of Baku-based Bolsheviks and geologists, believed that granting major concessions to foreign firms was a mistake and would jeopardize the security of the Soviet Union. The second group was based in Moscow and reflected the official Soviet position, supported by Lenin and Leonid Krasin. This group saw concessions as the only viable route to save the broader Soviet economy. The two camps, with their dramatically different visions, competed for influence over the reconstruction of the oil industry. The Baku-based communists successfully undermined Moscow's efforts locally, demonstrating that the industry did not need large-scale foreign intervention to recover.

Having eschewed immediate revolution in the East after Gilan and being refused a seat at the table in the West after Genoa, the Soviet leadership was looking for ways to establish a presence abroad. The Commissariats of Foreign Affairs and Foreign Trade wanted to do this by ensuring the integration of the Soviet Union into the world economic system through business deals and international trade agreements (and, when that failed, by undermining rivals). But behind these business transactions, particularly along the Soviet border with northern Iran in the Caucasus, was a deeper anxiety about the territorial integrity of the Soviet Union. Oil exports from Baku were one of the Soviet Union's few sources of hard currency, and the Soviet leadership was convinced that the location of the oil fields so close to the border made the Caucasus vulnerable to attack from the British. The Bolsheviks responded by leveraging oil in both regional and international politics. In Chapter 4, I reconstruct Soviet efforts in Iran to counter the perceived threat from the British, secure the border, and establish trade networks in the region. They did this through a series of business and trade deals. They also obtained an oil concession and founded an oil company in Iran. Although they had some success in establishing economic and political ties with their southern neighbor, the oil company led to decidedly mixed outcomes and exposed how ill-prepared the Soviets were as businessmen.

In Chapter 5, I return to Nariman Narimanov and the Communist Party in Azerbaijan in 1923. Narimanov, who had welcomed the Bolsheviks to Baku first as a Commissar in the Baku Commune and again as the head of the government of Soviet Azerbaijan, now denounced the Revolution. He sharply disagreed with the course of Soviet policy since the Bolsheviks occupied Baku three years earlier, on topics as varied as foreign policy to local religious accommodation. In early 1923, he submitted an antiparty manifesto titled *A History of Our Revolution in the Periphery* to the Political Bureau of the Central Committee of the Russian Communist Party (Politburo) detailing his grievances, which sparked an investigation into his activities by the party's disciplinary body. Increasingly, the party in Azerbaijan split into factions and Narimanov and his rivals sought to fill political posts with loyal cadres to cement their personal power. These local personality conflicts were exacerbated by Moscow's drive to institutionalize Soviet power and Iosif Stalin's increasing grip on the party in the South Caucasus. Questions about the place of the non-Russian republics and their relationship to Moscow gained urgency during this period. In this fraught environment, Narimanov linked Baku's oil to Soviet nationalities policy in Azerbaijan and argued that the two issues were different expressions of the same problem: Moscow's exploitation of Azerbaijan.

Like countless other revolutionaries and idealists of the Russian Revolutions and Civil War, Narimanov failed to see that the culture of open debate in Soviet political life was rapidly coming to an end. The party demanded adherence to official polices, which shifted depending on whose political bloc was in favor, and this was particularly so in Azerbaijan. As a border state with Muslim leadership and a valuable resource, ongoing instability there could have foreign policy and security implications. As a result, ensuring that the leadership would, at least publicly, toe the line was critical. What constituted sovereignty, the right to benefit from each republic's resources, and who should build the Revolution were all put on trial in the investigation into Narimanov. Over the course of 1923–4 the core of Iosif Stalin's power base—Sergo Orjonikidze, Anastas Mikoyan, and Sergei Kirov—partnered with like-minded Azerbaijani, Armenian, and Georgian communists in the South Caucasus and successfully isolated Narimanov from having any further influence over Soviet policy.

In the 1920s, an essential part of the Bolshevik project was to bind the periphery of the former Russian Empire to Soviet Russia and then the Soviet

Union. They succeeded in conquering first Baku, then Azerbaijan, and finally the rest of the South Caucasus. In Azerbaijan, this process was shaped by how the Bolsheviks used Baku's oil industry as a tool of state-building to keep the Revolution in Moscow's control and secure the Soviet Union's new borders. Far from irrelevant, the Bolsheviks understood the role that Baku's damaged oil industry could play in consolidating Soviet power.

This book begins in Baku when it was the heart of the imperial Russian oil industry and everything from tsarist decrees to petty bureaucratic disputes from the imperial capital in St. Petersburg shaped life there. But Baku was also nearly 2000 miles away from the capital. As the empire crumbled, war severed it from Russia proper. As part of the so-called periphery, the non-Russian regions on the borderlands of the empire, including Baku and the broader South Caucasus region, were left to grapple with the consequences.

The sketch of Baku and the oil industry in the late empire that follows illuminates the truly daunting challenges the Bolsheviks faced in rebuilding the industry and consolidating their power. It also highlights the numerous overlapping interests that had constructed the industry and the city and continued to lay claim to it. Many of these challenges echoed across the 1920s, from the legacy of foreign ownership and investment in the oil industry, the multiethnic and multi-confessional population of the city, to the undisciplined and decentralized Baku Bolsheviks and the consequences of relying on violence to secure the city.

Prelude: A Historical Sketch

Oil in the Russian Empire

For the better part of a century after the incorporation of Baku into the imperial Russian fold, oil extraction was a local affair. That changed when the tsarist government opened the fields to new leasing terms and introduced land auctions in 1872. The land auctions abolished the government monopoly and allowed investors to secure long-term leases.[1] Under the pre-1872 government monopoly, drilling rights had been granted to local Armenians while Azeris, called Muslim Tatars in imperial Russian sources, were relegated to refining oil.[2] With the new bidding regulations, a handful of Azeri oil magnates emerged on the scene, but ethnically Russian and Armenian entrepreneurs were the largest investors. Within a decade, international investment backed the bulk of Baku's oil, with British financing making up 60 percent of capital investment.[3] But there was no monopoly on the ground and there were over 100 smaller companies both drilling and refining.[4]

The Russian Empire's oil supply came overwhelmingly from Baku. It constituted 93 percent of the empire's output, with smaller fields developed in Grozny and Maikop.[5] The primary market for Russia's oil products—kerosene, initially—was domestic and the bulk of production made its way from Baku to Astrakhan, at first in barrels traveling by barge and then northward up the Volga.[6] In the 1870s, this was as much by necessity as by choice. There was no rail link connecting the Caspian Sea, where Baku's oil was extracted, to the ports of Batumi or Poti on the Black Sea where it could be shipped to Constantinople and then to the international market.

After the 1872 reforms, both Russian and foreign investors established oil companies in Baku. The largest were the Nobel Brothers Petroleum Producing Company (Nobel Brothers), founded and run by the Swedish brothers Alfred, Ludwig, and Robert; and there was the Caspian and Black Sea Petroleum

Company, run by the French Rothschilds. Solving some of these transportation challenges, Ludwig Nobel invented the oil tanker to replace the barrels and increase shipments. The Rothschilds funded the construction of a railroad in 1883 between Baku and Batumi on the Black Sea, which the Russian Empire had acquired in 1877 during the Russo-Turkish War. The Nobel Brothers and the Rothschilds rapidly expanded their operations to include drilling, refining, shipping, and marketing. Both companies built storage and marketing facilities in Batumi, tying the two cities together through the infrastructure of the oil industry.

With the construction of the railroad, Baku's kerosene entered the international market and England became the largest importer of Russian oil products.[7] But Russian kerosene also had markets in Germany, India, China, and Japan.[8] In fact, by 1901, Russian oil made up half of the world's output.[9] The export market consisted almost exclusively of kerosene and lubricating oil.

Even with access to Europe, the primary consumer of Russian oil products remained domestic.[10] And while kerosene was the main export commodity, at the turn of the century, Baku increasingly produced fuel oil rather than kerosene. Russia was an early adopter of fuel oil for transportation because the Caucasus had no ready source of available fuel in either timber or coal. Local engineers developed a method to use residual oil for steam power, and by 1900 40.5 percent of the Russian railroad ran on oil, 35.2 percent on coal, and the rest on lumber.[11] The Caspian fleet was converted from coal to oil in the 1870s followed by the bulk of the railroads a decade later. The Volga fleet, as well as the major metallurgical factories in central Russia and along the Volga, also switched from coal to oil around this time.[12] Only areas with easy access to the coal from the Donbas region still relied on it.

The Road to 1905

A series of compounding decisions and larger events between 1903 and 1905 reversed many of these gains and precipitated the swift decline of Russian oil production. The industry was both a catalyst and victim of these greater developments. In terms of policy, the auctions that had opened the industry to foreign investment were halted in 1903 in the face of a bureaucratic stalemate in St. Petersburg over land use. As a result, almost the entirety of Russia's exploitation relied on a small number of major fields in the Absheron peninsula, excessively concentrating this increasingly valuable resource in one, increasingly vulnerable, location. St. Petersburg's inability to reach an agreement hampered development in the industry at an inopportune time. Globally, there was a rapid drop in prices between 1901 and 1903 that led to surplus production. In Baku, as elsewhere, this drop in prices led to production cuts, unemployment, and decrease in capital investment.[13] By 1903, the wells were showing signs of exhaustion and drilling equipment was out of date. The industry needed new investment. As it turned out, 1901 had been the apogee of the imperial Russian oil industry and not a harbinger of things to come.

Although beholden to the strictures of imperial decrees on land use, the oil fields of Baku were a world unto themselves. Many of the governing structures present in much of the empire's other industrialized regions were absent. There were no land captains, no municipal administration, and no local landholding nobility. Instead, the Association of Baku Oil Producers oversaw the fields and everything in them. As the historian Nicholas Lund has explained "oil did not merely lay down the roads and build the schools in the oil fields in the manner that automobiles built Detroit or steel built Pittsburgh. Maintaining the roads and schools was not only ultimately paid for by the oil industry, but was subject to the purview of its main professional organization."[14] In other words, life in the fields was largely dependent on the oil companies, not the city administration. The oil districts were violent, crime was common, and Baku gained a reputation as a free-wheeling rough-edged frontier city.

For all the wealth that oil brought to the owners, life in the fields was unforgiving. There were critical housing shortages. Workers lived in crowded filthy barracks, breathed polluted air, and worked in dangerous conditions. The oil-worker districts, such as Black City, were overwhelmingly male and the majority of workers were transient labor migrants composed mainly of Russians from the central provinces, Muslims from the Volga region, Armenians, and immigrants from northern Iran, many of them speaking Azeri Turkish (today, Azerbaijani). Muslim workers, both from Baku and neighboring regions in the South Caucasus, made up a slight majority. Work was segregated by ethnicity. Russians and Armenians dominated skilled labor, the refineries, and office work; Azeris and people from Dagestan made up the majority of drillers and oil-field workers; and Iranian migrants conducted the most grueling labor.[15] By 1902–3, workers were continually striking in the fields and demanding better treatment. Socialist parties started agitating among the oil workers and successfully negotiated the first industry-wide labor contract in the Russian Empire, the so-called crude oil constitution, establishing labor rights, including the nine-hour workday.[16]

The city boomed alongside the oil industry. In 1872, Baku was a small walled city with a mostly Muslim population of about 14,500. By 1903, the population was nearly 156,000 and within a decade reached over 214,000.[17] This mass influx of people from across the Russian Empire and northern Iran changed the demographics of the city. The Russian and Armenian populations swelled, and while the Muslim population grew in real numbers, it declined proportionally. Baku expanded far outside the walled inner city and the larger city was divided into quarters, or mahalla, along ethno-religious lines.[18] The industrial outskirts encompassed the factory districts of Black City (extraction) and White City (refining) as well as the outer oil-field districts of Sabunchi, Balakhany, Bibi-Eibat, Surakhany and others.[19] The rapid expansion of the city combined with imperial under-governance and inequality. The ethno-religious division of labor exacerbated tensions between the Muslim and Armenian communities—tensions that eventually turned into outright violence.

In late January 1905, soldiers of the imperial guard opened fire on peaceful demonstrators at the Winter Palace in St. Petersburg in a massacre known as Bloody Sunday. The tragedy sparked the first Russian Revolution as demonstrations and strikes soon spread from the frozen reaches of St. Petersburg down to the Caspian and across the steppe to the Pacific as people took to the streets in protest. In Baku, the general atmosphere of labor unrest, discontent, and injustice led to interethnic violence in a series of massacres that came to be known as the "Armeno-Tatar War." This conflict overlapped with and cannot be separated from the empire-wide governing crisis of the 1905 Russian Revolution. The details are still in dispute. According to one account, in February, in advance of a demonstration protesting Bloody Sunday, word spread that a group of Armenians murdered an Azeri man in a public square. Bands of Azeris responded by randomly attacking Armenians to which Armenians responded by doing the same. Another account states the opposite, that an Azeri oil-field proprietor murdered an Armenian man setting off the spate of violence.[20] In this broader context of unrest, and a largely absent governing structure, ethnic violence spread throughout the South Caucasus in 1905 and into 1906.

During the conflict, there was also widespread destruction in the oil fields. Fifty-seven percent of the wells were burned, and 61 percent of drilling and deep wells were rendered inoperable. Exploitation fell by one-third and prices went up.[21] The price increase meant that Russian oil products were no longer as competitive on the international market and its share in England, previously the largest export market, rapidly lost ground to American products.[22] Baku, which already carried a reputation as a lawless frontier town, was now considered a risky investment; the imperial government had demonstrated it could not guarantee the security of the oil fields.

There were domestic implications as well. Low prices, combined with the governmental crackdown that ended the revolution, diminished the bargaining power of the oil workers. The strikes were firmly quelled by 1908.[23] Without new investment, the fields began a slow decline. The Rothschild family sold its interests in Baku to Royal Dutch/Shell in 1912.[24] Moreover, demand for Russian oil exports decreased. As a result, production shifted to fuel oil for the domestic market. On the eve of the First World War, 34.7 percent of the empire's railroads were reliant on oil as was 20 percent of the fleet, and 46 percent of factories.[25] A general fuel shortage took hold beginning in 1913 and once again a new strike movement burgeoned.

The start of the First World War in August 1914 did not immediately impact the oil industry in terms of production or development, but it did stop the renewed strike movement.[26] Within a year the war had increased domestic demand for oil and coal, and prices went up. Railway traffic grew year over year as did the demands of the military and metallurgical sectors of the economy.[27] In 1915, 70 percent of the Nobel Brothers' sales went to the Russian military.[28] The refineries increased production of fuel oil, and by 1915, 81.7 percent of Baku's production was fuel oil. The share of other products shrank with kerosene consisting of only 14.7 percent and lubricating oil 1.7 percent of production.[29] Defense production, centered in Petrograd (St. Petersburg), relied on coal imports from England, which quickly dried up. The government threw its energy and resources into developing coal in the Donbas region, but it was not enough to replace the lost English imports. Increasingly, the railroads, naval forces, ground forces, and aviation relied on oil from Baku. Under the stress of the war effort, the railways became bogged down by coal shipments. The delays led to massive bread shortages and sparked street protests in major cities which transformed into a social and political revolution.[30]

The February Revolution of 1917 was swiftly followed by dramatic declines in production as the ongoing war and disorder of the Revolution started to buckle the economy. The crisis in the coal industry rippled out from Ukraine and led to a collapse in oil production by summer of that year. In September, 1917 oil workers in Baku once again went on strike, and in November, the oil fields in Grozny were set ablaze.[31] By 1918, Baku's production declined 68 percent from its peak in 1901, and an energy famine spread throughout the region.[32]

The First World War and collapse of the Russian Empire brought catastrophe to the South Caucasus. The Russian occupation of several Ottoman provinces, the shifting front, food shortages, the 1915 Ottoman genocide of Armenians, and the resulting mass influx of refugees into the South Caucasus led to deprivation and suffering.[33] By the end of 1917, Russian and Ottoman troops stalemated, and Russian soldiers abandoned the front. During the Russian Civil War, from 1918 to 1921, many of the territories of the Russian Empire declared independence. In the South Caucasus, the Azerbaijan Democratic Republic (ADR), the Georgian Democratic Republic, and the Republic of Armenia were all established in this period, which irrevocably altered expectations about sovereignty and rights among the peoples and nations that experienced independence at this time. In the South Caucasus, 1918–20 had, and continues to have, a profound impact on the self-perception and national identities of the many nations there. The previous social and political structures of the region unraveled, and the people had to re-conceptualize themselves in light of these new events. These years are not the topic of this book but a basic grasp of some of the themes and events is important to understand the chapters that follow.

The Baku Commune

After Tsar Nicholas II abdicated and the autocracy ceased to exist in February 1917, most elites in the South Caucasus supported the new Provisional Government. They eagerly awaited the Constituent Assembly, where Russian subjects of all creeds and nations would have the opportunity to create a democratic Russia. But history did not wait. Instead, in late October 1917, the Bolsheviks seized power and, when the long-awaited Constituent Assembly was finally called into session a few months later in January 1918, they dissolved the assembly by force. In spring 1918, the Russian Empire began to tear itself apart in a civil war. Most of the liberal and nationally minded elites of Transcaucasia rejected the Bolshevik takeover. The provinces of the South Caucasus united first in the Transcaucasian Commissariat and then as a parliamentary body, the Transcaucasian Seim, whose delegates originally had been chosen to serve in the Constituent Assembly.[34] The Seim, which was based in Tiflis and formed in February 1918, did not declare independence from Russia. Although there was no unifying vision for the future, there was still a broad sense among these elites that the future of the region lay in some form of expanded autonomy in a reformed Russia.[35]

This hope was dashed when the Bolsheviks signed the Treaty of Brest-Litovsk with Germany just a month later in March 1918, withdrawing Russia from the First World War. The Bolsheviks ceded large swaths of territory across the lands that comprised the western borderlands of the Russian Empire. In the South Caucasus, they ceded the areas around Kars and Batumi to the Ottoman empire. The Transcaucasian Seim did not recognize Bolshevik authority or the treaty. Nonetheless, the Ottomans insisted on claiming the territories. These treaty's concessions confounded an already complicated situation and belligerents on all sides began making promises, and threats, to representatives in the Seim to gain access to the ports, railroads, and oil of the region. In a desperate attempt to fend off the Ottomans and conclude a separate peace, the Seim declared independence as the Transcaucasian Democratic Federative Republic in April 1918. This, too, was short lived. Under duress, Georgia, Azerbaijan, and Armenia all declared independence in late May and each newly formed state sought foreign sponsors to defend itself against further aggression as the Central Powers continued the war against a broken empire.[36]

The government of the ADR that declared independence in May 1918 was led by the liberal, national-minded Musavat and based in Ganja (Elizavetpol).[37] Baku was not under the control of the ADR, despite widespread support for the Musavat among the Muslim population of the city.[38] Unlike most other cities in the South Caucasus, Baku was governed by the Soviet of Workers Deputies (hereafter: Soviet), a coalition of various multiethnic Bolshevik, Socialist-Revolutionary, and Dashnaktsutyun (also known as Dashnaks, an Armenian national and socialist party) parties. The coalition cemented control of the city in April 1918 and formed the Baku Soviet of Commissars, or the Baku Commune. The Commune was led by Stepan Shaumian, and in addition to other Bolsheviks included prominent founders of the Muslim Social Democratic Party (known as the *Hummet*), Nariman Narimanov (Commissar of Social Welfare), Meshadi Azizbekov (Provincial Commissar), Prokopius Dzhaparidze (Commissar of Internal Affairs), as well as the Left Social Revolutionary Mir Hasan Vasirov (Commissar of Agriculture).[39]

The Commune was formed on the heels of violent events that became known as the March Days. On March 30, troops from the Savage Division (a majority-Muslim division of the Russian army) entered the port of Baku.[40] According to the historian Michael Smith, there were no more than 200 members of the Savage Division.[41] The Soviet feared that their arrival would inflame ethnic tensions because the Division had recently disarmed pro-Bolshevik forces in Lenkoran, in the south of contemporary Azerbaijan. In response, the Soviet demanded that the Savage Division disarm. They complied. The wider Muslim population of Baku, however, was infuriated by the news that the Muslim national unit was disarmed and set up barricades overnight throughout the city. On March 31, fighting broke out between Muslims and the Bolsheviks, and on April 1, the Bolsheviks shelled the Muslim section of the city leading to their surrender. This did not stop the fighting, however. Ronald Suny writes that, "When the acceptance of the committee's terms by the Moslem delegates was announced, shooting continued. The Armenian solders became more brutal as resistance subsided, and for a day and a half they looted, killed, and burned in the Moslem quarter."[42] There were around 3,000 casualties, the majority Muslim.[43] The resulting unrest was not limited to Baku nor was it limited to a conflict between Azeris and Armenians. Territories throughout the South Caucasus were contested, often violently.[44]

The Baku Commune was not able to hold the city for more than a few months. The government of the ADR allied with the Ottomans to take control of Baku from the Commune. From June to September, Ottoman troops and local armed detachments fought against the Commune. The Bolsheviks were pushed out, first by a temporary government known as the Centro-Caspian Dictatorship and then by the combined Ottoman and Azeri troops.[45] In September 1918, their troops marched from Ganja in the western region of contemporary Azerbaijan to Baku. In a tragic reversal of the March events, they carried out massacres against the Armenian population. Mere weeks later the Ottoman Empire surrendered to the Allies, withdrawing from the First World War and from Baku. In short order, the British army arrived from the Iranian port city of Enzeli to occupy Baku and secure the oil fields and railways of Transcaucasia for themselves and the Allied powers. The British stayed until August 1919 but were not interested in administering the state and allowed the Musavat to remain in power.[46] The ADR—like the other Transcaucasian republics—was unable to assert control over the territories it claimed during this period. The borders between them were ill-defined and disputed, leaving them vulnerable.

The bloody legacy of the first Bolshevik takeover, the Baku Commune, loomed large in the regional collective memory. Overcoming that legacy, or at least reimagining it, shaped Bolshevik policy when they returned two years later in 1920 to retake the oil capital. By this time the Bolsheviks were desperate for a reliable source of fuel. After years of war and shortages, and under pressure from an economic blockade by the Allied powers, the people of Moscow were on the verge of freezing to death and those in the Volga region were starving.

The recaptured oil fields and factories in Grozny, the north Caucasus, were in cinders, and the coal mines of the Donbas region in Ukraine were flooded and nearly inoperable. In April, as the Azerbaijani army fought with Armenia in the disputed territory of Nagorno-Karabakh, the Bolsheviks turned their attention to Baku and its oil reserves, stockpiled in cisterns.

1

The Soviet Invasion of Baku and the Reconstruction of the Oil Industry

The years 1918 and 1919 were long, cold, and hungry in the former Russian Empire and 1920 was not off to a good start. On February 28, 1920, Vladimir Lenin, the leader of the Bolshevik Party, sent a desperate telegram to the Revolutionary Military Soviet on the North Caucasus front of the ongoing civil war. He had an unambiguous message for the population: if you burn the oil fields, we will slaughter you.[1] The Red Army had been cut off from Russia's main oil reserves for nearly two years and was more than willing to follow through on the threat in order to hold Grozny and Maikop. One of the world's mightiest oil producers was reduced to an all-out scramble for resources.

A month earlier and nine hundred miles to the northeast, the Fourth Army of the Turkestan Front, already depleted from a debilitating typhus outbreak and recent battle with White Army forces, was ordered off the battlefield and into railroad construction. After taking the Emba oilfields in present day Kazakhstan, Lenin ordered Mikhail Frunze, the 34-year-old commander of the Red Army in Central Asia, to use the Fourth Army to build a rail connection and oil pipeline between Emba and Aleksandrov-Gai in a mad and completely unrealistic attempt to link Emba with Russia's main railroad lines to begin oil shipments.[2] More than just the Red Army, Moscow needed the oil. Facing several more months of winter without oil and kerosene, the city would freeze as well as starve. The situation was urgent and a rail link could not be built in time to help Moscow.

Lenin ordered Frunze to find a way regardless. Together, they enlisted the help of the Main Oil Committee, whose proposed solution was to assemble a series of camel caravans to traverse the snow-covered steppe. The so-called Camel Operation would cross nearly 330 miles from Emba to the nearest railway station in Uralsk and then on to Astrakhan and Moscow. The endeavor would be a logistical nightmare. Temperatures in January and February averaged around fourteen degrees Fahrenheit and harsh winter winds swept unimpeded over the flat steppe land. There were no food supplies and there was no road. Nonetheless, a call to locate as many barrels as possible was put out and an extensive search began, scouring the country for containers—from Moscow to Emba—capable of transporting oil. On the ground, Kazakhs were enlisted to collect wineskins to transport the oil. The committee estimated it would take two caravans of 100 camels each, carrying twenty-five to thirty tons of oil, to complete the operation. Lenin approved of the plan.

During the time it took to gather the material to outfit the camels and find the necessary barrels, the Red Army successfully took Grozny and its oil fields, followed by the coal mines of the Donbas region in Ukraine, rendering the caravan superfluous. The Bolsheviks completed their resource coup in April when they seized Baku in Azerbaijan, assuring that the Red Army, and the Revolution, would live to fight another day.[3]

The Bolsheviks considered the oil resources of the Caucasus essential to the survival of the state. They learned quickly that simply possessing oil fields was not enough to guarantee economic recovery. The exploitation of oil necessitates the maintenance of an expansive system of developed transportation, machinery, refining, shipping, and expertise. Beyond the needs of economics and logistics, it also requires certain political and social conditions, such as stability, a steady workforce, safe passage for crude oil to refineries, and in turn for refined petroleum products to enter the world market. In taking Baku by force, the Soviet leadership understood it would have to secure the whole of Azerbaijan and that this would entail the integration of Azerbaijan—and likely the entire South Caucasus—into the Soviet system. Soviet Russia needed political stability to achieve economic recovery, both of which were predicated on the procurement of oil and other fuel sources.

This chapter traces the effort to secure the fields, restart production, and begin the process of building a specifically Soviet oil industry. I explore the wider context in which Moscow subordinated and bound Azerbaijan's oil resources to the Soviet project. I argue that the needs of the oil industry shaped Soviet approaches to state-building in the South Caucasus, and some members of the Bolshevik Party, both in Baku and Moscow, pushed for the unification of Transcaucasia in part to exploit the oil industry and the infrastructure build to support it.[4]

Aleksandr Serebrovskii and Vladimir Ilych's Mandate

The 11th Red Army took Baku in early 1920 to secure the oil fields and establish a supply line that could sustain Soviet Russia to the north, fuel transportation networks to feed Russia's cities, and support the Red Army in the Polish-Soviet war, which had been renewed several days before the invasion of Baku. On May 1, the Azerbaijan Revolutionary Committee (hereafter: Revolutionary Committee) issued an appeal to the workers of Baku: "Soviet Russia is suffocating from a lack of fuel and every pound of oil infuses life and strength into the devastated economy of the country. Comrade workers! Our duty is to give oil immediately to the Russian proletariat and peasantry ... On May 1, stand at your revolutionary posts and work to send oil to Soviet Russia who thirsts for it."[5]

Lenin tasked Aleksandr Pavlovich Serebrovskii with the monumental endeavor of reviving the oil industry. In many ways, Serebrovskii's biography serves as a stand-in for an entire generation of elite Bolsheviks. He, like many of his comrades, pursued a technical education, joined the party as a disillusioned youth, was in and out of prison, and passed through Baku entering with one passport and exiting with a new one. During the course of the civil war and in the early years of Soviet power, a certain revolutionary pedigree was coming into being and where you were, at what time, and with whom was of tremendous consequence. These networks could save or devour, although this only became evident in time.

Serebrovskii, born in 1884, was a so-called old Bolshevik, the honorific given to members of the party who joined before 1917. He came from a family of revolutionaries and from an early age moved in the social world of the anti-tsarist underground. His father, Pavel Petrovich Serebrovskii, was a member of the populist People's Will movement, a group of revolutionaries who sought to overthrow the tsar and advocated for the use of terrorism as a tool of political change. He was sentenced to exile and hard labor in Siberia in connection with the famed Trial of the 193. Like his father, Serebrovskii rebelled against the tsarist autocracy and was arrested for the first time in 1902. He joined the Bolshevik wing of the Russian Social Democratic Labour Party in 1903.

After several more arrests, Serebrovskii moved to St. Petersburg where the Bolshevik commission assigned him to the Putilov factory as a machinist and organizer under the name Loginov.[6] The Putilov factory was a notorious hotbed of socialist and anti-imperial agitation, and Serebrovskii certainly became acquainted with other Bolsheviks and socialist organizers. On directives from the Bolshevik Party, he joined the followers of Father Gapon—the priest who famously led the march on the Winter Palace that ended in bloodshed and helped spark the Revolution of 1905—where he acquired the underground name of Gaponist.

Following the 1905 Revolution, the party sent him to Baku, where he hid in the underground, blending in as a fitter in the oil fields under the pseudonym Glazunov and maintained contact with Baku Committee Bolsheviks. He lived in Black City for a few months where he joined the Balakhano-Sabunchi Bolshevik organization. He left in September after a raid ended with the arrest of most of the Bolsheviks in the region.[7] He returned to St. Petersburg, again as Loginov, joined the Petersburg Executive Committee and was arrested under that name but released until the trial. In the interim, he changed names and began military work for the Bolsheviks smuggling weapons from Finland, yet another location of revolutionary legend. Several more years of arrests, narrowly avoided sentences, and passport changes followed. He fled Russia in 1909 and earned a degree in engineering in Brussels in 1911 while continuing his work with the Bolsheviks.

Lenin ordered him to return to Russia in 1913 where he worked in a factory in Moscow until he was once again arrested by the police and sent to the North Caucasus.[8] At the start of the First World War in 1914 he was conscripted into the army. In 1915, his command transferred him for detrimental influence on his fellow soldiers, to the South-West front and in Batumi. After the February Revolution in 1917, he returned to St. Petersburg (Petrograd) with a machine gun regiment and started working with the Vyborg Bolsheviks. At the time of the October Revolution, he led a company, and then a battalion, of the Red Guard, the militia that later became the Red Army. During the civil war, in autumn 1918, he was appointed deputy chairman of the Extraordinary Commission for the supply of Red Army, a post he held until 1919 when he became the deputy chairman of the Commissariat of Transportation. He was transferred again to help support the effort against Denikin, and in December 1919, he was appointed chairman of the Central Directorate of artillery factories for the Russian Soviet Federated Socialist Republic (RSFSR, or Soviet Russia).[9] These experiences cemented his reputation as a superior organizer who could move goods and people in the face of major obstacles.

On April 16, 1920, Serebrovskii was in Moscow, and Lenin requested that he come to his office. As Serebrovskii entered, Lenin turned to him and immediately inquired, "How do you feel about oil?"[10] The following day, ten days before the Red Army entered Baku, the Soviet of Labor and Defense, at Lenin's request, granted Serebrovskii an expansive mandate with three responsibilities. As a member of the Main Oil Committee and representative of the Baku Oil Committee, he was commissioned with the following tasks: (1) to organize the oil industry in Baku in accordance with the orders of the Supreme Soviet of the People's Economy (hereafter: Supreme Soviet of the Economy) and to increase productivity as much as possible, (2) to direct the shipping and transport of oil and its products, and (3) the right to use military, naval, and civil forces for the fulfillment of the aforementioned outlined goals.[11]

The mandate gave Serebrovskii the title Chief of the Garrison and stipulated that all military and civilian organizations follow his orders. The command of the 11th Red Army was instructed to obey and assist Serebrovskii in maintaining the security of the bays, ports, and factories in both Baku and elsewhere. Oil transport had priority on railroads, and his orders superseded those of Commissariat of Ways and Means. Those disobeying his orders would be sent before the Revolutionary Military Tribunal and sentenced under military law. The mandate allowed him use of any and all transportation as well as communication lines (priority in telegrams).[12] The Azerbaijan Oil Committee (later: Azneft) was formed to administer the industry and oversee nationalization, which he headed.[13]

The effects of this mandate, derisively referred to by Serebrovskii's later opponents as "Ilyich's Mandate," were far-reaching and shaped party politics in the South Caucasus for the next several years. The mandate effectively allowed Serebrovskii to work outside the official channels of bureaucracy, bypassing the authority of the Commissariat of Foreign Trade, and the Baku Communist Party, among others. This authority contributed to the creation of factions within the Azerbaijan Communist Party and led to accusations of Russian chauvinism.

Serebrovskii arrived in Baku together with Sergo Orjonikidze and Sergei Kirov, all of whom were deeply involved in the creation of the Soviet Union and the establishment of Soviet power in the Caucasus.[14] In 1920, the 34-year old Orjonikidze was the chairman of the Caucasian Bureau of the Central Committee of the Russian Communist Party (b) (hereafter: Caucasus Bureau) and Kirov, sent to the Caucasus as a representative of Moscow, and served as his deputy. The Caucasus Bureau strove to establish Soviet power (sovietization) and implement Soviet policy in the Caucasus.[15] The bureau was formed in April 1920, a few days before the creation of the Azerbaijan Oil Committee.

Orjonikidze, the future leader of Soviet heavy industry and longtime revolutionary, was known for his close relationship with Iosif Stalin, but for now, he was in charge of ensuring that Baku remained under Soviet control. Not unlike Frunze's initial task, the unrealized Camel Operation, Serebrovskii's first assignment in Baku was to ship oil to Astrakhan and up the Volga to Moscow.[16] Shortly after his arrival in April 1920, he toured the collapsing fields and found

Figure 1.1 Commanders of the 11th Red Army at the train station in Baku, May 1920.

that the reserve reservoirs were at capacity but that there was no way to ship the oil. The Caspian fleet was at the Iranian port of Enzeli, having fled with the approach of the Red Army. To begin shipping the oil, the Bolsheviks had to get the fleet back under their control and then return it to Baku. What remained of the Volga-Caspian fleet was ordered to proceed to Enzeli.[17] F. F. Raskolnikov successfully returned the remainder of the fleet to Baku and shipments began quickly thereafter (see Figure 1.1).

The Price of War Communism

Initially, oil from Baku sustained Soviet power, and the Bolsheviks were able to stave off collapse. Russia's strategic position also improved substantially over the first half of 1920. The RSFSR acquired the oil fields of Emba, Grozny, and Baku, as well as the coal mines of the Donbas.[18] Oil shipments from Baku to Soviet Russia via the Volga rose dramatically, and the Bolsheviks secured access to the port in Batumi on the Black Sea, the traditional point of export for Russia's oil abroad—all necessary prerequisites to assure oil supplies and begin economic recovery.

But conditions on the ground in Baku had deteriorated, and these military successes did not translate into success in oil production. Ongoing shortages and severed supply lines, due to both the war and ruined infrastructure, continued to hamper efforts to supply the oil industry with the machinery and materials necessary to restart operations. The region's success in supplying Russia and the Red Army between 1920 and 1921 was based on already existing reserves that had been extracted before the Bolshevik invasion and were sitting in the cisterns waiting to be shipped. The increased shipment of these reserves to the domestic market was a temporary victory that masked the more fundamental problem of drilling. Already in 1914, much of the machinery in the fields had fallen into disrepair. By the end of First World War and the civil war, the technology used in Baku was badly out of date, and initial Soviet attempts to restart production failed, which led to a steady decrease of an already severely curtailed output.[19]

By April 1921, Baku's oil workers faced chronic material and housing shortages, a debilitating food crisis, lack of proper clothing, and generally miserable working conditions. The oil workers protested their dismal conditions in that classic form so often agitated for by the Bolsheviks when they were in the opposition and feared when they were in power: a strike. The workers shut down the oil fields. Even bailers from Iran, the foreign workers who manually extracted oil and traditionally steered clear of strikes, participated under the slogan "bread or home."[20] Orjonikidze sent a telegram to Lenin that read bluntly: "Due to absolute hunger in Baku the workers went on strike." His follow-up telegram was equally to the point: "The strike has been liquidated, but if the food situation among the workers does not improve there is absolutely no guarantee that the strike will not repeat itself with a good deal more force and a good deal more undesirable consequences."[21]

The first year of nationalization had brought the industry to the verge of complete collapse. Correspondence and reports to Moscow uniformly told tales of catastrophe, hunger, shortage, and ruin. On top of the material scarcity, military discipline and harassment of technical specialists, where anyone viewed as a member of the prerevolutionary intelligentsia was targeted, had taken a heavy toll.[22] More broadly, War Communism, a policy that is often used as shorthand for the entire period between June 1918 and March 1921, replaced the market economy with the allocation of goods through the nationalization and state control of industry and trade. It also introduced military discipline for workers, compulsory labor, brutal agricultural requisitions that left people starving, centralized redistribution of agricultural products, food rations, and the elimination of private trade.

Despite these widely accepted tenets, War Communism varied substantially by region. Outside of Russia's traditional peasant heartland the policy was unevenly, if ever, implemented. Under the Azerbaijan Democratic Republic from 1918 to 1920 Baku, the only industrialized city in the region, was largely cut off from the remainder of Azerbaijan. The Bolsheviks hoped to reestablish trade links between the villages and the city when they took power in 1920 and knew that the harsh confiscatory policies of War Communism would undermine these efforts by alienating the peasantry and thus initially forewent its introduction. This approach, facilitating trade between the cities and the countryside, was introduced on a union-wide scale with the introduction of the mixed-market system known as the New Economic Policy (NEP) the following year. Only when the market failed to provide the needed surplus by September 1920, did the party leadership in Moscow force the introduction of requisitions of the peasantry familiar to those in Soviet Russia. Grain was seized and redistributed to the Red Army division stationed in Baku and to the oil workers. However, by November 1920, mere weeks later, it was clear that there was no surplus, either in grain or livestock, and the leadership abandoned War Communism altogether and requested food aid from Soviet Russia.[23] Despite these significant variations, the period between the Soviet invasion of Azerbaijan in April 1920 and the full introduction of the NEP, which in Azerbaijan was not until September 1921, was characterized by the same ideological militancy and harsh punishments that defined War Communism.

Recognizing a dire situation, the Azerbaijan Oil Committee, still under Serebrovskii's leadership, and the Baku Executive Committee established the Commission on the Clarification of the Needs of the Baku Oil Industry (hereafter: Commission or Baku Oil Commission) on January 2, 1921. According to the Commission's first protocol, it was formed to help the oil industry recover and emphasized "that the purpose of the Commission is not to interfere in the oil business ... but to provide the most comprehensive and systemic aid to those bodies" involved in oil production both in Baku and in Moscow.[24] The Commission divided the industry into sections based on function (drilling, refining, exploration, etc.). It assigned a representative of the oil committee, a representative from the trade unions, and a political representative of the Soviet government to each section to carry out assessments, the results of which the representatives submitted to a plenum of members from the Commission.[25] It compiled a series of these reports and in these reports offered recommendations to provide a clearer picture of what the industry was facing and where it believed the industry should be going.

These reports provide one of the most comprehensive views of the effects of the first year of nationalization in the oil industry and of the early period of Soviet administration in the oil fields. Nationalization was chaotic and ad hoc. The Commission struggled to reconcile an ideological commitment to the newly nationalized industry, which was supposed to be tightly centralized, with the strategic necessity of being flexible in the face of shortages. This created a tension seen throughout the reports, and, indeed, in the claim made earlier that the Commission would keep a distance from the day-to-day administration of the industry, which was essentially an attempt to mollify specialists who were reluctant to work with the Soviet government.

A Commission on the Needs of the Industry

The first report submitted to the Baku Oil Commission in January 1921 focused on the need to stop the hemorrhaging of workers. The Commission attempted to identify the areas where Baku's oil industry was most in need of assistance and then to get the peoples and materials in place.[26] The most serious problem singled out was the desertion of the bailers, the most grueling job in the field with a high mortality rate. These bailers manually extracted oil by directly entering the wells with buckets. Men suffocated from the gas fumes. In Baku's fields, these jobs were filled almost exclusively by Iranian subjects.

An abysmal state of production was exacerbated by the continuing bread shortage and the cold winter. In the second half of 1920, workers abandoned seven hundred wells, and in July 1920, only sixteen barrels of oil were extracted per day. Work in the fields had always been defined by the harsh environment because the wells were located in desert areas that were subject to extreme temperatures, strong winds, sandstorms, and winter snow. The complete collapse of infrastructure and the lack of goods and foodstuffs, not just in Baku but throughout the former Russian Empire, meant that workers were more vulnerable to the elements than ever. The author of the report urged higher food rations, industrial quality work clothing, and higher salaries to try and keep what workforce remained and attract those who left back to the fields. The report noted that workers were more frequently seen half naked and without shoes, huddled around the machines that gave off steam, than actually extracting oil. The only thing that would improve production, the author argued, was to make working conditions livable.[27]

The lack of qualified workers, especially in maintaining the heavy equipment, was felt in lagging production and constant breakdowns. But the distribution of qualified workers was also a problem. Just as reserves of oil were running low, so too were supplies—such as steel, glass, cement—and technical equipment was being exhausted throughout the industry.[28] The report pointed to the continual recall and transfer of skilled workers and specialists to various departments or assignment of additional duties as a major problem.[29]

Skilled workers were regularly accused of sabotage by militant and opportunistic workers or strivers and dismissed without warning and without informing the factory division in advance; they were deprived of ration cards and sometimes arrested.[30] According to the report, this persecution of engineers, combined with the interference of political representatives in the day-to-day running of factories, resulted in complete confusion about who was in charge and an absence of discipline among workers. Further, a "readiness to accuse [engineers] of sabotage and counter-revolution at every insignificant circumstance has led to a loss of initiative on the part of engineers to avoid being found guilty for the risk and bad luck that often accompanies initiative."[31] Engineers worked in constant fear of confiscation and relocation, a phenomenon that marked early Soviet culture throughout the emerging state. At the end of the day, their concerns were the same as the workers—trying to find flour, cabbage, and food for their families. Requisitions were not only disrupting the work of engineers and specialists but were also hindering the transport within the fields. Horses in particular were subject to requisition, which disrupted the entire production process.[32]

Not only was the nascent command economy failing, but the Bolshevik hold on the industry felt tenuous. The state of industry could not only be blamed on the neglect of capitalist owners and recklessness of the preceding years, which had allowed the industry to languish. By their own assessment, the problems were also political. The combination of low food rations, high prices, requisitions, diminishing reserves of both material and oil, and an overall destabilizing and aggressive work environment were to blame for the flight of workers and the inability to begin production.

The Situation Is Catastrophic

Reports from the Baku Oil Commission were not the only way Moscow was kept abreast of developments in the oil fields. Serebrovskii sent weekly updates to Lenin on the status of production from early 1920 through November 1921, and his findings echoed those of the Commission. A year after nationalization every sector was suffering from some kind of shortage. Serebrovskii oversaw housing, transportation, electricity production, goods procurement, maintenance, drilling, shipping, and every other subfield involved in the production of oil. The absence of unskilled laborers meant that the fields were not staffed, the lack of qualified workers and materials meant that machinery could not be repaired. Untrained and exhausted staff ran the accounting offices and discipline was difficult to enforce. Problems that had plagued the reconstruction efforts were especially noticeable by spring 1921 and were progressively worsening.[33] The strike was only the latest signal that they needed to change course.

Serebrovskii described the state of the oil industry in Baku in early 1921 as catastrophic. Too few workers, too little food, and poor technological know-how led to the decline in extraction. Little help was forthcoming from Russia. The oil industry was leaning heavily on the local Azerbaijan Regional Economic Soviet (Sovnarkhoz) for supplies, even though it was supposed to be a Moscow-led enterprise. Serebrovskii pointed out that all of the Azerbaijan Soviet Socialist Republic's (SSR) economic reserves were being used for the oil industry.[34] The only reason the industry, and by implication Russia itself, was surviving and showing even these slight improvements was because of the support of the Baku Executive Committee and the core of loyal Bolsheviks supporting the industry.[35] He concluded that the Soviet economy writ large was dependent on the successful recovery of Baku's oil industry and every Soviet republic would have to participate in its reconstruction.[36]

Serebrovskii's reports from the early 1920s devoted significant space to the crisis among the workers. The famine that struck the Caucasus, what Serebrovskii termed the food collapse, combined with the inability of Azneft to meet its salary obligations, meant that the basic food needs of the workers were not being met. Workers fled en masse back to Russia proper, or in the case of the bailers, to Iran, and those who remained showed signs of scurvy "due to systematic malnutrition."[37] Workers could not be persuaded to work overtime or complete their shifts. Many of them fell asleep at their posts and "negligence bordering on criminal sabotage" was everywhere evident to Serebrovskii. He used one example by way of illustration: in the engine room of one of the factories, a stoker poured water directly into four of the boilers and seawater gushed into the piping system of the electric station, which formed layers of scum and salt. The steam-powered safety controls that would have mitigated the situation were not functioning. As a result, all factories served by the boilers were forced to shut down and production dropped 60 percent. To correct the situation, the pipes needed to be completely dismantled, cleaned, and refitted. The plant was not in a position to do so for the foreseeable future.³⁸ Supply was so hamstrung that one careless, and likely starving, stoker shut down an entire production line.

The absence of proper clothing for workers in the fields during the harsh winter months led many of them to just stop working. The barrellers were not doing their jobs; in one of the refineries, the employees simply refused to work until they were provided with wool clothing, resulting in zero percent production for the month of April. Among the same group of laborers, Serebrovskii noted a "drop in labor discipline" presumably meaning that they stopped following orders because conditions were so poor. The factory needed qualified workers, and instead these people "approached their work with a cold and negligent manner." Workers set arbitrary goals for the day and refused to work beyond them, resulting in lowered production.³⁹ The oil committee reported to Serebrovskii that the biggest obstacle facing workers beyond the food crisis was the lack of transportation. Many workers had to travel up to an hour and a half to get to work and, because of the food situation, they were exhausted by the time they arrived. This resulted, Serebrovskii estimated, in a 50 to 60 percent reduction in efficiency among the workers.⁴⁰

Serebrovskii and the Baku Oil Commission needed Moscow to pay attention to Baku. This was a daunting feat when everywhere from Petrograd to Vladivostok was starving and in dire need of the center's limited favors. The Commission decided it had to convince Moscow that absent Baku's oil, Russia would not be able to pull itself out of the morass it was in. It recommended an information offensive, a sort of lobbying campaign, and sought to publish articles in newspapers, hold meetings, and appeal to the Central Committee in Moscow on behalf of the oil industry.

In addition to the lobbying campaign, the Commission called on local Central Committees to transfer workers, both qualified and unskilled, from Russia, Azerbaijan, Georgia, and Armenia, to work in Baku on the reconstruction of the industry. The Commission did not ask for volunteers, and there is no indication that workers had a choice. The Commission also compiled a list of specialists working in the 11th Division of the Red Army, then stationed in the South Caucasus, and had them sent to the oil fields to help with recovery.⁴¹

As part of this information offensive, Serebrovskii delivered a report, dated February 7, 1921, to the Third Congress of the Azerbaijan Communist Party titled "The Revival of the Oil Industry and Economy of the ASSR [Azerbaijan SSR]." He outlined the general state of fuel consumption and production in the RSFSR for the first ten months of Soviet power. He noted a significant improvement in 1920 over 1919. In 1919, the RSFSR exploited only 665.9 tons of coal versus 6,161 tons in the first 10 months of 1920. The change in oil was even more dramatic—in 1920, the RSFSR exploited 19,328 barrels of oil, while in 1919 the RSFSR had not exploited *any* liquid fuel. That fuel production improved at all speaks more to the proximity of collapse in 1919 than to any real success in 1920.

Serebrovskii's strategy was to link unequivocally and directly the success of the Revolution to the success of the oil industry. He sought to convince Moscow that if Baku failed, so, too, would they. After recounting marginal improvements in transportation, Serebrovskii continued that the "incipient revival of the RSFSR's industry demands huge reserves of raw materials and fuel. From this point of view, Azerbaijan is of special importance as a source of incalculable reserves of liquid fuel."[42] Expressing what was already becoming a common refrain, Serebrovskii declared that "it is not a secret to anyone that the entire world revolution depends on the successful functioning of oil extraction."[43]

Despite gains for Russia, the industry in Baku and extraction in particular had been declining since nationalization. As Serebrovskii presented it, the future of the Revolution hung in the balance. He had an overriding interest in linking the success of the Revolution and oil extraction because he was responsible for the realization or failure of the largest oil industry in what would soon become the Soviet Union. He, and his colleagues in the Commission, repeatedly argued that the fate of the oil industry and the fate of the Revolution were fundamentally connected, and they treated the reconstruction of the industry as an integral part of carrying out the Revolution, replete with forced mobilization and forced labor. What was on the line was for more than the amount of oil extracted. It was a vision of a Soviet future and the Revolution itself. The reconstruction of the oil industry was a revolutionary task; this was the message that Serebrovskii sought to convey repeatedly over the next five years.

Serebrovskii's campaign was successful and his demands, and the terms of his mandate from Lenin, were largely met. The Third Congress of the Azerbaijan Communist Party resolved to improve working conditions and granted the request that workers from Russia, Armenia, and Georgia, as well as the 11th Division of the Red Army, be sent to the oil fields. The party congress ordered the military to assist the oil committee and to fulfill all economic tasks assigned to them. All able-bodied members of the population not already involved in "productive work" were reassigned to the oil industry per his request.[44] Such compulsory labor was a feature of the oil industry until the introduction of the NEP in Azerbaijan in September 1921. The party in Azerbaijan thus abetted Serebrovskii's demands and aided the reconstruction of the oil industry by placing at his service Red Army units stationed in and around Baku and through the voluntary and involuntary transfer of workers to the oil fields.

Despite the extraordinary measures to shore up the industry, including enlisting the military, the initial Soviet takeover aggravated an already dire situation. In accordance with directives from Moscow, and despite the crippling material shortages, the Azerbaijan Oil Committee shipped Baku's oil to other Soviet organizations free of charge. The industry received no compensation, even in the form of barter, for the oil it sent. The industry was not regularly supplied with new equipment and, perhaps most damagingly, it was not in charge of the ration cards its employees received, so "the size of rations had absolutely no connection to labor input."[45] The result was widespread hunger. Workers returned to their extended families in the regions, and, despite orders that no one working in the oil industry was allowed to desert their posts, workers fled in droves and production plummeted throughout mid-1920-1.

The food supply crisis was not isolated to the South Caucasus. Famine struck the Volga region from 1921 to 1922 as the confiscatory policies of War Communism, years of war, and a debilitated railway system laid waste to the region; as many as 6 million deaths were attributed to hunger and disease during this period. Further, the grain and bread supplies for Transcaucasia were shipped in from the north, and the shipments were not arriving. Within this maelstrom, the fight for the improved rations and supplies for the oil industry was in full swing.

Baku Is Not Enough

When the 11th Red Army invaded Azerbaijan in April 1920, the political leadership in Moscow and Baku had understood that to consolidate Soviet control over the oil industry, they would have to reestablish the shipping, trade, and supply lines of the Russian Empire. Domestic shipping relied on access to the Caspian Sea. Baku's oil products were shipped to Astrakhan and then northward along the Volga to the rest of Russia. With Astrakhan and Baku in Soviet hands, this supply line had been secured. But export to the international market took place via a rail line and the kerosene pipeline that traversed the South Caucasus. A flat desert corridor stretched between the North and South Caucasus Mountain ranges connecting the Caspian and Black Seas. The reconstruction of the oil industry would be impossible without this crucial link between Baku and Batumi.

Immediately after the invasion, a faction of Bolsheviks in the Caucasus, including Nariman Narimanov, Iosif Stalin, Sergei Kirov, and Sergo Orjonikidze had argued that taking Azerbaijan in isolation would not be enough to eliminate anti-Bolshevik activity along the borders, which was needed to ensure stability. In an obviously expansionist bid, Kirov and Orjonikidze pushed for the occupation of Armenia and Georgia, in part citing the need to control the rail lines to supply Azerbaijan and the North Caucasus.[46] Georgii Chicherin, the Commissar of Foreign Affairs, opposed the imminent invasion of the two states, fearing the retaliation of European powers and forbade Orjonikidze from invading either of Azerbaijan's neighbors in the immediate future.[47] The push to invade was risky. Both Armenia and Georgia had ongoing boundary disputes with Turkey, and Batumi was occupied by Turkish troops. And the situation in Azerbaijan was far from stable.

Talk of invading Azerbaijan's neighbors came to an abrupt halt on May 25-6, 1920, when the deposed Musavat government started a major counter offensive against the Soviet occupation in Azerbaijan's second largest city of Ganja (Elizavetpol). The fighting lasted six days before the Red Army suppressed the Musavat's Azerbaijani forces.[48] The Soviet army killed as many as 4,000 Muslim civilians during the six-day battle. Bodies were later found in gardens, homes, and entryways where civilian had sought shelter from the fighting.[49] The Musavat-led army killed around 1,500 Red Army soldiers. Interethnic fighting between Muslims and Armenian soldiers also started as both groups attacked each other. In the midst of the uprising, a commander Gittis instructed the Red Army to intervene in the interethnic clashes only if it did not interfere with holding the oil fields.[50] Under the direction of the Azerbaijani Commissar of Internal Affairs, Hamid Sultanov, the Red Army executed an additional 4,000 suspected Musavat sympathizers in Ganja and Baku in the following days.[51] Although the Red Army quelled the Azerbaijani uprising in Ganja by May 31, conflict continued at a lower level of intensity throughout the countryside.

In a letter to Lenin and Lev Trotsky, dated June 3, 1920, Orjonikidze reported that they had nearly lost all of Azerbaijan outside of the oil fields. He confessed that the Red Army was the only thing keeping the former Azerbaijani army from turning on Soviet power and that the Soviets still were in very real danger of losing both Baku and Dagestan.[52] On June 5, 1920, the Red Army began disarming the Muslim population throughout Azerbaijan, as well as the Armenian population of Ganja.[53] The disarmament of Muslims began in the village of Mashtag not far from Baku. When the villagers refused to turn their weapons over by a 2 p.m. deadline on June 5, Nesterovskii, the Chief of the Garrison of the Baku Red Army, executed four hostages in the public square.[54]

The Soviet Azerbaijan Revolutionary Committee quickly released an article denouncing the uprising, the so-called "Ganja events," as a Musavat and Dashnak provocation.[55] The Red Army succeeded in stopping the uprisings in Azerbaijan. The Red Army invaded Armenia in December 1920 and Georgia in February–March 1921, incorporating the entirety of the South Caucasus into the Soviet sphere. There were now three ambiguously but formally independent Soviet republics connecting the Black and Caspian Seas.

The New Economic Policy

In the midst of the occupation of Georgia, Lenin outlined a major policy shift at the Tenth Party Congress in Moscow in March 1921 with the introduction of the NEP. The NEP replaced the confiscatory policies of War Communism, ended grain requisitions, allowed free trade on a local level, and even opened the door to foreign concessions on Soviet territory. But it kept the oil industry under central state control. On the last day of the party congress, March 16, 1921, Moscow cemented its control over the South Caucasus when it signed a treaty with Turkey, agreeing to the Turkish withdrawal from Batumi.[56]

Some effects on the oil industry were apparent immediately after the introduction of the NEP. Serebrovskii connected free trade on the local level with an increase in desertion in the fields.[57] The addition of the markets in Batumi and Tiflis, which had desperately needed European goods, made these tensions even more evident as speculators engaged in price gouging and hoarding. The situation was exacerbated tremendously by competing foreign trade commissariats in the separate republics.[58] In scenes foreshadowing those made famous by Soviet propaganda over the ensuing years, Orjonikidze described the presence of the so-called bagmen at the markets,

> a representative of one of the foreign trade agencies appears in some store—it doesn't matter which representative—Azerbaijani, Armenian, Georgian, or Russian—and literally carries in a bag of money and says, well come on [nu-ka], give me what you have, I'll buy it. The buyer puts it in the bag and carries it out. If the vendor offered 2 thousand he, to avoid a loss, offers 4–5.

Orjonikidze continued and offered an example, relayed to him by a representative of Serebrovskii, "If before 4 o'clock you buy nails for a certain amount, let's say 2–3 thousand, then after 4 o'clock., if you please, pay 100% more."[59] The markets in Batumi and Tiflis, however, were in a precarious position. The entry of Soviet troops into Georgia alarmed foreign merchants, many of whom fled with their goods as the Soviets approached, fearing confiscation.[60] Much like the sovietization of Baku only provided temporary respite from the fuel famine, so too the sovietization of Tiflis and Batumi failed to alleviate the economic crisis.

Crisis and Unification

Several concurrent developments spurred the push for the economic and political unification of the Transcaucasian republics. Major military and political changes at the top—the Red Army's invasion of Georgia beginning in February 1921 and the NEP announced at the Tenth Party Congress in March—combined with consistent and ongoing local supply crises and competition at the markets overdetermined economic unification.[61]

Multiple proposals intended to ease the economic strains in early 1921 were circulating among the leadership in the South Caucasus. On March 1, Narimanov, via his deputy Beybut Shahtakhtinski, suggested making Transcaucasia a constituent part of Russia while the Georgian Communist Party proposed the unification of railroads.[62] On March 16, 1921, the Azerbaijan Central Committee (hereafter: Azerbaijan CC) sent a proposal on unification to the Central Committee of the Russian Communist Party, which formed a commission to discuss the issue, although it came to no firm resolution.[63] Then, on March 18, Orjonikidze suggested to Narimanov and the Azeri Bolshevik Mirza Davud Huseynov, the Azerbaijan Commissar of Finances, that they create a unified foreign trade organization as well as coordinate the administration of the railroads and asked both of them for their opinions on the matter.[64]

Two days after Orjonikidze telegraphed Lenin to report the suppression of the April strike, Lenin instructed the Caucasus Bureau to unify and coordinate the policies of the Transcaucasian republics with the RSFSR and that the Azerbaijani, Armenian and Georgian Soviet republics should "create a regional economic body for the whole of Transcaucasia."[65] But he did not tell them how to do this. The ultimate interpretation of Lenin's decree on unified action was left to the members of the Caucasus Bureau, many of whom disagreed with one another about the best way to implement it.

The following day, April 10, 1921, the Azerbaijan CC met with the Caucasus Bureau to discuss how to interpret the decree on coordinated action between the republics.[66] Underlying the debate that ensued was a central paradox that plagued the Bolsheviks in Transcaucasia—they needed oil to feed the workers but could not feed the workers without oil. That is, oil was the only source of currency in terms of both barter and trade contracts, but the workers could not produce the oil until they obtained goods—such as clothing, food, and shoes—that would allow them to work in the fields. As long as oil remained in the ground, in storage houses, and unrefined, it was only potential wealth, and the workers would remain unfed and unproductive. Any consideration of foreign trade, therefore, was implicitly referencing oil. Four days later, on April 14, Lenin instructed the Caucasus Bureau to coordinate the economic policies of the Transcaucasian republics with the RSFSR, later viewed as the first official step toward the creation of the Transcaucasian Soviet Federative Socialist Republic (Transcaucasian Republic) in March 1922.

Lenin hoped that economic unification would solve intersecting problems, beginning with helping to mitigate the confusion at the markets in Batumi and Tiflis, outlined earlier on. He also tied coordination directly to the oil industry and urged Serebrovskii to get as much of Baku's oil to Batumi as soon as possible so that it could be traded abroad for heavy equipment and food, a task that required a unified policy to be effective.[67]

Given later developments with the rise of Iosif Stalin and the absolute intolerance of dissent, coupled with Lenin's announcement on the ban of factions at the Tenth Party Congress in March 1921, historians assumed that there was no discussion of Lenin's decree in Baku and that the Politburo hammered it out in Moscow and sent it whole cloth to Azerbaijan.[68] Moreover, the personality and policy conflicts surrounding the so-called Georgian Affair, a scandal over Stalin and Orjonikidze's abrasive treatment of the Georgian CC during debates on the unification of Transcaucasia, have overshadowed the Azerbaijan CC's role in the process.[69] It was not the case that Moscow crafted unification without local involvement. Initially, the Azerbaijan CC helped facilitate both the economic and political unification of Transcaucasia—even as they disagreed with the policy—in part by keeping their disputes, and later power struggles, internal.[70]

The idea to unify Transcaucasia did not originate with Lenin, although Soviet-era histories certainly give that impression. The South Caucasus had briefly emerged as an independent state, the Transcaucasian Democratic Federative Republic (or the Transcaucasian Commissariat), from February to May 1918, and party circles had been discussing the status of the republics since 1917. It is safe to assume that unification of some sort was on Moscow's agenda before the Red Army ever set foot in Azerbaijan and the leadership of the republics were aware of this.[71] How this would be implemented was still up for debate, however.

Furthermore, there *had* to be discussion of Lenin's decree because the Caucasus Bureau could not carry out Moscow's policies without active support from the local leadership. It simply did not have the resources or the support of the local population to do so alone. In Azerbaijan, Orjonikidze could not act without the agreement of the Azerbaijan CC because it could, and in the early 1920s often did, simply refuse to carry out Moscow's orders.[72] The joint meeting between the Caucasus Bureau and the Azerbaijan CC from April 10, 1921, centered on economic questions, primarily access to Western European goods and the question of social and political stability.[73] In response to Orjonikidze's request from March 18, Huseynov had written a proposal to create a confederated foreign trade agency between the republics that would make contracts contingent on joint decisions.[74] Orjonikidze, in contrast, pushed for a formal union that would eliminate the individual foreign trade councils and form one unified (*ob'edinennyi*) foreign trade council in Transcaucasia.[75] It was Huseynov's proposal and Orjonikidze's counterproposal that set the parameters for discussion about how to implement Lenin's decrees in Azerbaijan.

During the discussion, Orjonikidze argued that each republic in Transcaucasia had national borders that, roughly, reflected the ethnographic make-up of the republics. This was not really true, but it was an acknowledgement that Azerbaijan, Armenia, and Georgia had recently been independent states and that there were national claims to the territories. The railroad, completed in the 1870s–80s, had not been built with the new national divisions in mind. It had not been constructed with the idea that these republics would someday be ripped apart by war.[76] The railroad, he argued, and the economy more broadly, did not accommodate national distinction. By implication, if they wanted to save the economies of the Transcaucasian republics then they had to unify, regardless of national sentiment. This was a tall order after years of interethnic infighting. The logistics of the oil industry were much like those of the railroad—the pipelines, the location of the refineries, and the ports were all built to serve an integrated economy in the Russian Empire and only bolstered Orjonikidze's argument.

The Azerbaijan CC agreed in principle that foreign trade and the railroads needed to be administered jointly and voted in favor of Orjonikidze's proposal. Oil was a different matter, however. Even though Moscow was already in charge of regulating international oil shipments from Baku's petroleum industry—Azerbaijan and Russia signed a treaty in 1920—it still had to be produced locally.[77] Further, the terms of the treaty stipulated that Soviet Russia would receive the petroleum it requested before the remainder went to market, preventing Western Europe from getting it first. In fact, preventing

Europe from using Azerbaijan's oil was one of the main reasons the head of the Azerbaijan Soviet of People's Commissars and member of the Caucasus Bureau, Nariman Narimanov, had endorsed Russian control over shipping and distribution.[78]

But Soviet Russia did not yet have an agreement with Georgia, nor did Azerbaijan and Georgia have foreign trade arrangements. As noted earlier, Baku's oil could only reach the international market through Batumi, but even once the oil arrived numerous contracts with refineries had to be concluded and the refined products had to be shipped abroad.[79] In the prerevolutionary period, the Nobel Brothers and Manteshev factories shipped the products in concrete, but those factories were no longer running. While there was a market waiting, the Turkish government, for example, was willing to trade kerosene for bread; there was no way to even get the supplies to Turkey. Orjonikidze concluded, "In any case, don't ever think that because we have oil that we can buy everything."[80]

The members of the Azerbaijan CC, and Narimanov in particular, understood that oil was the key to Azerbaijan's political future, but they also understood and feared that the population would protest if it realized how the Soviet government was distributing oil products. The Bolsheviks considered Baku's oil collective property that they could distribute to those points that would most benefit the overall economy of the Soviet republics.[81] If Moscow believed that Nizhnii Novgorod or Samara needed Baku's oil more than Astara, then that is where it would be shipped. The only thing that was visible to the larger population was the flow of goods and resources to Baku in a time of severe shortage. The Azerbaijan CC feared this would lead Georgia and Armenia to accuse Moscow of favoritism vis-à-vis Baku and Azerbaijan.

On the other hand, after supplying the Red Army and oil industry, Moscow planned to distribute the products and profits of the petroleum industry to Armenia, Georgia, and the Mountain Republic in the North Caucasus in the form of food and supplies. The allocation of the fruits of Baku's labor to their recent enemies, the Azerbaijan CC warned, would lead the population of Azerbaijan to accuse Moscow of stealing its natural wealth and dispensing it to its neighbors. While the Bolsheviks controlled Transcaucasia militarily, the communal peace that held remained precarious and the distribution of oil products could easily spark conflicts.[82] The Azerbaijan CC feared another uprising.

Narimanov believed that the Caucasus Bureau was moving too fast and, just as importantly to him, believed that the center of any unified Transcaucasia—both economic and administrative—should be in Baku.[83] Political or even administrative unification would shift the locus of power from Baku to Tiflis, the prerevolutionary governing and cultural center in the South Caucasus that already had the necessary bureaucratic infrastructure. He understood that relocating the center of power to Tiflis would diminish his own position — that he would have far less leverage over Baku, as well as the neighboring states of Turkey and Iran, if the seat of power was moved from a Muslim capital. Ultimately, this is exactly what happened.

Nevertheless, in a public speech delivered shortly after the closed-door discussion, Narimanov explained the necessity of binding Azerbaijan, and now Georgia, to Soviet Russia, justifying unification thus: "Comrades, you have to get it into your heads that when I say the life of Azerbaijan depends on the life of Soviet Russia these are not empty noises." He pointed out that Azerbaijan's oil had already played a vital role in forcing the British to negotiate with Russia, claiming "without question, it was oil. When we announced that our oil belongs to Soviet Russia, it was a trump card in the hands of Soviet power. This, comrades, revolutionaries, and communists is how you should reason: what is more important to us—the life of Soviet Russia or oil?"[84] This quote also contains a thinly veiled threat. Narimanov was making it clear that Soviet Russia would not simply walk away from Baku's oil and that it would be better for Azerbaijan to try to get what it could out of the situation.

Narimanov saw a choice between aligning Azerbaijan with unification or collapsing altogether. Members of the Azerbaijan CC, and most certainly Orjonikidze, argued that Georgia had to unify with Azerbaijan if the economy of the republics and the oil industry was to recover. In a July 1921 protocol from the Caucasus Bureau, Stalin noted that the three Transcaucasian states were granted full independence for two reasons. First, each had been independent for three years and the republics were therefore accustomed to a national state. This experience made it impossible for the republics to immediately cooperate with one another. Second, in contrast, was the international market. Once Armenia and Georgia had come under Soviet control, the port in Batumi began supplying all of Transcaucasia. Stalin argued that "we must use Georgia as an open path to foreign firms. A recognition of Georgia's complete independence will make trade that much easier."[85] Businessmen who refused to deal directly with Soviet Russia had no problem doing so through the auspices of the Georgian Soviet Republic. Maintaining a degree of independence and later autonomy was a way to keep those trade connections open and goods flowing.[86] This was an explicitly economic argument, and it was not just a pretense but part of the purpose behind the creation of the Transcaucasian Republic.

Baku's Oil Goes to Constantinople

Much as Narimanov warned of potential conflicts embedded in the unification of trade and the economy, so too did Serebrovskii quickly understand that a unified trade organization would undermine Azneft.[87] Just a week after these unification meetings, on April 16, 1921, Lenin gave the Azerbaijan Oil Committee, in the person of Serebrovskii, the right to trade oil products in Iran, Turkestan, and Europe in exchange for equipment, food, and clothing for oil workers.[88] This partially bypassed the Commissariat of Foreign Trade monopoly.[89]

Not wasting any time, Serebrovskii and Orjonikidze departed from the newly sovietized port of Batumi on the steamship *Georgia*, which was loaded with oil and kerosene, and headed for the Dardanelles to purchase goods on behalf of the Azerbaijan Oil Committee. At the same time, a large order of heavy machinery bound for Baku's oil fields was held up by customs in Constantinople and it refused to release the equipment. The equipment belonged to oilmen whose companies had been nationalized by the Bolsheviks in 1920. The oilmen were biding their time in the hopes of a Bolshevik collapse and sought neither to move the equipment nor to ship it to further ports. Serebrovskii and Orjonikidze went to retrieve the goods as well as sell the oil.

Constantinople, having been defeated in the First World War, was divided into zones of occupation, and English, French, and Italian personnel policed the ports on a rotating weekly basis. When Serebrovskii and Orjonikidze arrived, the British were patrolling. Fearing a hostile reception, they refused to dock the ship and insisted on holding negotiations in Serebrovskii's cabin aboard the *Georgia*. While they held court on the steamship, they also entered into negotiations with Turkish customs officials over the seized equipment. After several days of boat-side talks, and a new more accommodating French patrol, the *Georgia* finally docked and Serebrovskii entered into serious negotiations with French firms for the oil and kerosene.

On May 9, they concluded an agreement for the ship's contents with the French trading company *Societe Commerciale Industrielle financiere peur la Russie* (hereafter: Sosifross), which the Bolsheviks preferred, for ideological reasons, over offers from Shell and Standard Oil. They used the money from the Sosifross deal to convince Turkish customs officials, by way of "very moderate" bribes, to let the Bolsheviks quietly remove the machinery and ferry it back to Soviet territory.[90] Serebrovskii also brought over nearly 3,000 workers to staff the fields, factories, and warehouses in Baku. A second run increased the number of workers by a total of 4,615. The workers were there on six-month contracts and only 10 percent them were skilled, but the more urgent needs of the Soviet oil industry—both in terms of equipment and supplies for workers—were satisfied in the spring of 1921.[91]

But the transition to the NEP also confused and complicated the recovery of the oil industry. Throughout 1921, the administration of industries was reorganized into trusts, replacing a system set up around so-called chief administrations, or glavki. The glavki system was centralized and dictated from Moscow. While trusts remained nationalized under the NEP—known as the commanding heights of the economy—the administration of trusts was decentralized. Further, the trusts were expected to turn a profit to help fund their own recoveries (called *khozrazchet* in Russian).[92] Theoretically, decentralization allowed trusts to pursue independent policies, such as Serebrovskii did when he traded abroad, but in practice this was hampered because they were required to fulfill unprofitable orders from other state bodies and were not allowed to charge fees for services or materials, causing shortages.

Soviet trusts were run differently from their counterparts in the West. Soviet trusts were not in charge of the marketing or distribution of their products.[93] Azneft oversaw oil production, extraction and sometimes refining, but under the trust reforms the marketing and sale of Soviet oil domestically and internationally went through the Oil Industry Syndicate (hereafter, Oil Syndicate). The Oil Syndicate was part of the Main Fuel Administration under the Supreme Soviet of the Economy, formed in April 1921. In other words, the Oil Syndicate worked for Moscow not Azneft.[94]

This meant that the allocation of Azneft's production was several steps removed from the control of the trust. For example, if Azneft needed to ship oil and/or oil products it had to go through the Oil Syndicate. The Oil Syndicate had to conclude a separate contract with the Commissariat of Ways and Means for the use of oil tankers or railroads and only then could the oil be shipped.[95] Because all of these commissariats were in competition with each other for resources, and they had to coordinate independently, distribution was slow, and orders went unfulfilled. Serebrovskii later argued that divorcing production and trade, and introducing the Oil Syndicate as an intermediary, would harm the recovery of the industry. He asserted that the disruption between production and trade, both domestic and foreign, was entirely artificial and would mean that Azneft would not be able to verify the success of its products or to make accurate budgets.[96]

Serebrovskii's first attempt to trade abroad and turn a profit for Azneft did not go according to plan and had to be amended by the Soviet Labor and Defense.[97]

The RSFSR Commissariat of Foreign Trade objected that Lenin's support for the Azerbaijan Oil Committee was counterproductive. The Azerbaijan Oil Committee did not have an established trade apparatus and it undermined the planned merger of the three Transcaucasian foreign trade commissariats. Indeed, the unification of the Transcaucasian foreign trade outlined earlier on was approved on April 26 and signed on June 2, 1921. From that date, the individual trade organizations were united under the Unified Foreign Trade Commissariat (hereafter, Unified Commissariat).

In late September 1921, the Commissariat of Foreign Trade revoked the Azerbaijan Oil Committee's right to trade abroad. Leonid Krasin, the foreign trade commissar, informed Serebrovskii that past experience with the oil committee had demonstrated that it was incapable of negotiating reliable deals and that it had nearly granted a monopoly to "a questionable Greek speculator."[98] The Azerbaijan Regional Economic Soviet, under Narimanov, sided with Serebrovskii and petitioned to reinstate Azerbaijan Oil Committee's right to trade, which was granted on a limited basis.[99] But this small concession was not likely to keep control with Baku. Circumventing the new unified trade organization, on September 13, 1921, Serebrovskii instructed Azneft's office in Constantinople to trade independently "in direct subordination to Azerbaijan" and to continue working in their previous positions.[100]

The newly established Transcaucasian trade representative in Constantinople reported to Tiflis that the relationship between the new unified foreign trade organization, the Unified Commissariat, and the Azerbaijan Oil Committee "daily becomes more abnormal" and could disrupt the work of the Commissariat of Foreign Trade completely. The representative placed the blame for the situation squarely on the shoulders of the oil committee's workers, whom he claimed were absolutely lacking in discipline.[101]

He outlined several examples to demonstrate Serebrovskii and the oil committee's behavior. First, the foreign trade office in Constantinople was granted a reserve account by the Soviet of Labor and Defense for the oil committee, but the committee used far more money than it was allotted and aggressively demanded more. The foreign trade workers were afraid to deny the demands because they were aware of Serebrovskii's mandate from Lenin. The Azerbaijan Oil Committee workers screamed at and bullied the foreign trade workers "and that noise will immediately roll into Batum, Baku and all the way to Moscow itself all because comrade Serebrovskii has that letter from Ilich [Lenin] in his pocket."[102] The Azerbaijan Oil Committee also had a larger staff than the foreign trade office and spent money without regard to budgets. He reported "such a blatantly unceremonious, even more, criminal, relationship to the national wealth I have never seen."[103] He accused Serebrovskii of paying far above market prices, and in a further bid for personal control, "appoint[ed] his wife as Executive Authority to the Oil Committee here [in Constantinople] with a salary of 400 lira a month."[104] He also complained that the oil committee kept no accounts. When he asked the oil committee workers what their salaries were, they replied that they did not have fixed salaries but "take what they need."

He was also concerned about the state of shipments from Batumi, which were completely disorganized and not fit to sell on the foreign market. The prices had to be reduced and they lost money. But, he complained, the most egregious offense was that some of the barrels arrived empty, indicating not only incompetence but corruption. As a final note, he claimed that "comrade Serebrovskii has special symbols that he puts on letters for his workers and by these symbols they know which of his decrees they actually have to follow and which they do not, regardless of whether his signature is on the letter."[105] Through these symbols, Serebrovskii allegedly countermanded orders from the Unified Commissariat and pursued his own policies.

Complaints that Serebrovskii instructed his workers to proceed as if the Unified Commissariat were not in the picture continued unabated, and his staff in Constantinople were simply unwilling to follow orders from Tiflis.[106] F. Ia. Rabinovich, the Transcaucasian trade representative in Constantinople, was summoned to Baku in late October to address the situation before the Caucasus Bureau and claimed that Serebrovskii, without directly lying, consistently misrepresented the situation between the oil committee and the Commissariat of Foreign Trade.[107] Serebrovskii, in turn, wrote to Orjonikidze and Narimanov at the Caucasus Bureau on January 26, 1922, blaming inefficiencies in the Unified Commissariat for the problems.[108]

Serebrovskii was protecting the institutional prerogative of the Azerbaijan Oil Committee in light of the restrictions from the new Unified Commissariat, but he was also operating in a situation of severe and ubiquitous shortage, which is why Lenin granted him a mandate in the first place. He was using his mandate to circumvent official institutions—a practice with a long history in the Russian Empire and one to be institutionalized in the Soviet Union as well—to get the supplies he needed. In the process he was undermining the establishment and smooth functioning of the institutions he was bypassing.

The wide-ranging tensions in Azerbaijan over unification with the other republics in the South Caucasus and over control of the oil industry reflected the inherent contradictions in Soviet policy writ large. Soviet ideology espoused a liberatory radical ethic, but its practitioners relied on pressure and violence to achieve those goals. The tensions specific to Azerbaijan illustrate a wider emerging state practice. Baku was vital to the Soviet cause, but it was far away from Moscow, which faced its own, often overwhelming crises. Russia could not send the kind of financial and material support needed to fix the oil fields or to supply the population with material goods. The result, reproduced throughout the Soviet republics, was that local leaders, together with political agents sent by Moscow, had to tackle crisis after crisis on their own. Moscow handed local leaders decrees and told them to fulfill the decrees without instructions and without supplies. The actual means of achieving success, and by extension of carrying out the Revolution, was highly discretionary.

The tensions and contradictions between the utopian ideals and policies emanating from Moscow and the reality of what was possible on the ground, in this case the larger context around the politics of oil, is precisely where the relationships and practices between Moscow and the periphery were established. This system came to rely on a merging of personal and institutional power and fostered fierce competition for control over these institutions.

2

Revolution in the Muslim East: The Bolsheviks and a Soviet Republic in Iran

In April 1920, as the Bolsheviks prepared the overthrow of the Azerbaijan Democratic Republic (ADR) and troops from the 11th Red Army amassed along the southern Russian border in Derbent, Vladimir Lenin struck a deal with the Azeri Bolshevik Nariman Narimanov for the future of Soviet Azerbaijan: oil in exchange for a government. Narimanov agreed to do what he could to help supply Soviet Russia with oil and in return Lenin put Narimanov in charge of the Soviet government of Azerbaijan. On the eve of the invasion, Lenin appointed him Chairman of the Soviet of People's Commissars of the Azerbaijan Soviet Socialist Republic with the understanding that he could shape Soviet policies in Azerbaijan. He charged Narimanov with facilitating connections between the industrial stronghold of Baku and the rural countryside of Azerbaijan. Economic and social connections between the peasant countryside and Baku were virtually nonexistent after years of civil war but were essential to the stability on which the shipment of oil depended. This understanding between Lenin and Narimanov created the foundations of Soviet power in Azerbaijan.[1] It also sowed the seeds of chaos and strife as it became increasingly clear that the locus of power in the new Soviet state lay firmly with the Communist Party, not the state.

From the beginning, Narimanov understood the connection between his mandate and the accessibility of oil.[2] In the pivotal early years of Soviet power, he granted desperately needed legitimacy to the Bolshevik presence in Azerbaijan among the majority Muslim population, as well as to the outside world.[3] While the Caucasus Bureau, under the chairmanship of Sergo Orjonikidze, oversaw political and military policy, Narimanov hoped to bring Azerbaijan, and the wider Muslim East, into the communist future. Narimanov had worked with the Bolsheviks since 1905. He was a commissar in the Baku Commune in 1918, and in 1919 was appointed head of the Near Eastern Section of the Commissariat of Foreign Affairs in Moscow and then Deputy Commissar of the Commissariat of

Nationalities, which was run by Iosif Stalin. But his aspirations were embedded in a long-standing Muslim reform movement that predated Bolshevism and spanned the Russian, Ottoman, and Persian Empires.[4]

Narimanov was part of the Russian Empire's Muslim cultural elite and promoted a heterodox socialist modernist vision of the future that sought mass education and political and economic liberation from Russian colonialism. Muslim regions in the Russian Empire all had unique political and social circumstances. Thanks to Baku's oil industry, it had a multiethnic industrial base and a rich political tradition of radicalism that was missing both in Russia's recently acquired periphery of Central Asia and in the long-established territories of the Volga Tatars. As a result, Narimanov had to navigate multiple cultural landscapes—from rural mullahs and Iranian revolutionaries to radical Russian and Armenian oil workers. The presence of Baku's oil on the borderland between Soviet Russia, Iran, and the Ottoman Empire, all worlds with which Narimanov to one degree or another possessed ties, was decisive in elevating him to a position of influence in 1920.

In the upheaval of 1918–20, Narimanov presented himself as the guardian of both the interests of the Revolution and of Azerbaijan. In the highly personalized politics of the early Soviet period, Narimanov understood that ensuring the success of his policies depended on his own ability to gain power. Rather than seeking independence or influence through claims to national identity or nationalism, Narimanov sought to secure Azerbaijan's future by leveraging Baku's oil. He understood that the Red Army was not simply going to walk away from Baku. It was too vital to winning the Civil War. He viewed a Bolshevik takeover, in some form or another, as both inevitable and desirable. Narimanov envisioned that he could walk a line where Azerbaijan was tightly bound to Russia out of ideological affinity and economic necessity even while maintaining a degree of independence.

Narimanov also wanted to use Baku's oil to foster revolution in Iran.[5] The prospect of bringing revolution to the Muslim East was one of the key reasons that Narimanov and others like him supported Bolshevik power and helped secure the Red Army's initial entry into both the city of Baku and its oil fields. This chapter examines how the integration of Azerbaijan into the Soviet family became intertwined with a separatist movement in northern Iran. Soon after the Red Army's invasion of Azerbaijan, local Baku-based Bolsheviks took advantage of the opportunity to spread the revolution to Iran and helped establish the Gilan Soviet Socialist Republic in the northern Iranian province. A combination of Soviet Red Army and Azerbaijani troops occupied sections of northern Iran, set up political parties, and supplied weapons to guerrilla fighters. It did not take long before the attempt to spread revolution spiraled out of Moscow's control. This chapter argues that the doomed experiment in the Gilan Soviet Republic, and the broader context of Eastern policy, trade politics, and economic policy, illustrated to the leadership in Moscow that the Baku comrades had their own agendas. Consolidating Soviet power in the South Caucasus, and securing Baku's oil, would mean curbing the ambitions of the Baku comrades. The South Caucasus ultimately would be bound both tighter together and to Moscow but not as Narimanov had envisioned.

Nariman Narimanov and the Revolution in the East

The Soviet Red Army invaded Baku on April 28, 1920, because it needed access to the oil fields on the outskirts of the city, but a military victory would not guarantee long-term success. Acutely aware of this fact, most of the Bolshevik leadership, and Lenin in particular, had been hesitant to invade Azerbaijan. They wanted Baku's resources, certainly, but would have really preferred if the oil city was in a more central location, connected to the international market already, and not surrounded by hostile peasants. More importantly, Moscow was apprehensive about seizing Baku because of what happened to the short-lived Bolshevik Baku Commune two years prior.[6]

In that case, local Bolsheviks took control of Baku in April 1918 and formed the commune. Tensions within Baku increased between Bolsheviks, Muslims, and Armenian Dashnaks as order broke down in the countryside outside of Baku with the collapse of the Caucasus front and threatened to bring violence to the city. The Bolsheviks, led by soon-to-be immortalized Stepan Shaumian, took advantage of the tension and aligned with the Dashnaks in the hopes that their alliance would prevent the Muslim population from taking control of the city. Narimanov, who was part of the Bolshevik coalition, attempted to negotiate a truce between the Bolsheviks and the Azeris to no avail. Initial skirmishes between Soviet troops and Muslims escalated when Dashnaks joined the Bolsheviks and the clashes turned into a slaughter. The Baku Dashnaks led a series of massacres against Muslims in the city and Bolsheviks lost control of the situation in a series of events known as the March Days.[7]

When the fighting stopped, the Bolsheviks held the city with a coalition with other left parties and declared the formation of the Baku Commune. Knowing that they had lost the support of the Muslim population, the commune appointed several Muslim Commissars, including Narimanov as Commissar of Social Welfare in part hoping to calm the situation. The Commissars coordinated policy with Moscow via telegram. They nationalized land and the oil industry and fostered class warfare. Their coalition was precarious, however, and they lost control of the commune in July. The new city government declared a military dictatorship and allied with the British, hoping to prevent an Ottoman advance. The remaining commissars (Narimanov had evacuated to Astrakhan) were arrested and thrown in prison.

It was at this point that two consequential events for the future of Azerbaijan occurred. In September, Ottoman troops combined with troops from the ADR marched toward Baku. The young Bolshevik Anastas Mikoyan, who was based in Baku, secured the release of the commissars as the Ottoman troops approached, and they fled the city via the Caspian hoping to make it to Astrakhan. Instead, their ship sailed eastward across the Caspian. When they landed, the commissars and their supporters were captured. Not long after, all of them, except Mikoyan, were executed by the local government. Their deaths turned them into Bolshevik martyrs, the so-called twenty-six commissars.[8] While their fate cemented the legacy of the commune in Bolshevik lore, back in Baku the Bolsheviks would be associated with a different legacy. The combined Ottoman and Azerbaijani troops retook Baku, this time slaughtering Armenians. The Bolsheviks, who had capitalized on ethno-national tension between Armenians and Muslims to advance their own agenda, were permanently associated with the bloody events that bookmarked both ends of the commune.

After the collapse Narimanov noted, "We must acknowledge that our exit from Transcaucasia [then] did not elicit any particular regret among the local population."[9] He argued that the Bolsheviks would never create socialism in the Muslim East without first acknowledging that policies must be adapted to local tradition and not rely on coercion. Otherwise, a second invasion of Baku would simply repeat the bloodshed of 1918 and alienate the Muslim population, making it impossible to govern.

Nariman Karbalayi Najaf oglu Narimanov was born into a poor family in Tiflis (Tbilisi), the present-day capital of Georgia and the cultural and administrative center of the Caucasus in the Russian Empire. He attended the Russian-Tatar school at a Gori seminary, and after several years of teaching, earned a medical degree in Odessa. During the mid-to-late 1890s, he was radicalized, frustrated by his experiences growing up in poverty and chagrined at having to rely on the charity of others to receive an education. He became a socialist and a member of the Muslim Social-Democratic Party the *Hummet* during the

Russian Revolution of 1905.[10] During this period, the *Hummet* worked with the Baku Committee of the Bolshevik Party, including Orjonikidze, Shaumian, and Meshadi Azizbekov, to conduct revolutionary work in Iran, which was in the midst of its own constitutional revolution.[11] Narimanov was also associated with the Iranian social-democratic group the *Adalat*, which was composed primarily of Baku-based Iranian oil workers and more explicitly intertwined socialism and Islam than the *Hummet*.[12] While spreading international revolution was a core tenant of the Leninist worldview during Russia's Civil War, for Azeris, northern Iran held a unique attraction. The majority population across the border was also Azeri, sharing both language and religion.[13]

The Muslim socialist parties worked with the Russian-dominated socialist parties, including both the Menshevik and Bolshevik wings of the Russian Social Democrats, and some held memberships in both but insisted on remaining independent. Alongside his political work, Narimanov concentrated primarily on teaching, advocacy, and play writing while continuing to work as a medical doctor.[14] Most of his political writings before the 1917 Revolutions were broadly socialist, agitating for an eight-hour working day, social benefits, and workers' rights, but he sided with the Bolsheviks after the collapse of the Empire.

The period 1918–20 was dominated by territorial conflicts between the nascent Azerbaijani and Armenian nation states, part of the larger regional reconfiguring after the collapse of the Russian Empire and the ongoing partition of the Ottoman Empire. They fought over multiple contested regions, each laying claim to Nagorno-Karabakh, Zangezur, and Nakhchivan. There was also a mass influx of refugees into the South Caucasus in response to the Ottoman genocide of Armenians during the war, which further destabilized the region.

Angered by the violence against civilians in 1918, Narimanov was critical of the Baku Commune. In a speech he gave in 1919, he blamed the collapse of Soviet power on the Bolsheviks' single-minded quest for oil and power.[15] He argued that Bolshevik behavior toward Muslims resulted from the party's prioritization of oil over community work and consensus-building with the local population. Narimanov pointed out that the failure of the Bolsheviks to protect Muslims from attacks by Armenian nationalists during the March Days, when thousands of Muslim civilians were slaughtered, had alienated local support for the party. Bolshevik failure to protect Muslims, he asserted, is why the ADR invited the Ottoman army into the city and directly resulted in the loss of oil resources for the Bolsheviks.

A new Soviet invasion, Narimanov explained, would be no different if the Bolsheviks did not take into account the importance of local politics and the cultural traditions of the Muslim population. Achieving a lasting national peace between Armenians and Caucasian Muslims was also a prerequisite to achieving the stability the Bolsheviks desired. There was no soul-searching about how Bolshevik policies contributed to their own collapse; instead, Narimanov pointed out that "everyone was united in thoughts and ideas. At that time, from September to October of 1918, there was no discussion in Baku about the Soviet system; all anyone could talk about was Baku's oil."[16]

While preparing for the invasion, the Red Army and the Commissariat of Foreign Affairs debated whether to occupy only Baku or all of the ADR.[17] Narimanov emerged as a champion for the occupation of all of Russian Azerbaijan, arguing that Baku could not be held without the rest of the country, as the 1918 failure demonstrated.[18] He reiterated that Baku was an industrial island with a dramatically different demographic composition than the rest of Azerbaijan. Believing that Baku needed to be tied to the countryside or it would remain vulnerable and unstable, Narimanov likewise felt that the Azerbaijani countryside must be integrated into the economy and culture of Baku. Using his authority as a respected educator and politician, Narimanov portrayed himself as the person who could deliver the support of the countryside and in the process make the workers and peasants codependent.

Narimanov's lobbying efforts to ensure that the leadership of Soviet Russia, and Lenin in particular, would implement this vision of a unified Azerbaijan paid off. Having fled Baku for Astrakhan with the collapse of the commune, nearly all of the Muslim social democrat *Hummetists* became members of the Commissariat of the Affairs of the Muslim Caucasus within the Commissariat of Foreign Affairs and worked to carry out revolution in Azerbaijan from across the border in Bolshevik-held territory.[19] He argued that a Muslim-led political party *within* the Bolshevik Party must establish Soviet power on the ground.[20] Over the objections of several of his *Hummetist* comrades—including major figures in the future Azerbaijan SSR such as Dadash Buniatzade, Ali Heydar Qarayev, and Mirza Davud Huseynov—Narimanov sought the formal incorporation of the *Hummet* Party into the Bolshevik Party. Succeeding where many others had failed, in July 1919, the Politburo agreed that the political party *Hummet* would be an autonomous Muslim wing of the Bolshevik Party.[21] As the Red Army prepared for invasion, Narimanov was appointed Commissar for the Affairs of the Muslim Caucasus.[22] He and his fellow *Hummetists*, now Bolshevik-*Hummetists*—all held posts in the new Soviet government.[23] He had convinced Lenin to follow his policy, and in April 1920, Lenin sent him back to Azerbaijan with a specific mandate to facilitate the connection between the oil city of

Baku and the overwhelmingly rural Azerbaijani countryside. Narimanov's own political agenda was thus facilitated by the Soviet desperation for oil.

In spite of Narimanov's success in positioning himself as head of Soviet Azerbaijan, he resented that he had no real institutional power over the oil industry or the infrastructure it depended on, which reached far beyond Azerbaijan's borders. .[24] In fact, his authority was rendered local even before he arrived in Baku. Newly appointed Chairman of the Caucasus Bureau, Orjonikidze, together with Stalin intervened to constrain Narimanov's role. They urgently petitioned Lenin to ensure that his influence be limited to the confines of the Azerbaijani territory. In other words, they asked Lenin to to strip Narimanov of any say in the foreign affairs of Soviet Azerbaijan and Lenin acquiesced.[25] This fact, of which he was likely unaware, did not mitigate Narimanov's ambitions.

The Bolsheviks Look South

Immediately after the Soviet invasion of Azerbaijan, a faction of Bolsheviks, including Narimanov, Stalin, and Orjonikidze, argued that taking Azerbaijan in isolation would not be enough to eliminate anti-Bolshevik activity along the borders. They pushed for the occupation of Armenia and Georgia. Georgii Chicherin, the Commissar of Foreign Affairs, opposed the imminent occupation of the two states, fearing the retaliation of European powers and, with the backing of Lenin and Lev Trotsky, forbade Orjonikidze and the Caucasus Bureau, from invading either of Azerbaijan's neighbors for the time being.

Talk of establishing Soviet power was not limited to Transcaucasia, however. The same logic that led to the invasion of the South Caucasus extended to northern Iran. Orjonikidze wanted to push the Red Army further south into Iran. On May 18, 1920, the Caspian-Volga Red fleet docked at the Iranian port city of Enzeli (Bandar-e Anzali) in the Iranian province of Gilan to seize the White naval fleet. The White fleet was headquartered in Enzeli under the protection of the British troops that had occupied northern Iran after the collapse of the Russian Empire in 1918. Orjonikidze accompanied the fleet and telegraphed Lenin, Stalin, and Chicherin that the Red Army could easily occupy the neighboring Iranian province of Azerbaijan.[26] Orjonikidze proposed that the Bolsheviks, together with the local revolutionary Kuchuk Khan, proclaim Soviet power "and go from city to city chasing out the English."[27]

The Commissariat of Foreign Affairs replied quickly and firmly to Orjonikidze's telegram that Soviet troops were not under any circumstances to go beyond the borders of Enzeli. The Red fleet was supposed to ensure that the British and the White Army could not attack Azerbaijan or Russia. With the Caspian cleared of the British, the borders of Soviet Azerbaijan would be secure and protected against a possible future seizure of Baku's oil fields. It would also guarantee shipping routes for oil and other goods to Russia proper. Trying to contain international reaction, the Commissariat of Foreign Affairs instructed Orjonikidze to announce that Enzeli was part of Iran, end of story.[28] The commissariat, however, held limited sway so far from Moscow, and official policy was followed only insofar as Bolshevik leaders on the ground saw fit.

Bolsheviks in Iran

For many Bolsheviks from the South Caucasus spreading the communist revolution to Iran was an integral aspect of revolutionary policy and one rooted in years of experience. Bolshevik involvement in Iranian politics can be traced to the revolutionary movements that swept both the Russian and Iranian Empires in 1905.[29] Many radical Social Democratic revolutionaries operated on both sides of the river Araz—the border dividing Russian Azerbaijan and Iranian Azerbaijan established with the 1828 Treaty of Turkmenchai. The core of the revolutionaries in northern Iran was made up of Iranian immigrants who worked in the oil fields of Baku and Caucasian revolutionaries who crossed the border.[30]

At the turn of the twentieth century both the Russian revolutionary movements and Iranian constitutional movements faced violent reaction from their governments, forcing revolutionaries to go underground. During the years of Stolypin's repression after 1905, hundreds of revolutionaries from the Caucasus fled to Iran, usually to the provinces of Gilan and Azerbaijan.[31] The Bolsheviks forged strong ties in northern Iran in this period that would prove vital in the establishment of Soviet influence in Iran in the 1920s. Narimanov and Orjonikidze also met during this period. In 1908, Narimanov was funneling weapons to Iran from Tiflis to assist revolutionaries in an uprising against the Shah. Orjonikidze, meanwhile, fled from exile to Tiflis where he was put in contact with Narimanov. Narimanov used his network to help Orjonikidze flee across to the border and hide in Gilan, where he spent the next two years, a connection that led Orjonikidze to support Narimanov's bid to head the Soviet Azerbaijan government in 1920. Narimanov himself was arrested in 1909 and exiled to Astrakhan.[32] While in Gilan, many Bolsheviks—particularly Georgian Bolsheviks—had worked for the entrepreneur and concessionaire Akakii

Khoshtariia. Under the auspices of his Russo-Persian company, Khoshtariia had interests in forestry, railroads, agriculture, and, most importantly, oil. He reportedly held great sway with the Russian consul, maintained his own police force, and issued passports.[33] But it was his relationship with the Georgian revolutionary Polikarp "Budu" Mdivani, who had worked for Khoshtariia in Enzeli, that would later prove useful when Mdivani vouched for Khoshtariia in the reestablishment of his oil concession with Soviet aid in 1924.[34] This was precisely the kind of cross-border network on which the Bolsheviks came to rely.

Along with exporting socialist and nationalist ideologies, activists from the South Caucasus organized terrorist acts and distributed arms and explosives to Iranian revolutionary groups. For example, in 1909, the Georgian Sergo Gamdlishvili, together with a group of Georgians and Iranians, assassinated the governor of Resht, the capital of Gilan region and the same city that would fall to a Bolshevik coup eleven years later.[35] The Bolsheviks fled Gilan in 1911 when the Iranian government cracked down on the region and returned only with the outbreak of First World War in 1914, when the imperial Russian army occupied Iran.

In 1915 and 1916, several Bolsheviks, including Mdivani and Orjonikidze, returned to Iran disguised as Georgian refugees, reestablished contact with other revolutionaries, and carried out political work in Resht.[36] Among those revolutionaries was Mirza Kuchuk Khan, the populist revolutionary and leader of the Jangali movement that Orjonikidze wanted the Bolsheviks to ally with later in 1920. The Jangalis began as a guerilla force organized against the tsarist Russian occupation of northern Iran, which had occurred with the outbreak of the First World War. Russian troops left in the wake of the Bolshevik Revolution and British troops took their place. The Jangali movement then shifted its aim from fighting the Russian troops to ousting the British from Iranian territory. The Bolsheviks and the Jangalis both wanted the British out of northern Iran. Seeing an overlap in interests, Kuchuk had first attempted to contact the Bolsheviks for help in fighting the British in the summer of 1918 and even went to Lenkoran in summer 1919 to try to connect with them. Although that attempt was unsuccessful, he was able to communicate with members of the Communist International (Comintern) and was already acquainted with Orjonikidze and Mdivani.[37]

Invading Iran

Fedor Raskolnikov, the commander of the Volga-Caspian fleet of the Red Army, arrived in the port of Baku on May 1, 1920, and soon after telegraphed Moscow requesting permission to pursue the remainder of General Anton Denikin's White Naval fleet to the port of Enzeli in northern Iran. Raskolnikov wanted to seize the warships and, if necessary, to follow Denikin's troops onto Iranian territory. The White fleet was in Iran seeking shelter under cover of friendly British troops based in Enzeli. Concluding that the Shah's government in Iran would not disarm the White Guards and that Britain was unlikely to interfere, Trotsky and Lenin approved the request up to and including the entrance of Soviet troops into Iranian territory.[38] The Shah's government held little sway in its northern provinces—the Iranian province of Azerbaijan was in revolt and had even declared itself an independent state of Azadistan— and it was undergoing its own crisis in the wake of the First World War.[39]

Raskolnikov claimed personal responsibility for the Red fleet invasion in order to shield the government of Soviet Russia from culpability in the event that things went poorly. On May 18, 1920, he arrived in Enzeli and announced to the Iranian government and the British ships in the harbor that the Red Navy had no aggressive intentions and simply wanted to recover the military equipment that Denikin had stolen from Soviet Azerbaijan and Soviet Russia. He continued that "to avoid any misunderstandings," the British commander should immediately withdraw his troops from the city.[40] Regardless of what Raskolnikov claimed, landing 2,000 Soviet marines in Enzeli could not reasonably be interpreted as anything other than hostile by the Iranian government.[41] The Soviet invasion sparked fears of a "Bolshevik threat" in Tehran and, despite Raskolnikov's protestations to the contrary, that the Soviet government was indeed giving him orders.[42]

Raskolnikov was pleased with the expedition and noted, "We secured much booty at Enzeli. Besides the naval ships and aeroplanes our trophies included numberless guns, machine-guns, shells and rifles, with stocks of cartridges."[43] He seized all of the White fleet and the British, more concerned with Mesopotamia than Iran, evacuated quickly under the condition that its troops be allowed to maintain its arms.[44] Having reclaimed the fleet and returned the tankers (although not yet the marines) to Baku to transport oil up the Volga, Raskolnikov instructed his commanders to cooperate with Kuchuk Khan if such assistance was desired on Kuchuk's part. It was in fact desired and Kuchuk contacted Raskolnikov almost immediately.[45]

After Raskolnikov and the Red fleet docked at Enzeli, the Iranian Prime Minister Vosuq issued a formal protest against the Soviet presence on Iranian territory, thus entering into formal diplomatic correspondence with the Bolshevik government. Before the Bolshevik landing at Enzeli the government under

Vosuq had been strongly allied with the British. Vosuq's government signed the 1919 Anglo-Persian Agreement, which essentially rendered Iran a protectorate of Britain and was spectacularly unpopular at home. Despite Vosuq's support for the British, he realized within a few months that the British did not intend to defend Iranian interests, despite the vociferous claims of Britain's representative in Iran, Lord Curzon. No longer trusting the British, Vosuq's government reached out to the Bolsheviks mere days before the landing at Enzeli.[46] Although the presence of Soviet troops on Iranian territory caused great anxiety in Tehran, it also gave Vosuq's government the opportunity to establish relations without the consent of the British.

In reply to Vosuq's protest, Chicherin confirmed the landing of Soviet troops on Iranian territory and reiterated Raskolnikov's claim that Russian troops were there primarily out of military necessity and harbored no aggressive intentions. Soviet troops were there to "liquidate from the shores of the Caspian the base of hostile movement against the RSFSR," that is, the British fleet. Officially, Russian troops were evacuated almost immediately, on June 6, 1920. In reality, numerous soldiers remained, or returned, ostensibly as volunteers through October 1921.

Chicherin distanced himself from the troops that remained in Iran after Raskolnikov's evacuation and claimed that they had no official ties to Soviet Russia.[47] Technically, this was true; the remaining troops were there under the flag of the Azerbaijan Soviet Republic. Chicherin indicated that Azerbaijani troops were forced to occupy Enzeli and the neighboring city of Resht in order to protect peaceful trade and secure the Azerbaijani border from the British threat to Baku, and the Caucasus more broadly. Chicherin claimed that the troops would be withdrawn "as soon as the Azerbaijani government has confidence that the threat to its borders has passed and the British troops begin their evacuation of Persia."[48]

The Commissariat of Foreign Affairs maintained Azerbaijan as an independent state in 1920, rather than incorporating it directly into Soviet Russia. This allowed Russia to carry out its foreign policy with a much freer hand than would have been the case under the flag of the Soviet Russia. It could maintain Azerbaijani troops on foreign territory without too much international condemnation. This abundance of caution preserved the image of noninterference for the British, with whom the Soviets, despite events in Iran, were negotiating a trade deal that would eventually become the Anglo-Soviet Trade Agreement. The British would only agree to a trade deal with the Bolsheviks if the Soviet government agreed to stop hostile propaganda and actions against British interests. The Bolsheviks were walking a thin line, lending support to Kuchuk while trying to establish trade ties with the British. This tension between revolutionary policy and economic necessity was characteristic of Soviet foreign policy from the beginning. There was an acute awareness that if events in Enzeli got out of hand, it would jeopardize a possible trade agreement and the security of the Caucasus more generally. The British were furious that the Soviets sent troops into Gilan but too busy elsewhere to push the issue. A nominally independent Azerbaijan provided a pretext for both British and Soviet diplomacy.

The Bolsheviks only wanted to engage Kuchuk Khan to the extent that it did not interfere with the overall Soviet foreign policy of regularizing trade relations with the economic powerhouses of Western Europe.[49] Despite recent gains in the Caucasus, Chicherin reminded Raskolnikov that the Bolsheviks would not even be able to hold Baku without the Red Army, let alone hold Iran. Lev Karakhan, the deputy commissar at the Commissariat of Foreign Affairs, instructed Raskolnikov that Soviet policy was active and there was enthusiastic support of revolution against the Shah and the British presence in Iran. But this came with limits. Crossing the line in Iran could lead to a new blockade or even the loss of Baku.

A Soviet Republic

Kuchuk wanted to cooperate with the Bolsheviks, but his support for the communists was not unconditional. Unlike the Bolsheviks, he was not hostile to local landlords or merchants and he sought local control, not a full-fledged social and political transformation. As the head of the Caucasus Bureau, Orjonikidze was in charge of establishing an agreement with Kuchuk and, somewhat disappointed by his limited ambitions, he telegrammed the Commissariat of Foreign Affairs that Kuchuk Khan was not interested in establishing Soviet power in Iran. Orjonikidze further informed the Politburo that Kuchuk Khan's supporters hated communists and that there was no proletariat in Iran, making a real Soviet-style government impossible.[50]

Despite these ideological disparities, the Politburo and the Commissariat of Foreign Affairs saw a common goal between Kuchuk's Jangali movement and the Bolsheviks, that of wanting the British out of northern Iran. It was a solid enough basis for cooperation. When Kuchuk Khan heard about the Bolshevik arrival in Enzeli, he, together with his close collaborator Ekhsanulla Khan, left his his forest base and headed to the port city to negotiate with the Soviet representatives. Meeting aboard the steamship *Kursk*, Kuchuk spoke with Orjonikidze, Raskolnikov, and members of the *Adalat* (Justice) Party, the Iranian Communist Party based out of Baku. The *Adalat* sought to form a Revolutionary Committee that would be in charge of coordinating actions between the Bolsheviks and the Jangalis. The *Adalat* representatives distrusted and were openly hostile to Kuchuk Khan from the outset, making it clear that the organization would not willingly work with Kuchuk Khan, whom they considered bourgeois.[51]

In response, Orjonikidze returned to Baku and then sent Mdivani, a member of the Caucasus Bureau, to meet with Kuchuk Khan in place of the earlier *Adalat* representatives. Kuchuk and Mdivani quickly found they could work together, and upon the latter's return to Baku they formed the Iran Bureau of Communist Organizations (Iran Bureau). Members of this second Iran Communist Party included Anastas Mikoyan, Beso Lominadze, and Mdivani.[52] The Politburo, Caucasus Bureau, and Commissariat of Foreign Affairs all hoped that the Iran Bureau would act as a second Iran Communist Party, which would obey Moscow and cooperate with Kuchuk, unlike the *Adalat*.

After Kuchuk negotiated a deal with Orjonikidze on the *Kursk*, the Politburo ordered Raskolnikov to provide Kuchuk Khan with goods and instructors. On May 26, 1920, Raskolnikov was ordered to leave Enzeli and make sure any areas under Bolshevik control be passed to Kuchuk Khan. He finally departed on June 6 and, when leaving, made a public statement that the Soviet government did not wish to interfere in Iran's domestic affairs. He left behind enough troops, under the flag of independent Azerbaijan, to ensure Kuchuk Khan remained in charge of Enzeli.[53]

These two Communist parties in Iran, the *Adalat* and the Iran Bureau, were both based out of Baku and had close ties to the Russian Communist Party. The first party, the *Adalat*, was originally founded with the help of Narimanov and Sultan Majid Afandiyev as the Social Democrat Party of Iran (SDI).[54] The SDI was composed primarily of Iranian immigrants and workers who had experience in the oil fields of Baku. Its political program largely mirrored the leftist social democratic Muslim party the *Hummet*. During the First World War, the SDI became increasingly radicalized and more closely aligned itself with the Bolsheviks. A group of radical members of the SDI split off and formed the *Adalat* in 1916. The *Adalat* viewed the success of the Revolution in Russia as an important part of spreading the revolution to Iran. They actively organized and fought alongside Bolsheviks in the South Caucasus and set up party branches throughout Iran.[55] At a congress from June 23 to 25, 1920, about five weeks after Raskolnikov landed in Enzeli, the *Adalat* created the Iranian Communist Party (ICP), and thereafter the ICP and the *Adalat* were used interchangeably.[56] At this same conference, the *Adalat* was technically subsumed into the Russian Communist Party. In practice, however, the *Adalat* continued to pursue its own policies, namely that of a Communist revolution in Iran.

The second communist party, the Iran Bureau, like the Caucasus Bureau, was directly subordinate to the Central Committee of the Russian Communist Party. The Iran Bureau, together with Kuchuk's men, formed the Revolutionary Committee, mentioned earlier, to direct the Iranian revolution. The personnel of these various organizations overlapped, creating a complex bureaucratic tangle that was in constant flux. By the end of July 1920, the Iran Bureau was composed of Mdivani and Narimanov from the Caucasus Bureau, Lominadze and Mikoyan under the Central Committee of the Azerbaijan Communist Party, and Buniatzade and Aga-zade from the Central Committee of the Iran Communist Party.[57] In theory, each of these bureaus and parties were subordinate to the Central Committee of the Russian Communist Party and directly under Orjonikidze, although in practice this was virtually impossible to enforce. The conflicting interests of these parties—and the individuals backing them on both sides of the Araz river—would wreak havoc on any unified action.

A Revolution within a Revolution

Forming a coalition of sorts with the Bolsheviks, Kuchuk declared a Soviet Socialist Republic of Gilan on June 4, 1920, and the Soviets immediately began providing arms and training to the Jangalis. Kuchuk and the Bolsheviks departed for Resht to set up a new base, as the British retreated to the nearby city of Kazvin.[58] It was never clear who was in charge—Kuchuk Khan, the Iran Bureau, or the Bolsheviks. Kuchuk had to balance the demands of his erstwhile Bolshevik allies with those of local elites, mostly merchants who feared the Soviets. In addition, the more militant communist presence of the *Adalat* continued to disrupt Kuchuk's plans.

Within six weeks, the coalition fell apart and a radical faction of Bolsheviks, led by the Bolshevik Mikoyan, and a faction of the Jangalis, led by Ekhsanulla Khan and the Kurdish revolutionary Khalu Kurban, overthrew Kuchuk. On August 2, 1920, Mikoyan, in his capacity as a representative of the Azerbaijan CC to the Iran Bureau, sent a telegram to the Eastern Department of the Commissariat of Foreign Affairs in Moscow with the simple title, *Revolution in Persia*.[59] He reported that the night before they had carried out a coup in Enzeli and Resht, following which they took power. The Revolutionary Committee seized control of the entire province of Gilan. Mikoyan declared that among the goals of the Revolution were to form an Iranian Red Army and overthrow the Shah, to destroy feudal privileges, to help the peasantry, and to reestablish trade between Russia and Azerbaijan, which had come to a halt when the British consolidated a hold on northern Iran.[60] He stated that "Kuchuk turned out to be a spokesman for the merchants of Gilan. But the presence of his main forces, the Baku workers, Persians, Azerbaijanis, and sailors fueled the revolutionary movement."[61] Kuchuk, having had a falling out with Ekhsanulla, had already left for the forests outside of Resht on July 19 to lead his guerilla troops from there.[62]

Orjonikidze gave an abbreviated account of why the Bolsheviks had fallen out with Kuchuk—an inevitability that could not have surprised anyone. He noted first that Avetis Sultanzade's Iranian communists, the *Adalat*, were partly to blame for the uneasiness that developed between Kuchuk and the Bolsheviks. Sultanzade refused to cooperate with Kuchuk and sought to overthrow him.[63] Another point of contention was the treatment of Iranian merchants, whose goods were confiscated by the Azerbaijani government in Baku. These merchants were friendly with Kuchuk and an essential part of his power base. Nonetheless, the new Bolshevik government in Soviet Azerbaijan seized all goods at customs, including those of the Iranian merchants who formed part of Kuchuk's support network. The merchants pressured Kuchuk to force the Bolsheviks to return their confiscated goods, but to no avail. In Gilan, the merchants then began denouncing the Bolsheviks in public squares and at mosques. Kuchuk appeared at these meetings and promised those gathered that the Bolsheviks in Iran would not behave as they had in Baku. According to Orjonikidze, "Despite this announcement, something in the Baku-manner [*po bakinski*] ... nonetheless happened there."[64] In other words, the Bolsheviks used violence to requisition goods and foodstuffs in Gilan, exactly as Kuchuk feared they would. Orjonikidze continued that because the Soviets had brought two to three thousand people into Iran without Iranian, or any other currency, and no resources to procure food or other goods for them, they were forced to "impose a tribute on the merchants and knock the money out of them."[65]

Three weeks after Kuchuk was overthrown, on August 20, 1920, Mdivani attended a meeting of the Iran Bureau in Baku together with members from the Caucasus Bureau. Both Mdivani and Mikoyan wanted to use Russian Red Army troops to march on Tehran and overthrow the Shah. Mdivani argued a strong show of force would unite the peasantry behind the Bolsheviks. The members of the Iran — and the Caucasus Bureaus—nearly unanimously approved the proposal, with only one objection. After they ousted Kuchuk, however, popular sentiment swung sharply against the Bolsheviks throughout Gilan as it became increasingly clear that the new coalition of Ekhsanulla and the Baku Bolsheviks were pursuing their own agenda. The Baku Bolsheviks were multiethnic and were based in or connected to Baku prior to or during Russia's Civil War.[66] Some members of this group included Sergo Orjonikidze, Anastas Mikoyan, and Nariman Narimanov. Mikoyan, for example, was part of the Baku underground organization during the Russian Civil War. In 1919–20 he was chairman of the Baku Bureau of the Caucasian Regional Committee of the RCP(b), a member of the Caucasian Revolutionary Committee, and from May 1920 he was chairman of the Soviet of Trade Unions of Azerbaijan. Baku Bolshevik was also a term used for party members who were part of the Baku organization and pursued their own policies in defiance of Moscow's orders. This coalition of Bolsheviks also included Mdivani, and although he was based in Tiflis, he often worked closely with them.

A Comintern report later claimed that the Baku Bolshevik's actions in Iran had been so blatantly colonial that it would have been difficult for Moscow's enemies to have planned the situation better. The report also expressed concerns that irresponsible actions, such as overthrowing Kuchuk and seizing goods, would spark a holy war against Soviet power in the Caucasus and Turkestan, resulting in the loss of vital oil and cotton resources.[67]

The south Caucasian Bolsheviks, including Narimanov, Mikoyan, Mdivani, and Orjonikidze, continued to attempt to usurp the course of events in Gilan by reorganizing the leadership of the Iran Bureau. Worried about the growing influence of Sultanzade's *Adalat* and their own declining popularity in Iran, the Baku Bolsheviks used the First Congress of the Peoples' of the East to take advantage of the fact that representatives from all over Iran were in Baku. The congress was organized by the Comintern and held in the first week of September 1920 in Baku. During the congress, the Baku Bolsheviks created the Action and Propaganda Council in the East, which they hoped would push through their own policies on Iran.

The Action and Propaganda Council voted, under pressure from Narimanov and Orjonikidze, to form a new Central Committee of the Iran Bureau that was more in line with Azerbaijani Bolshevik policies and support Ekhsanulla's government. Narimanov pushed through his unpopular candidate Haidar Khan, who Iranian communists such as Sultanzade viewed as an amateur and adventurer.[68] The Azerbaijani Bolsheviks were the only ones who recognized this second Central Committee to the Iran Bureau. Neither the Politburo nor the ICP acknowledged the Baku Bolshevik's new Central Committee, leading to multiple power centers. The Politburo even ordered the Baku Bolshevik's to accept Sultanzade as a member of the Iran Bureau's Central Committee, acknowledging that the Azerbaijani Bolsheviks were unpopular in Iran.[69]

A Treaty with Iran, A Treaty with Great Britain

In spite of the plotting by the Baku Bolsheviks, the Commissariat of Foreign Affairs in Moscow set a goal "to liquidate Soviet survivals in Resht" after concluding that the revolutionary government of Ekhsanulla was a liability to both Soviet prestige and Soviet foreign policy.[70] The Commissariat of Foreign Affairs thus decided to abandon the revolution in Iran and the Gilan Republic as well as remove both Russian and Azerbaijani troops from Iran. Despite Moscow's intention to stop supporting the Gilan Republic by late 1920, it took until October 1921—and some rather dramatic political infighting and military bumbling—for Soviet troops to evacuate completely.

The Commissariat of Foreign Affairs' message of national self-determination was popular in the Near East as a voice against colonial oppression. In 1918, Trotsky renounced a series of secret agreements between tsarist Russia and England that had included the partition of Persia, Afghanistan, and the Ottoman Empire into spheres of influence. Trotsky also recognized the right to the political independence of each of those states, particularly from England. The deputy commissar of Foreign Affairs Karakhan reaffirmed Soviet Russia's position advocating the right of self-determination of Muslims in the Near East in a June 1919 note to the Iranian government.[71] By late 1920, however, the Commissariat of Foreign Affairs was seeking conciliation with Great Britain in the hopes of securing a trade agreement. The evacuation from Gilan has been framed as the exemplification of the abandonment of the Eastern policy, positioning the Congress of the Peoples' of the East held in September 1920 as the culmination rather than the beginning of formal Soviet endorsement of revolution abroad. But the Bolsheviks left Gilan because it was a fiasco and they had a state to secure, not because they had attenuated their radicalism.

Making it abundantly clear that events in Iran were far beyond the control of the Jangalis or Bolsheviks, the Iranian politicians Reza Khan and Aqa Seyyed Zia' od-Din Tabataba'i seized the capital on February 21, 1921, precluding the advance of Soviet troops to Tehran that had been planned by Orjonikidze and Narimanov. The situation again changed dramatically when Soviet Russia and the new Iranian government concluded the Russo-Persian Treaty of Friendship on February 26, 1921. This was followed not long after by the Anglo-Soviet Trade

Agreement signed on March 16, 1921. The histories of these two agreements were intertwined.

The Russo-Persian Treaty of Friendship formalized Soviet Russia's commitment to renounce tsarist-era concessions and privileges. It also stipulated that all Soviet troops leave Iranian territory, an aspect of the treaty that was not fully resolved until seven months after its ratification.[72] Despite Moscow's claims that the treaty was a complete break with tsarist-era policies, it contained two articles that would undermine Iranian sovereignty.[73] The first was Article 6, which gave the Soviet government the right to intervene in Iran if its territory were ever used as a base of attacks against Soviet power by a third party as it had been during the Russian Civil War. In the context of 1921, this was an assurance from the Iranian government that it would not allow England to use northern Iran as a staging ground for attacks on Azerbaijan or the Caucasus.[74] The second was Article 13, which stated that any concession relinquished by Soviet Russia could not be granted to a third party but must be owned and run by Iranian subjects or the Iranian government. The consequences of Article 13 played out in the competition among oil companies from the United States, Great Britain, and Russia over the former concessions.

The Russo-Persian Treaty of Friendship was followed within weeks by the March 16, 1921, Anglo-Soviet Trade Agreement. Negotiations between Soviet Russia and Great Britain had been stalled on two fronts: outstanding tsarist-era debt and hostile Soviet propaganda against Britain in Iran, Turkey, India, and Afghanistan. The British tied the conclusion of a trade deal to the cessation of Soviet propaganda in the East, something greatly complicated by the Soviet invasion of Gilan (not to mention Britain's own hostile stance toward Soviet Russia). The condition to cease hostile propaganda was a constant source of conflict between the commissariats. The Commissar of Foreign Trade, Leonid Krasin, negotiated the details of the Anglo-Soviet Trade Agreement. The Commissar of Foreign Affairs, Georgii Chicherin, however, argued that he, not Krasin, should be defining the terms of the agreement. Chicherin accused Krasin of making promises to the British on political matters and not strictly confining his discussions to economic affairs, a fine, and likely unrealistic, distinction.[75] As late as December 23, 1920, Chicherin wrote Lenin, expressing his fear that agreeing to a cessation of propaganda against the British before an actual agreement was signed—something Chicherin repeatedly accused Krasin of doing—would put Soviet Russia in the probable position of losing Baku to the British.[76]

Despite ongoing ideological differences, representatives from Soviet Russia and Great Britain signed the trade agreement. On the international stage, this signaled a new Soviet policy that favored foreign economic ties and domestic reconstruction over ideological politics. It also marked a shift by Western governments toward accepting the Bolshevik-led state on the international stage. While the Anglo-Soviet Trade Agreement did mark a shift it was not, as claimed by later its detractors, the cause of the pivot toward economic practicality over revolutionary zeal. The decision to seek pragmatic alliances had much more to do with the fact that the Civil War was winding down and the Soviets needed to consolidate power at home. Furthermore, Lenin, the Politburo, the Commissariat of Foreign Affairs, and the Commissariat of Foreign Trade had sought ties with Britain and other Western powers long before the actual signing of the trade agreement. They were also negotiating the Russo-Persian Treaty of Friendship, the terms of which the Bolsheviks, especially the Commissariat of Foreign Affairs, took seriously.

Many other factors coalesced in early 1921 that led to a shift in Eastern policy. Significant changes in the Near East, including the rise of Ataturk in Turkey and Reza Khan in Iran, combined with the desperate material state of the Soviet republics, the severe energy shortage, the need to get Baku's oil to market, and mounting famine all played a role. That this shift was also driven by domestic needs was clear in the Tenth Party Congress of March 1921, which introduced the NEP. The NEP included a policy allowing foreign concessions on Soviet territory as well as outlined the Soviet position on nationalities policy, two positions which came to loom large in the following years. At the time, however, many Azerbaijani Bolsheviks, foremost among them Narimanov, viewed the trade agreement with England and the simultaneous shift away from revolution in the Near East as an ideological betrayal.

A Betrayal in the East

Narimanov sharply disagreed with the Commissariat of Foreign Affairs' treatment of the Eastern question, which he argued was virtually ignored in favor of a fixation on Europe. He dismissed its policies as insincere and wrong-headed. Beginning in 1919, he urged Moscow to give greater attention to the Muslim East, which he argued was where questions of imperialism and colonialism would finally be decided. He advocated for an active policy in Iran and prodded his comrades to cooperate with Kuchuk Khan against the British. He had hoped that he would be able to shape policy after he was appointed to head the Commissariat of Foreign Affairs' Department of the Muslim Near

East but was quickly disillusioned when he realized that he was merely a policy advisor to Chicherin and would not be making policy himself, a consequence of Orjonikidze and Stalin's intervention with Lenin to keep Narimanov out of foreign policy.[77]

For Narimanov, larger questions about the future of the revolution in Russia and Azerbaijan could not be separated from policy in the East. He argued that the Commissariat of Foreign Affairs' position of compromise with Britain, which he interpreted as sacrificing Iran, was based on a fundamental misunderstanding of Muslim cultural and political traditions and practices.[78] Narimanov argued that it had only a superficial view of Muslims and simply did not take Muslims seriously as political actors and revolutionaries. Narimanov, as a seasoned revolutionary and organizer, obviously disagreed with the assessment. Most importantly, he argued that Muslims had no institutional place in the Soviet government and were edged out of shaping policies in the East. Speaking as the head of the Department of the Muslim Near East, Narimanov argued that Soviet foreign policy should not treat the Eastern policy separate from its policies with the West. Somewhat incongruously, he also argued that he should be considered a full member of the Commissariat of Foreign Affairs and in charge of policy *because* the Eastern policy was part of policy toward England.[79] Understanding the bias of his audience, he still validated the importance of the Eastern policy's worth through its relationship to the West.

Narimanov noted that the surest way to bring revolution to Europe was by undermining the economic base of England—the Near East. He argued that the British connected lifting the economic blockade against the Bolsheviks to an evacuation of Gilan "mainly to distract our attention from the East in general and in particular, from Persia."[80] Narimanov viewed these policies in his characteristically Manichean way: either trade with the West or carry out Eastern policy.[81] He did not think they could do both, and he argued that the Bolsheviks were capitulating. He believed that a stronger policy in Iran would give them more leverage against Britain in the long run. He had expressed such views earlier as well. In early 1920, he wrote to Lenin in frustration noting that if Moscow was prepared to sacrifice the rest of Azerbaijan to Denikin in order to secure oil reserves in Baku, then it would be at the cost of having an Eastern policy.[82] Narimanov held that Soviet support for the revolutionaries in Iran was just a bargaining chip for Russian foreign policy with the British.[83] He was not wrong in practice, but his perspective differed dramatically from that of Fedor Aronovich Rotshtein, the Soviet representative to Iran.

Evacuating Gilan

Rotshtein was a journalist and historian who had spent thirty years in England prior to his return to Russia in the summer of 1920. The Commissariat of Foreign Affairs appointed him Soviet Russia's representative to Iran on November 15, 1920, and recognized as such by the Iranian government on January 10, 1921. Rotshtein was an expert on British expansion in the Near East, fluent in English, and he had petitioned for a position abroad, finding conditions in Moscow difficult. He had wanted to go to Sweden, not Iran.[84] Rotshtein departed for Tehran via Turkestan after the Russo-Persian Treaty of Friendship was signed on February 26, 1921. He was turned away at the Iranian border because the Soviets had still not withdrawn troops from Gilan, however. After a several-week delay, Rotshtein and his entourage were allowed to enter Iran, and they arrived in Tehran in late April.[85]

A later report by the Information Department of the Comintern's Action and Propaganda Council pinned responsibility for the more brazen proposals, such as the desire to sack Tehran and capture the Shah, on Orjonikidze and attempted to distance overall Soviet policies from these schemes. But it noted the main reason Soviet troops were withdrawn from Gilan was to abide by the terms of the treaty signed with the Iranian government.[86] Conditions in Gilan had deteriorated, and the only active troops in Gilan were Russian and Azerbaijani—the Red Army had completely lost contact with local Iranian revolutionaries, presumably after Kuchuk fled to the forests of Resht. It was time to let the Iranians take over the revolution. They saw little choice but to evacuate. As Soviet popularity plummeted, rumors of forced disarmament, looting, and general intrigue surrounding the evacuation nearly led to armed confrontation between the Red Army and the inhabitants of Gilan. In conclusion, the report cautioned that Moscow and Baku needed to "seriously reflect [*podumat'*] on the level of revolutionary consciousness of the troops in Persia."[87]

The situation was even more tenuous than the report outlined. Two months before, on May 6, 1921, the People's Commissar for the Military and Navy for Soviet Azerbaijan, Ali Heydar Qarayev, and the chief of staff of the 11th Army, Alexander Remezov, ordered the disbandment of the Iranian army, but Orjonikidze—issuing verbal orders—countermanded the order immediately before leaving Baku for Moscow. Rotshtein denounced Orjonikidze as a criminal when he found out about the order; he accused Orjonikidze of "fanaticism" and of interfering with orders from the Commissariat of Foreign Affairs.[88] Indeed, the contradictory orders led to further uncertainty as rumors spread that, with the withdrawal of Soviet troops, the radical left faction of the Gilan revolutionaries would kill the Iranian revolutionaries who had sided with Kuchuk. Minor skirmishes broke out over the next few days and discipline largely evaporated. On May 17 and 18 in Moscow, the Politburo confirmed that Soviet troops should evacuate Gilan as soon as possible. The Politburo noted that Soviet troops were destabilizing the situation as antiforeign sentiment increased in Iran.

On May 20, the Politburo's Central Committee ordered the Red Army to evacuate Gilan. A week later, the Central Committee also ordered that the Iranian army, formed by the Baku Bolsheviks, be evacuated to Baku together with Soviet troops.[89] Despite these orders, the evacuation did not begin until the beginning of June. Reports from Gilan, in what became known as the July events, chronicled looting and significant desertion by the Azerbaijani troops, many of whom preferred to join Kuchuk Khan in the forest than return to Soviet Azerbaijan and face possible starvation as the bread shortage continued throughout the Caucasus.

When news reached Chicherin that Soviet troops were deserting en masse, he sent Orjonikidze a frantic telegram warning him to evacuate before the entire army melted away. There would be scandal if they defected to Kuchuk. He asserted, "No one will believe us that this was done without our consent. It will compromise us, undermine our relationship with Persia, ruin the treaty, play into the hands of England and lead to her troops returning to Tehran."[90] Despite Chicherin's warning some troops remained in Enzeli, waiting for evacuation to Soviet Azerbaijan.

While the Bolsheviks began the evacuation of Gilan, Rotshtein became embroiled in negotiations between different factions of Iranian politicians and revolutionaries. He had developed a relationship with Reza Khan as well.[91] By September, Rotshtein was deeply invested in the power struggle among Kuchuk, Ekhsanulla, Haidar and Khalu Kurban. As Soviet troops evacuated Gilan over the summer of 1921, Reza Khan and his troops were reasserting control from Tehran over the northern provinces.[92] Reza Khan arrived in Resht to quell Kuchuk Khan's uprising, altering the power dynamic once again. Immediately upon Reza's arrival in Gilan, Khalu Kurban abandoned his negotiations with Rotshtein and joined Reza Khan. Khalu Kurban went to Reza Khan and "presented him [Reza] his mauser with both hands. Riza-Khan returned his mauser together with a Colonel's stripes."[93] With Khalu Kurban now working with Reza Khan, the Soviet endeavor carried even less weight.

Reza Khan successfully concluded separate agreements with other local notables throughout the north, including the leader of the Talysh,

Zargam-us-Saltane, and various Kurdish leaders. To entice local tribal leaders to help put down Kuchuk Khan's rebellion, Reza Khan offered both amnesty and bribes. Once Reza was in Gilan, Rotshtein also sought negotiations with him. Rotshtein sent his advisor comrade Khavin to Resht to meet with Reza Khan and negotiate a guarantee of amnesty for local Iranians who had been fighting alongside Kuchuk Khan in Gilan, which Reza Khan granted.[94] In fact, Reza Khan was directly involved in the Soviet evacuation. As preparations to evacuate Kuchuk's supporters to Baku from Enzeli were underway, Azerbaijani troops that had been stationed in Enzeli since May 1920 began causing serious unrest because they had not received their salaries for months.[95] Further, the Azerbaijani troops demanded that they be returned to Baku as soon as possible. The Bolsheviks on the ground proved incapable of handling the situation, and it was Reza Khan who resolved the disorder, preventing the chaos Rotshtein had feared.

To facilitate the Soviet withdrawal and calm the increasingly anxious Soviet troops, Reza Khan paid Soviet Azerbaijani troops their back salaries. He formed a troika that consisted of Khalu Kurban, who acted as his proxy, a representative from the Azerbaijani consul, and a representative from disaffected Azerbaijani troops. Each troop boarded one of Reza Khan's steamers, surrendered his weapon, received his salary, and was then transferred to a new ship to depart for Baku.[96]

In total, approximately 3,500 people took advantage of the amnesty and fled north. On October 20, 1921, the remaining Soviet troops finally departed. When Kuchuk Khan learned of Khalu Kurban's new position, he and his men attacked Resht. Kuchuk's troops lost, and he once again returned to the forests, eventually heading to the Khalkhal mountains (where Khalu's men served as guides). Kuchuk and his companion Gauk died of frostbite after being caught in a snowstorm. A local man found their bodies after the storm, and Kuchuk's head was severed. Khalu Kurban delivered it to Reza on December 10, 1921.[97]

The occupation of Gilan was a disaster for the Commissariat of Foreign Affairs and revealed how little control Moscow had over the Baku Bolsheviks in 1920–1. The Baku Bolsheviks, including Narimanov, Orjonikidze, Mikoyan, and Mdivani, drew on their prerevolutionary connections in northern Iran and sought to incorporate Gilan into the Soviet sphere. To extract themselves from their entanglement in Iranian politics, the Commissariat of Foreign Affairs and the Baku Bolsheviks had to rely on Reza Khan. The mess of Gilan demonstrated another point to the Commissariat of Foreign Affairs and Moscow: it needed to centralize power and subordinate the Baku Bolsheviks.

Dissention within the Ranks

Interests both within and beyond the borders of Gilan persuaded the Politburo to change course in Iran and abandon support for Kuchuk Khan's revolution. Although Soviet Azerbaijan was fully allied with Soviet Russia and many members of the Azerbaijan Communist Party were also members of the Russian Communist Party, on the matter of revolution in Iran the Azerbaijani leadership disagreed sharply with Moscow. For the Baku Bolsheviks, revolution in Iran was linked directly to the success of the revolution in Azerbaijan.

The Baku Bolsheviks defied orders to disband, promoted revolution, and directed Iranian troops without permission.[98] Narimanov, Orjonikidze, Mikoyan, and Mdivani undermined decrees from both the Politburo and the Commissariat of Foreign Affairs time and again. Even after the Politburo agreed that Rotshtein should follow a policy of "scrupulous non-interference" in Iranian alliances, Azerbaijani representatives in Enzeli refused to follow his orders "and openly worked against [his] policies."[99] Mikoyan overthrew Kuchuk Khan, Orjonikidze worked with Ekhsanulla and wanted to kidnap the Shah, and Narimanov kept funneling weapons to Kuchuk after Rotshtein's orders not to take sides. This was not just simple adventurism but a consequence of the fact that many Bolsheviks in the Caucasus had a vision of the revolution that was informed by local circumstances, and it differed significantly from Moscow's understanding of the situation.

After the evacuation of Enzeli, Lenin took Rotshtein to task for not following the policy of noninterference to the letter, but reports to Chicherin reveal a beleaguered diplomat unable to reign in the persistent recalcitrance of two of the most prominent Bolsheviks in the Caucasus: Orjonikidze and Narimanov. Rotshtein argued that Orjonikidze was blinded by his friendships with Ekhsanulla and Khalu Kurban as he continued to smuggle Soviet funds and materiel to them after the Politburo ordered Orjonikidze to stop funding the revolutionaries. Rotshtein was incredulous that Orjonikidze could fail so absolutely to see the bigger picture, noting, "I acknowledge that I absolutely do not understand how it is possible to irresponsibly sabotage our huge game of chess against our English partners. It is really possible that comrade Orjonikidze doesn't see the unsuitability, I would say the worthlessness of these people."[100]

As an advisor to Rotshtein in Iran, D. Gopner sent updates to Chicherin at the Commissariat of Foreign Affairs. In a letter written on November 4, 1921, Gopner addressed allegations that Rotshtein disobeyed directives from the Politburo and the Commissariat of Foreign Affairs by hindering the activities of the Gilan partisans. Echoing Rotshtein, Gopner redirected Chicherin's attention to Orjonikidze and Narimanov. Gopner noted that "from all corners of Baku and Enzeli traces of activity by the Bakuvians on behalf of the partisans stand out. The only difference is that Orzhenididze [sic] is supporting Ekhsanulla Khan's 'communist' faction at the moment, and Narimanov, the 'democratic' faction of Kuchuk Khan, whom they earlier supported together."[101]

Gopner implied that Moscow was partly to blame because the Commissariat of Foreign Affairs knew that the Gilan Republic did not have wide support and was "at all times completely established and maintained by Caucasian workers/ Medevani [sic], Orzhenikidze [sic], and others/. The Caucasian comrades acted during a period of the intensive expansion of our borders, during a period of revolutionary war on all fronts."[102] They had been sent to Iran to push the British out and secure the region as a rear base for Baku. But everyone knew they had their own agendas. Insistence on party discipline was not enough to control the Baku Bolsheviks. He recommended that the Caucasian workers be replaced as there was no one around with enough influence to curb the "activism" of the Baku members.

Gopner was not arguing that the activism of Orjonikidze and Narimanov was difficult to understand. Rather, he was arguing that different jobs required different personnel. The transition from the wartime tactics to which the Bolsheviks were accustomed to a peacetime policy of conciliation was a shift that Gopner imagined would cause problems throughout the former Russian Empire.[103] That a peacetime government should have different goals than a government at war touches on one of the most fundamental aspects of Soviet governance. Rather than demilitarizing the government, the Bolshevik government militarized its interactions with civilian society. The 1920s Soviet Union became an era of fronts to be stormed, borders to be crossed, and enemies to be vanquished.

Rotshtein assumed he had Moscow's full support in "taming the obstinate Bakuvians," and his reports to Chicherin revealed his deep frustration with Soviet policies and Moscow's inability to control these prominent communists in the Caucasus. He did not see how he was supposed to fulfill his duties with men like Kuchuk Khan or his supporters. Nor did he trust Orjonikidze or Narimanov. While preparing to evacuate Enzeli, Rotshtein noted that he chose Astrakhan as a place to send insurgents over Baku because, even considering the famine in the Volga, Rotshtein "had absolutely no confidence in Baku, where the refugees could be reorganized and rearmed for quasi-revolutionary activities in Gilan." He complained that "our Caucasian comrades" did not follow orders and he had no expectation that they would.[104]

Moscow, Rotshtein asserted, had made the proper decision in abandoning Kuchuk Khan and any additional support of insurgent khans or revolutionary uprisings would serve only to weaken the Soviet position. He wanted to know why the Soviets decided to "tamper about" in Iran in the first place and what, if any, interest they had in Iran

> What would we even care of Persia if the English weren't here, of general intrigue and uncovering the intent of our enemies? Who laid the guardianship of the Iranian people at our feet, the mission to free them from feudalism, Shahism, capitalism and other evils? In general, I don't understand why we should be more interested in Persia than in say, some Guatemala, or in some Timbuktu? … I suspect and am even convinced that this imperialistic instinct lives in our Bakuvian and, even partly in our Tashkent, [comrades].[105]

As a Soviet representative, Rotshtein viewed his task as limited to the eradication of British influence from the north, not in transforming Iran. This view combined a patronizing dismissal of Iran with a sincere desire to curb imperialist policies, as he saw it.

Chicherin was sympathetic to Rotshtein's account of what happened in Enzeli and was aware of the problems that the Baku comrades were causing. He repeatedly questioned the wisdom of establishing an Iran Bureau made up of Caucasians and Russian Iranians when a Iranian Communist Party already existed.[106] He wrote a letter to Lenin defending Rotshtein's actions in obtaining amnesty for the rebels; the front fell apart because it could not maintain itself without Soviet support, not because Rotshtein was supporting the Shah's army, Chicherin asserted.[107] Rotshtein achieved the goals laid out for him by the Politburo and Commissariat of Foreign Affairs in Iran: to undermine British hegemony. Any more joint projects with rebels, such as Orjonikidze proposed, could "lead to the collapse of Rotshtein's policies and to the return of the British."[108]

In contrast to Rotshtein, Narimanov argued that the evacuation of Gilan was a concession to the British after the Anglo-Soviet Trade Agreement of March 16, 1921. The trade deal with Britain was unquestionably an important consideration, but not the only one. Chicherin and the Commissariat of Foreign Affairs sought to show the world that Soviet Russia was strong, while hiding the fact that it had largely lost control of its troops in Gilan (not to mention that it even had troops in Gilan). Narimanov, whose own power base was weakened considerably by abandoning revolution in the East, ignored the fact that the Bolsheviks had no popular support among the population in Gilan and that developments in Iran were heading in a different direction with the rise of Reza Khan. While Narimanov was correct that some Bolsheviks, especially in the Commissariat of Foreign Trade, were perfectly happy to trade revolution in Iran for a trade deal with the British, the situation was not as clear cut as he would have preferred.

From Moscow's view, and from the view of the Commissariat of Foreign Affairs, the main purpose of Soviet policy in Iran was to ensure the safety of the Caucasus—especially Baku and its oil—from a possible British invasion. By early 1921, Bolshevik policy had successfully cleared the Caspian of the British presence, restarted oil shipments, established Soviet power in Armenia, and was well on its way to taking Georgia.

In order to pacify the newly acquired Caucasian territories, Soviet Russia had to feed and supply them, which required trade agreements, ideally with wealthier states like Britain. The increasing power of Reza Khan and the near-complete failure of the Baku Bolsheviks to foment revolution across Iran coincided with Britain's decreasing interest in the region. Taken together, this meant that the Soviets had little incentive to remain in Iran, Narimanov's protests aside.

These intra-party conflicts spilled over into Iran in no small part because in the local imagining the security and success of the revolution included Iran. For Narimanov, the abandonment of revolution in Iran, made formal in the 1921 treaties with Iran and Great Britain and Lenin's announcement of Peaceful Coexistence, was not only a betrayal of Eastern policy but of his personal power.

When the Bolsheviks took Baku, they saw an opening in Iran, but for Moscow it was always opportunistic. They coupled the military necessity to seize the warships and tankers in Enzeli with the political agenda of spreading communist revolution to the East. The Commissariat of Foreign Affairs in Moscow hoped an alliance with the populist anti-British revolutionary leader Mirza Kuchuk Khan would push the British out and possibly lead to a wider revolution against the Shah. It cautiously allowed the Caucasus Bureau to pursue revolution in Iran because it would have been a propaganda victory, not because it ever considered Iran essential to the Bolshevik revolution.

The gamble in Gilan did not pay off, but it unequivocally showed Moscow that the Baku comrades had their own agendas and that securing the South Caucasus, and its resources, would require asserting more control over the region. It re-enforced the need to keep control of foreign policy firmly in Moscow's hands. From now on, the Baku Bolsheviks, including Orjonikidze and Narimanov, would have to defer to central policy in foreign affairs if they wanted to stay in Moscow's favor. To do this, Azerbaijan, Georgia, and Armenia needed to be bound more tightly together and then in turn bound to Moscow. Bolshevism was a revolutionary movement, not a governing party, and the transition was messy. The real questions centered on who ultimately got to decide what the revolution meant, what those meanings were, and how they changed over time. Whomever was able to marshal the resources to give those meanings currency, would be successful. In this round, it was not the Baku Bolsheviks.

3

Bolsheviks on the World Stage: Soviet Concessions Policy and the Oil Question

The radical American journalist Anna Louise Strong traveled to the Soviet Union in 1923 to witness the Soviet project firsthand. On her journey to the USSR, she visited Baku, Azerbaijan—Russia's primary source of oil and noted, "I have spent two weeks in Baku. It is desolate, and fascinating as hell." She observed that Baku was "an industrial oil city, modern, mechanical, ruthless. In it live children orphaned by famine, and veiled women of the East, and men, Russians and Tartars [sic] and Persians and Armenians and the tribes of Central Asia who have not yet learned to read and write but who can produce oil for rebuilding a nation."[1] Strong visited Baku at a tumultuous time when the city, and the oil industry, were still recovering from years of war and occupations. In early 1923, Baku was a relatively well-known city because it had been in international headlines for the past year in connection with the Genoa Conference. As the *New York Times* reported, "Baku has literally moved to Genoa, and Azerbaijan has been put on the map for diplomats who formerly had little idea where that republic on the Caspian was located."[2] Indeed, the Soviet leadership firmly viewed the Bolsheviks as participants in the international quest for oil.

The Genoa Conference convened in the spring of 1922 to reestablish economic relations and resolve outstanding claims between Soviet Russia, Germany, and Western Europe following the conclusion of the First World War.[3] The Supreme Allied Council established the basic agenda for the conference in the Cannes Resolution of January 6, 1922, which stipulated that Soviet Russia recognize all debts and obligations of the Russian Empire and Provisional Government in exchange for the reestablishment of full diplomatic recognition and the extension of loans to the Bolsheviks for reconstruction. This included compensation for the nationalization of private property, such as oil companies, after the 1917 Bolshevik Revolution. The Soviets likewise sought compensation for Allied interference in the Russian Civil War.

While different worldviews on private property and nationalization were obstacles to an agreement from the beginning, two events defined the conference. Soviet Russia sent shockwaves through Genoa when it concluded the Treaty of Rapallo on April 16 establishing diplomatic and trade relations with the then pariah state of Germany.[4] A few weeks later on May 3, 1922, the *New York Times* reported an inaccurate rumor that Soviet Russia had concluded an oil concession with Shell further upending negotiations.[5] The first ignited the ire of Britain and France, the second prompted denunciations from Britain, France, and the United States. Shortly thereafter, the German and then the Soviet delegation rejected Allied (French) demands for the restoration of private property. The conference thus came to an ignominious end with an agreement that negotiations would be resumed in June 1922 in the Hague.[6]

Disentangling Genoa from Rapallo and the failure to conclude agreements makes a few things clear beyond the conference's importance to international relations. Reviving the oil industry was essential to the economy and security of the new Soviet state. But the official pursuit of concessions provoked strong opposition at home. This chapter argues that the prospect of appearing on the world stage forced the Bolsheviks to confront a number of fraught domestic questions—about foreign participation in the Soviet project, economic reconstruction, the structure of the energy sector, and the political status of the ostensibly independent Soviet republics of Azerbaijan, Armenia, Georgia, and Ukraine—that they had been able to postpone until that point. In Azerbaijan, the prospect of giving away Baku's oil to outsiders sparked a debate about who was most able to make decisions about the industry—oil specialists, local communists, or diplomats in Moscow. The failure of Genoa left these questions unresolved, but through the process the Bolsheviks learned another lesson. Informal backroom channels, with both governments and businesses, was a more productive way to conduct foreign policy than official diplomatic conferences.

Russia's oil industry dominated the conference despite its absence on the formal agenda, and offering oil concessions was pivotal to the overarching Bolshevik strategy.[7] Initially, the Bolsheviks believed that success at Genoa hinged on negotiating wide-ranging concessions. In a typical concession, a foreign company contracts directly with a host country to exploit a region or resource using the company's equipment and capital. In exchange, the company reaps the profits, and the host country taxes those profits. But the Soviets used the term concession more broadly and considered joint ventures between foreign firms and the Soviet government to be a form of concession. It also considered technical assistance, or technology transfer contracts, a form of concession, and it pursued all three types.[8]

The Soviet delegation arrived in Italy with expansive plans for concessions in the fuel and mining sectors of the economy, focused on Baku, Grozny, and the Donbas region. A year earlier, at the Tenth Party Congress, Lenin had invited former owners—capitalist oil magnates—to begin negotiations for the exploitation of Soviet oil, and he hoped to realize this goal at the conference. What potential concessionaires didn't know was that Baku's oil industry was teetering on infrastructural collapse throughout 1920–1. When Genoa was announced in early 1922, amidst a major famine, the situation in the oil fields was critical. The former owners, based in Britain, France, and the United States, lobbied ceaselessly to undermine the normalization of relations with the Soviet republics. They organized economic boycotts of Soviet oil and other products abroad. They pursued legal recompense in courts abroad making would-be concessionaires think twice before agreeing to do business with the Bolsheviks. But behind the scenes they were ready to talk.

Soviet Oil after the War

The importance of oil to war-making, to the economy, and to wielding power was as clear to statesmen as it was to oilmen by the end of the First World War. Recently established British control over vast territories in the Middle East (Mesopotamia) believed to contain oil deposits, combined with new open-door policies in the United States that saw American-owned companies like Standard Oil of New Jersey (Standard) and Sinclair cross the oceans in search of new markets, dramatically shifted the political and economic landscape by introducing new competitors.[9] The Bolsheviks wanted to leverage oil's potential to bring in profits and foreign capital. They saw the fight over Soviet oil within the framework of a global competition to control reserves. Genoa was preoccupied by the oil question—who would control it and who would reap the profits of a rebuilt Baku?

Before the conference began, former owners asserted a series of claims and counterclaims over shares that had been lost to Bolshevik nationalization, engaged in backroom deals, and proposed strategies to recover losses and regain control of Soviet oil in Baku and Grozny.[10] Foremost among those with claims or interests were Royal Dutch Shell, Standard, and the Anglo-Persian Oil

Company. Royal Dutch Shell had the largest claim against the Soviet Union as it had purchased 80 percent of the Rothschild's shares in the years leading up to the world war. Standard, meanwhile, purchased all of the Nobel Brother's shares in 1920. This claim was far more dubious than Shell's because Nobel sold its shares to Standard *after* the Bolshevik nationalization of Baku's oil in spring 1920 and the deal was clearly predicated on the assumption that the Communist government would be overthrown in short order. Anglo-Persian's interest was more indirect but no less insistent.[11]

These companies and governments were often competing for control over potential deposits, not already productive fields. Outside of the former Russian Empire, France and Britain concluded an agreement in April 1920 known as the San Remo Agreement. Under the agreement, France would receive 25 percent of the oil produced in British-controlled Mesopotamia (Mosul) through the Turkish Petroleum Company.[12] Although the announcement of the San Remo Agreement initially outraged both US oil companies and the US government, Standard Oil and Anglo-Persian reached a joint agreement in relation to northern Iran before Genoa.[13] In 1922, no major oil reserves had been discovered in these locations—Mosul or northern Iran—and these ventures were highly speculative. The relevance of guaranteed oil reserves in Baku and Grozny, in comparison to the then undiscovered reserves in the Middle East, were therefore extremely attractive.

The Soviet position going into Genoa was informed by the Russian State Planning Committee's (later, State Planning Committee USSR: Gosplan) understanding of the global oil market. As Gosplan—the advisory committee that coordinated economic plans—viewed the situation, the United States drove the market for petroleum products. It argued that the rapid growth of American domestic consumption, which was virtually guaranteed with the expansion of the personal automobile, would outpace extraction, and that the United States would become an importer nation in the near future.[14] The assumption was that increased US extraction, with its corresponding declining reserves, would force the United States abroad in search of new reserves, putting it in conflict with Shell and the British, something already evidenced in Mesopotamia.[15] Gosplan predicted that this would put Soviet Russia in an advantageous position by creating an outlet for Russian oil products and also playing the companies off one another.[16] It concluded that the increased demand for oil products would mean a "bitter global struggle for oil" that would lead to limited supplies and high prices.[17] Gosplan understood this and asserted that "the value of our oil wealth is so great and the race for the fields will be so energetic that the oil industry is one of our biggest trump cards in the international game."[18] Soviet domestic growth and development, diplomatic overtures to normalize relations with the West, and re-integration into the international economy were thus inextricably linked. At the center of these projects was oil.

Western oil companies hoped to create a united front against Soviet Russia at Genoa with the aim of pressuring Russia into a general settlement on nationalized private property. Competition among them hindered any possible unity, however. Lenin was counting on these rifts. He observed that the war over reserves and emerging markets between Shell and Standard was intense enough that Standard would enter into a concession with the Soviets exclusively to push Shell out of the market.[19] Unofficial meetings between oil representatives and Soviet delegates took place, both leading up to and throughout the conference, giving the Soviets cause to believe a deal might be possible.[20]

Lenin's view was representative of a fundamental problem going into Genoa: the Western powers and the Soviet delegation were essentially preparing for two completely different conferences. The oilmen and their various backers busied themselves with sorting out who had a legitimate claim to what territories, while the Soviets were proceeding from the premise that nationalization of these industries was nonnegotiable.[21] This disconnect characterized the preparations for the conference and persisted beyond the conference itself.

Preparing for Closer Scrutiny

After the Soviets accepted the invitation in the Cannes Resolution, the Commissariat of Foreign Affairs formed the Preparatory Commission to develop materials for the Soviet representatives to the conference on major positions, including diplomatic recognition, loans, compensation for former industrialists/owners, credit, and technical questions. The commission was housed within Gosplan, which determined losses, by industry, incurred by the Soviet government due to Western intervention in the Civil War. Gosplan was responsible for compiling technical information and offering expertise on a range of topics, but its role was advisory and it was not in charge of formulating policy. Lenin was the nominal head of the Soviet delegation, but the Commissar of Foreign Affairs, Georgii Chicherin, who served as the deputy head, was in charge of organizing the delegation and actually attended the conference. Chicherin had leeway to make decisions for the delegation on a day-to-day basis at the congress, but policy remained firmly in the hands of the party apparatus, the Politburo.[22]

Initial protocols noted several goals the Soviet government hoped to accomplish before the conference began, including the conclusion of an economic agreement with Germany, which it hoped would stipulate compensation for Brest-Litovsk in return for a refusal to recognize the Treaty of Versailles.[23] Another pressing question was the legal status of the other Soviet republics, which remained in limbo. Ultimately, the USSR was not formed until December 1922 and included the Russian Soviet Federated Socialist Republic (RSFSR), the Transcaucasian Republic (Armenia, Azerbaijan, Georgia), the Ukrainian SSR, the Belorussian SSR, the Far Eastern Republic, and the People's Republics of Bukhara and Khorezm. In the period between the end of the Civil War and the creation of the USSR, the status of the other Soviet republics was ambiguous and fiercely debated. Chicherin asserted that "by the time the conference begins it is desirable to carry out the federation of all the fraternal Republics and include them in the RSFSR [Russian Soviet Federated Socialist Republic]. Formal close-union ties with the FER [Far Eastern Republic] is also desirable, although its sovietization is premature."[24] When one of the Italian delegates inquired about whether the Russians would be representing the allied republics, Chicherin wrote to the Politburo informing them that they had to have some sort of answer soon.[25]

How to formalize the relationship between the RSFSR and the other Soviet republics remained unclear, but there was certainly no agreement that they should be directly incorporated into the RSFSR. In terms of the conference, the RSFSR had no legal mandate to negotiate on behalf of the nominally independent republics and achieving any concrete results at the conference would be virtually impossible if they were not legally bound to one another. Chicherin wrote to Viachislav Molotov at the Politburo that the "question of the inclusion of the fraternal republics into the RSFSR before the conference" was a matter of extreme importance because concluding several parallel treaties would only create confusion and complications. Chicherin argued, likely correctly, that that international situation was such that their swift incorporation into the RSFSR would not cause serious problems on the world stage and it was in the interests of Soviet Russia "to present to the Great Powers with a fait accompli."[26] This was easier said than done, of course. To give just one example, he was concerned that including Bukhara and Kiva in the RSFSR would make them look like imperialists and make things very difficult for the Soviets in Tashkent, where he worried that Muslim nationalism would undermine Soviet power.

Regardless of what Chicherin and the Commissariat of Foreign Affairs hoped, the incorporation of the republics into the RSFSR, either directly or through a confederation, would be impossible to organize in three short

Figure 3.1 Georgii Chicherin and Nariman Narimanov, 1922.

months. But Moscow's campaign to unify the three South Caucasus republics Armenia, Azerbaijan, and Georgia was in full swing. During this period, Sergo Orjonikidze, the head of Caucasus Bureau, aggressively pushed for the unification of the republics based largely on economic needs. Chief among those needs was the imperative to get Baku's oil to the international market through Georgia's port in Batumi. This required unification of the railroads and the foreign trade between the republics, a precondition to formal unification, which took place just in time for the Genoa Conference in March 1922 as the Federative Union of Soviet Socialist Republics of Transcaucasia.[27] The exact role of the conference in pushing for unification and confederation, either as catalyst or determinate, remains somewhat unclear, but it indisputably served as a pressure point, accelerating the discussions about what form unification should take and how the republics should interact with foreign powers. The need to come to a concrete conclusion was largely obviated when they realized they could appoint delegates from the republics—Narimanov for Azerbaijan, Mdivani for Georgia, and Aleksandr Bekzadian for Armenia. Despite their presence, they were part of the Soviet delegation and did not take part in negotiations independently of Russia (see Figures 3.1 and 3.2).

Figure 3.2 Narimanov, Mdivani, Bekzadian, 1922.

Chicherin had a keen sense that the image the Bolsheviks portrayed would be as important to the success of the conference as the technical details. He was particularly anxious about controlling the flow of information in the Soviet press about the actual state of the economy leading up to the conference. On January 12, days after the commission was formed, he wrote to Lenin and urged him to prevent articles like one that had recently appeared in *Ekonomicheskaia zhizn'*, openly admitting that 50 percent of Soviet enterprises had closed, plans were left unfilled, and that the domestic market was shrinking. He cautioned, "Excessive frankness about our devastation worsens our international position" and "seriously strengthens" the position of their opponents in the upcoming negotiations. It would be best, he argued, if the press were told to be careful about what it writes, and that Soviet economists be given instructions about how to answer questions to ensure that they take into consideration Soviet Russia's international interests.[28] Delegates were instructed to never disagree with one another in front of others and always show discipline.[29] Chicherin wanted all aspects of the Soviet presentation to the outside world to be monitored to the extent possible, likely fueling the credibility problem he was seeking to address.

He was also monitoring foreign press coverage leading up to Genoa and was concerned that the international community was not taking Soviet Russia seriously as a business partner. Chicherin asked the Politburo to instruct the Soviet delegation that the Genoa Conference was an economic venue and not to be used as a platform for Soviet propaganda or as a "revolutionary tribunal for agitation."[30] Chicherin cautioned it needed to look at the situation "as Marxists and as realists" and understand that there were direct negative consequences in the realm of trade to successful Soviet propaganda campaigns abroad. He noted, for example, that the US press had largely ignored the Bolsheviks until large labor strikes convinced the right that communism was a real danger. Likewise, in Britain, Soviet trade delegations were viewed with suspicion when British labor movements were strong. Chicherin reminded the Politburo that it had already decided to maintain a distinct separation between the Soviet government (the Commissariat of Foreign Affairs) and the activities of the Comintern, "The Soviet government defends the political and economic interests of the laboring masses of Russia." By implication, not the toiling masses of the world, "If, going into Genoa, we forget this strict division we will put in jeopardy all of our economic achievements that make up the tasks of the moment."[31] He compared Genoa and the question of concessions to the decision to sign the Treaty of Brest-Litovsk. At Brest, the Bolsheviks had to choose between refusing to compromise with Germany and perishing because of their own intransigence or falling back and continuing the revolution. At Genoa, he argued, they faced a similar dilemma—allow the economy to collapse or enter into an agreement "for the sake of maintaining the political power of the proletariat."[32] Other tasks, he emphasized, must not interfere with Genoa. The main goal of the Soviet delegation must be "to find an acceptable middle line between the demands of the Entente and our demands. The aim of our trip must be this kind of deal."[33]

Despite his initial optimism, Chicherin increasingly understood that economic incentives would not be enough to persuade European governments of Russia's goodwill. He explained to his fellow comrades that no matter how tempting their offerings to the European powers, "if the table covered with goodies is in a predatory lair then no one will go there because they will be sure that they will be robbed or killed there."[34] He insisted that brash statements and uncompromising nationalization would not win them any allies, or business deals. He told them that they had to stop scaring concessionaires and act more approachable. Essentially, he was arguing that the Soviet delegation needed to professionalize to gain trust and credibility. In addition to being revolutionary communists, the members also needed to be diplomats and learn to tailor their language, their clothing, and their demeanors to satisfy their capitalist counterparts and reach a deal on reconstruction.

Leonid Krasin and Soviet Capitalist Joint Stock Companies

As the Soviet delegation prepared for negotiations over leasing Baku's oil to foreign interests, it was still trying to get a handle on actual conditions on the ground. During the tsarist period, hundreds of small companies had conducted their own surveys of wells, and each kept the results secret from its competitors. This vital information became state property with the nationalization of the industry in 1920, but many of the company records and archives had burned, or were intentionally burned, during the Soviet invasion. The result was that "in the hands of the geologists there were only a comparatively small amount of data on drilling wells, their condition, on their productivity etc."[35] Until autumn 1921, the collection of data on individual wells had been completely dependent on the participation and cooperation of workers in the fields who would gather information and relay it to the geologists. The clearest message coming from the fields was that the oil industry was suffering from crippling material and personnel shortages. To improve conditions in the fields and understand what was happening on the ground, the Soviet of Labor and Defense formed a commission in late 1921 to investigate the state of the individual wells. The commission found extensive flooding that threatened the prospects of restarting production.[36] Going into Genoa, Moscow was highly skeptical of the prospects of Baku recovering on its own.

To avert a potential disaster, stop flooding, and boost recovery, Leonid Krasin, the Commissar of Foreign Trade and member of the Soviet delegation, proposed joint ventures between foreign capitalists and the Soviet government in the energy sector. He prepared a detailed proposal that served as the basis for talks at the Genoa Conference and convinced Chicherin, and most importantly Lenin, that concessions were the surest way to ensure recovery of the industry. The economists within Gosplan countered that they could turn the industry around without foreign help, but Krasin dismissed these predictions as unrealistically optimistic. The ruination of the energy base was too thorough and complex to save without serious outside assistance (see Figure 3.3).

Krasin outlined his position in a report marked top secret to the Central Committee of the Politburo, submitted on March 1922. He argued that the energy sector was fundamentally different from the other sectors of the economy,

Figure 3.3 Leonid Krasin.

"In our current economic situation, in the absence of organized knowledge and competency, it is vital that we save our fuel industry by any means necessary as the basis of our entire industry and transportation system."[37] He continued that, unlike other sectors of the economy, which could grant concessions on an individual basis, they had to approach the energy sector as an indivisible economic unit. The consolidation of oil fields and elimination of previous company boundaries under nationalization fundamentally altered the landscape of the oil fields, both literally in their exploitation and figuratively through their combined administration. During the imperial period, the oil fields in Baku were a veritable patchwork of ownership, with noncontiguous wells spread out over large distances and cross-sectioned with plots from other owners and businesses.[38] Consolidation of the plots allowed for centralized administration. Reconstituting previous borders, as former owners and potential future concessionaires wanted, would seriously cripple any broader reconstruction efforts. Any interested concessionaires would therefore have to accept the new administrative units as a precondition for an agreement.

According to Krasin, he never entertained the proposition of returning the enterprises to their former owners, which in his opinion would not have worked in any case. The coal and oil industries relied on an integrated infrastructure of production and transport that was no longer functional. If the Nobels, the prerevolutionary magnates of Baku's oil industry, returned to the fields, they would find their wells seeped with water, little to no electricity, and roads and pipelines in desperate need of repair. The Donbas was in a similar state and "not even its [the Soviet powers] most bitter enemies can deny the reality that, in these industries, all concepts of ownership have been hopelessly confused and all boundaries erased."[39]

The Soviets were not willing to negotiate over nationalization, but they were willing to negotiate over foreign participation in industry. As one historian has argued, the Soviets were willing to negotiate in the oil sector because "oil was the most readily available source of desperately needed revenue for the new regime, but it could not be sold worldwide without a proper distribution network." Those networks held titles to expropriated lands and sought to prevent the Soviet government from entering the international market. "Soviet oil had to pass through the Dardanelles. Turkey lay in the hands of the capitalist Allies, and the Soviets had to consider that the commercial antagonism of Standard Oil and Royal-Dutch Shell could translate into an oil blockade at this geographic chokepoint."[40] Much like the Bolsheviks had found themselves at the mercy of geography in the Caucasus—bound to the existing infrastructure of rail lines and pipelines—domestic policy was also constrained by the international structure of the oil industry.

Adding a further consideration, Krasin's plan was based on the thesis that "nationalized oil should help rebuild the nationalized coal industry."[41] The recovery of the coal and oil industries were treated as interdependent processes. Profits from oil exports could theoretically be reinvested in the more economically precarious business of coal extraction. In this context, coal was synonymous with the Donbas in Ukraine, and oil was, of course, synonymous with Baku. Of the two, oil was in a more favorable position for development because there was demand on the international market and, if managed properly, oil could be exported. The situation with coal, however, was more challenging because the market, both domestic and international, was less certain. Krasin pointed out that "if some wizard suddenly, magically, gave the hundreds of millions of necessary rubles for the recovery of the coal enterprises, the question is then how and where to dispose of the coal?"[42] Soviet industry had not recovered to the point that it would even be able to use the coal, or export it. He did not see how they would reap any profit relative to the amount of capital that they would have to invest to rebuild the Donbas. The Soviet industrial base could not support the coal industry, he asserted, nor could the railroads, and the government did not have the resources to subsidize it.

Krasin's solution was for the oil industry to subsidize the coal industry and facilitate its reconstruction. He advocated consuming the absolute minimum oil possible for domestic needs and exporting the remainder. Oil scarcity, the argument went, would create a domestic market for coal, and because coal burned more inefficiently than oil, a greater amount of coal would be necessary, that is, for the 200 million poods (24,009,603 barrels) of oil exported, 350 million poods (4,375,000 tons) of coal would have to be produced. He went so far as to advocate that Soviet Russia should intentionally convert more efficient oil-based machinery and engines *back* to less efficient coal to create an outlet and a stable state market for the coal produced in the Donbas.[43] Further, because oil sold at a much higher price than coal, the 200 poods (24,009,603 barrels) of oil sold abroad would more than pay for the 350 poods (4,375,000 tons) of coal coming from the Donbas.

This broader position—to favor coal over oil domestically, and to slate oil as a commodity for foreign exchange rather than domestic consumption—had lasting consequences for the energy system of the Soviet Union.[44] Railroads, factories, and electric stations were reconverted to coal and hydroelectric power while oil was exported. The Soviet turn to coal after the First World War, largely dismissed as wrong-headed, was heavily informed by the need for the industrial base to recover cheaply and quickly while providing a much-needed market for the coal industry, which would not be competitive on the international market. Krasin's arguments dovetailed with the then popular belief that *all* countries of the world were on the verge of running out of oil and if Russia saved its reserves for future use, it would be the only one with any oil left at all.[45] This belief was encouraged by the fact that many major oil fields had not yet been discovered in Texas, California, or the Middle East. One of the biggest proponents of this view was the prominent thermal engineer Leonid Ramzin (later arrested in the fabricated Industrial Trial) who was working on the electrification plan in the early 1920s. Taking this further, he asserted that the Soviet Union did not even need to look for new sources of oil because they would not find anything. His conclusion was that "the basic source of energy for the next 200 years will be coal."[46] Krasin emphasized this point again at Genoa, noting that the export value of oil was the only hope of saving the Donbas.[47]

Krasin doubted that Soviet administrative and technical bodies could rebuild the energy base. Nor was he convinced that international capital, for example, potential investors, had any faith in Soviet know-how or Soviet capability to use money effectively even if loans or other resources were granted for reconstruction. He saw little other choice, however. The first assumption proved to be untrue, but the second was well-founded. To overcome disputes about ownership and Soviet counter claims vis-à-vis Western interests for intervention in the Russian Civil War, he proposed the formation of joint trusts between Soviet owned enterprises and international capital. He argued that once former owners understood the extent to which the war uprooted and rendered unrecognizable the oil and coal industries, they would see that the Soviet government could not honor its claims even if it wanted to. Misjudging rather badly the entrenched position of the former owners, Krasin expressed readiness to grant compensation without any discussion of a return of titles.[48]

In this plan, the Soviet government, and likely Krasin himself, would have been responsible for working out the details of the proposed compensation. The foreign participants in the combined trusts would be responsible for bringing in new capital—machinery, in particular. Krasin argued that the benefits reaped by both sides would prove far more profitable than a simple return of property, a prospect Krasin hoped would guarantee participation of the former owners and mollify calls to return their enterprises. The Soviet government, for its part, would own a percentage of the shares and be guaranteed a part of the profits, the output, or a combination thereof.

Krasin conceded that the actual administration of the trusts would be trickier. Although the Soviet government would own the fields, the ultimate administration would be "in the hands of representatives of capital." This carried with it some danger, namely that the capitalists could sabotage the recovery of the Soviet economy. But, he said, "One must, finally, at some point acknowledge that in terms of managing production outstanding revolutionaries and eminent experts and theoreticians of communism turned out to be somewhat unfit masters."[49] Relying on the practicality of Western businessmen, he asserted that they would not waste the time and capital required to do real work in the coal and oil industries only to sabotage their own efforts and profits. Given the proper surveillance and precautions—using the trade unions and local militias—any threats or intrigues by the capitalists could be controlled. If it came to such a serious situation as war, the Soviet government could simply take over the administration of the trusts, exactly what former owners feared.

Krasin hoped the proposal would be compelling but was unsure whether Western capitalists would accept the conditions. He pointed to the continued "distrust of the professional qualities of Soviet power" among potential takers. He counted on the prospects of significant profits and a share of the Russian market as sufficient incentive, not to mention that reestablishing the industrial base of the former Russian Empire would allow the Soviets to fulfill early debt obligations. The organizational and legal questions were a hurdle and Standard, Shell, and Royal Dutch were notoriously combative among themselves. These "global plunderers" would have to be balanced against each other by granting concessions to multiple trusts in both the Don basin and the oil regions. For example, "British participation in one of Grozny's trusts would require from them a formal renunciation of claims to the Baku region so that it would be possible to attract American or French participation in the Baku trust without interfering with the British."[50] The Commission for the Preparation of the Genoa Conference (as the Preparatory Commission was renamed) debated Krasin's proposal and adopted his position on March 16, 1922, with the added condition that the Entente powers officially recognize the nationalization of Soviet industries.[51]

The condition tied Krasin's plan to the overall outcome of the conference. This restricted his ability to make guarantees to foreign companies or conclude agreements that did not explicitly acknowledge the official Soviet position. The exact reasons for the addition of the condition are unclear, but it may have indicated a hesitancy to endorse Krasin's plan fully, or, possibly, an overconfidence in the Soviet position going into Genoa.

Reactions to Krasin's plan were mixed. It would be tempting to argue that positions broke down into ideological positions versus pragmatic solutions driven by economic expediency, but those distinctions are not clear cut. The goal of the Bolsheviks was to retain political power, and Krasin presented his proposal as the surest way to do this. Some of his comrades disagreed, not because Krasin's proposal was not ideologically sound but because they did not think his plan would work. Despite four out of five votes in favor of Krasin's scheme (Maxim Litvinov, Chicherin's deputy, abstained) there were some reservations. Evgenii Preobrazhenskii, the economist and soon to be member of the Left Opposition, objected that the entire policy of concessions could not be solved "only in relation to Baku and the Donbas."[52] He noted that the Central Committee remained skeptical of Krasin's plan and argued that Krasin had not proven that granting concessions in Baku would facilitate the reconstruction of the Donbas. Andrei M. Lezhava, the trade representative to the Soviet of Labor and Defense, was also hesitant to back Krasin, and asked the Politburo to reconsider its support for the proposal. Although it sounded good, Lezhava noted, it was not achievable because Krasin had provided no concrete evidence.

Litvinov, Chicherin's deputy, also had reservations and was correctly concerned that not directly addressing the question of ownership from the beginning would cause confusion. He advocated coming to the table with a clear refusal to recognize the rights of former owners and to propose the concessions in that context. Chicherin, in contrast, was a staunch supporter of Krasin's view on concessions. By late February, he was convinced that the Soviet economy, and in particular major branches of industry, would not be able to recover without the help of foreign capital.[53] He was confident going into the conference that the Soviet government would be able to negotiate some form of capital, even if it was not the ideal amount of investment. Acutely aware of the problem of loans and former owners, Chicherin was convinced that Krasin's plan was the most likely to succeed in persuading former owners to participate in these industries and/or placate them enough so that others would be able to participate.[54] Krasin's proposal for joint Soviet-capitalist trusts was presented as the only reasonable option available, despite a steady flow of information from Baku arguing for another approach altogether.

Gosplan Objects

The possibility of foreign concessions on Soviet territory, especially in such essential areas as coal and oil, was met with fierce resistance from within the Bolshevik Party and from geologists on the ground. This backlash resulted in a campaign from within Gosplan, and from Baku Bolsheviks, to counter Krasin's plan and seek to minimize foreign interference in the Soviet project.

In January 1922, Gleb Krzhizhanovskii, chairman of the Soviet of Labor and Defense, submitted a report to the Politburo titled, "Why We Should not Offer the Industrial Regions of Baku or Grozny for Concessions."[55] His report laid out major objections, detailed further on, of the Gosplan economists and geologists. Foremost, he argued that because oil is one of the fundamental sources of energy—both in its raw and in multiple refined forms—it must "be completely and indivisibly under the control of the government."[56] It was irresponsible, he argued, to allow capital, particularly foreign capital, to have a controlling interest in such a resource. He further argued that the trusts should be allowed access to their profits and then the industry could fund its own reconstruction. These points became standard objections to official concessions policy.

Gosplan argued that Soviet Russia could handle the situation itself. According to the report, the oil industry was the most profitable sector of the economy, and as such, it could feed, clothe, and supply the 50,000 workers and their families attached to the industry. It could also, in the form of a loan floated on gold or refined petroleum products, replace outdated equipment. The second major objection was that concessions would prohibit the Soviet government from gaining any profit from the oil industry in the short term. The report claimed, rightly as it turned out, that the industry required a recovery period of at least four to five years to return even to prewar levels of production. Concessions would mean that the Soviet government would be sending any profits to foreign companies rather than reinvesting it in the industry and building the Soviet economy. Concessions were also viewed as untenable because when the Bolsheviks nationalized the oil industry, they eliminated the patchwork system of individual plots and consolidated the fields into large individually administered units, thus allowing Soviet geologists and engineers to restructure the process of drilling and refining.

There was a clear argument coming out of Gosplan that concessions in oil and coal would be an infectious political element. Concessions "[are] the introduction, in the form of one strong or forgotten wedge or in the form of overlapping ownership, a thorn in our economic body around which there will be a permanent festering."[57] Krzhizhanovskii warned the Politburo that it was, in his estimation, forgetting the fierce global competition for oil resources currently underway. This objection was firmly ideological. Concessionaires may have been interested in profits, but they would not have a vested interest in aiding the Russian economy. A strong Russian economy would have propped up the Bolshevik government and thus run directly counter to the interests of international capital. Discounting Krasin's argument that foreign capitalists would protect the Soviet economy by protecting their investments, Gosplan worried that foreign oil companies could use concessions to undermine Soviet control of its own resources. Standard Oil and the Shell group had millions of barrels of oil at their disposal, "What interest does our 300 million pood [36,014,405 barrels] offer? But the contested point about the future domination of Baku and Grozny is of interest to them."[58]

Krzhizhanovskii pointed to past experience as a warning. In the tsarist period, he argued, the industrialist plundered the fields. Krzhizhanovskii laid the blame for the dire state of the industry at their feet: "The current threat of flooding in our oil regions is the heavy legacy of past rule by capitalists. It is hard to believe that the capitalists will come to us with new methods of work. They were predators and that is how they remain."[59] This was only partially true. The heavy machinery and infrastructure of the fields were outdated for over a decade by the time the Bolsheviks took the fields. But mismanagement of the oil industry by the Bolsheviks, particularly in 1920, harmed production, alienated specialists, and exacerbated flooding.

Ivan Strizhov and Alternate Futures

One of the Gosplan strategists in charge of formulating the Soviet position within the confines of official policy was the geologist Ivan Nikolaevich Strizhov. Before the Revolution, Strizhov worked in the oil industry, primarily in Grozny in the North Caucasus. He was a respected geologist who was sympathetic to ideas of planning and centralized administration. In the Russian Empire, only mining engineers or those with extensive technical backgrounds could act as administrators in the oil fields, and Strizhov was one of these experts. After having served in multiple posts, he participated in the Administration of the Caucasus Mining Okrug and was appointed head of the oil industry in Grozny. After the Bolsheviks came to power, he worked as an engineer at the trust in Grozny, Grozneft. Soon after, he was sent to Moscow to work as deputy chair and then as chair of the Production and Technical Department of the Main Oil Committee. From Main Oil Committee he was promoted to the Main Fuel Administration, and by February 1924, he was appointed director of the Baku Oil Industry, where he was ordered to help boost production. He worked from Moscow and coordinated with Serebrovskii, who worked from Baku. In 1926, he was promoted again to senior director of the Oil Industry at the Supreme Soviet of the Economy of the USSR.[60]

In early 1922, Strizhov authored much of the Gosplan material on the oil industry submitted to the Preparatory Commission. He wrote a report in February 1922, "Oil Business. Mistakes of the Past and Signposts for the Future," to give the conference delegates a clear understanding of the history of the industry and a sense of the macro-organizational problems confronting the oil business.[61] Baku's oil industry, he began, had existed for fifty years and Grozny's for thirty years. During this period, the shortcomings of the established system became clear, and while oilmen accumulated a great deal of knowledge, they made many mistakes. He argued that the engineers and geologists did not manage the wells rationally and that the industry did not meet its obligations before the state. The oil industry could have corrected some of the inefficiencies, he emphasized repeatedly, *gradually*, but the Revolution rendered this evolutionary process moot. Now, he said, they have a "cleared ground on which they can build new buildings." The mistakes of the past, he asserted, would not be in vain.[62]

Strizhov belonged to a cohort of professionals in the early Soviet Union, among them scientists, theorists, and revolutionaries, who viewed the sciences as something to be rationally planned and directed by the state. They argued that the exploitation of natural resources and the mechanization of labor would be most productive and beneficial for society when centralized. This view regarded the state as an engine of historical progress and believed that working through the state would contribute to progress. Planning and the rationalization of productive forces, as they were termed, played a major role in the making of the Soviet Union.[63] For Strizhov, first identifying inefficiencies and pinpointing ways of correcting them was the key to the rationalization and reconstruction of the oil industry.

In his initial report, Strizhov outlined a litany of past mistakes made in the exploitation of oil and the issues he believed the Soviets must address for recovery to be successful. He complained of fierce competition between companies for contiguous plots that resulted in excessive derricks along the boundaries of plots. There had been insufficient mining regulation from the state and unsatisfactory provisioning of fire safety in industrial areas resulting in burning fountains and significant losses, both of oil and human lives.[64] The other problems he highlighted were broader in scope. He pointed to a lack of initial capital investment from companies—a problem that was easily connected to Krasin's plan to bring in capitalist investors. Most important to him was the lack of scientific and technical know-how among geologists and the absence of higher training. Geologists had not surveyed much of the country, and those parts that had been surveyed would likely need to be reexamined because geological methods were technologically undeveloped.

The solution, for Strizhov, was clear. State control of oil would mean that the oil industry would be obligated to put oil to good use. The industry must be planned and it must be in the hands of the state, "I think that the oil industry is the type of branch that in particular/by its very nature [*preimushchestvu*] demands a plan that takes many years ahead into account, the kind of branch that must be a unified state industry, and must be built according to a specific, complete plan."[65] The alternative would be a jumble of competing interests.

In addition to providing the Preparatory Commission with a clear understanding of the state of the oil industry, Strizhov also submitted a lengthy commentary against the official line on concessions policy in oil. He argued that inviting foreign companies into the industry was short-sighted. He acknowledged that flooding was a serious problem and that nearly 3,000 of 3,650 wells were currently inoperable.[66] The question then was how to fix the problem and who was going to fix it. The industry had faced a similar situation in 1905 and 1906 when the fields were burned and largely destroyed during the so-called Armeno-Tatar War—a conflict in the South Caucasus primarily between the Armenian and Muslim populations.[67] In fact, flooding was never resolved, even fifteen years after the unrest. Instead, private companies "just moved to the wells that were easiest. They just expanded and found new wells leaving the old ones in disrepair because it wasn't profitable." He emphasized, "State interest did not lie with the duties of private firms. No one compelled them to do it [fix the wells] and they didn't do it themselves because it wasn't profitable."[68]

He cautioned that the Soviets had to learn from this experience or face the consequences in the form of a stagnating industry. They needed to restore drilling in the fields, but in the final reckoning they could not depend on private capital to take the overall development of the Soviet state into account because their primary motive was profit. Instead, the state must take the initiative. In 1905–6, he argued, the state stood by and left the recovery of the industry up to private capital, a mistake that loomed large fifteen years on, "Thus, the struggle with the flooding of the oil fields was, is, and must be a problem for the state ... I think that the struggle with flooding is a difficult struggle that we will inevitably have to lead, that we will have to put in the hands of the state because otherwise it will be a ruined business."[69]

Thus, Strizhov located deeper roots to the flooding crisis. The problem was not exclusively a result of the Russian Civil War and foreign invasions. Nor were the problems only the result of harsh Soviet policies in the fields, although the aforementioned issues certainly exacerbated existing shortcomings. The crisis in the oil industry, according to Strizhov, was built into the fields from their inception and lay in the structure of the industry, in the disorderly arrangement of derricks, the placement of factories, and the incentive to abandon damaged property.

He argued that he had dealt with flooding in 1905 and could deal with it again. He had direct experience working with foreign owners and knew them to be unreliable in general. He positioned the geologists and the engineers as laborers in opposition to capitalists "if those at the top side with defenders of the concessions and decide to give oil concessions to foreigners then the state will still have to vigorously follow these problems." He implied that oil concessions would not work and that it would be left to specialists—loyal to the state—to fix the problems.

Binding the Periphery

Where he located the state was also very clear. Refined products, which were intended for use by the centralized state, should be manufactured in Russia proper, not the periphery where they were extracted. The production of subsidiary goods and the concentration of refining products on site only cluttered the fields. He explicitly named the imperial power dynamics between Baku and Moscow and asserted that Azerbaijan had to be bound to Russia. In an explicitly colonial argument, he asserted that Soviet Azerbaijan should be stripped of its control of Baku's oil, not only through a series of treaties, as it already was, but by physically dismantling the infrastructure of the oil industry and binding Azerbaijan to Russia irrevocably:

> We need to respect the interests of the center and ensure that the regions have no advantage and would not be able to live a complete, independent industrial life. The regions must be dependent on the center. Only the fact that Baku, in addition to the oil fields, also has refineries, chemical factories, machine-building factories, cotton factories, cable factories, and various other sorts of production, not only for the oil business but for other industrial life, allowed Baku to tear itself away from the State and for a short time to live as an independent state.[70]

He understood that the oil industry had the potential to form a power base outside of the direct control of Moscow and he argued that it should be prevented from ever developing. He saw Azerbaijan's brief independence as evidence that the infrastructure built to support the industry could also support a separate state under the right conditions. If Moscow wanted to control Azerbaijan, it had to control the oil industry. He concluded, "We have to make it so the regions cannot live without the state for even a minute. Therefore Baku should only extract oil and refining it should be done in the Center of Russia, and everything that is necessary for Baku's oil industry, all of the pipes, cables, sulfuric acid, belts, etc.—all of it should be produced in RUSSIA."[71] He astutely understood the intertwinement of state power and the extraction and production of petroleum products. As it turned out, he understood the implications of leaving the infrastructure intact far better than policymakers.

Strizhov's advice to dismantle the industry's infrastructure did not become policy, but his views were not singular and the drive to subordinate and bind the periphery was not necessarily based in Bolshevik ideology as much as technocratic utopianism and extractive colonialism. From 1918 to 1924, the Bolsheviks, in partnership with prewar experts such as Strizhov, advocated for competing paradigms to structure the new Soviet state, one based on nationality and one based on economic expediency. Gosplan pushed for the economic paradigm that would have divided the state into economic-administrative districts based on local "productive forces." In this vision, the Caucasus would have been a region structured around the procurement of oil and valuable minerals. It was envisioned as one economic unit, the arguments also laid out by Sergo Orjonikidze and Iosif Stalin in the push to unify the railroads and economy of the South Caucasus. Despite the outward primacy of the national model, the result was actually more of a series of compromises between the two, and the needs of the oil industry did shape policy.[72]

Offering his opinion on concessions policy and the structure of the industry, however, was not Strizhov's main task on the commission. He could state his objections, but he did not make policy. Instead, he needed to articulate a position for the Soviet delegates to present at the Genoa Conference that would win over hostile European powers. His strategy was to frame Russia's reconstruction as the source of European economic recovery. Strizhov, and other uncited authors, laid out this line of argumentation in a Gosplan report "The Role of Russia in Global Fuel Supply." First, Gosplan argued that Europe, and England in particular, needed Russia to buy its coal. If England helped increase Russia's purchasing power, it would be guaranteeing a market for England in the process, and it was thus in everyone's best interest to rebuild the Russian energy sector. Russian and European interests would also be served through an exchange of this coal for Russia's oil and its products. More specifically, by "exporting its oil through southern ports, Russia would be able to supply the needs of the Mediterranean coast; conversely, England could supply north-west Russia with its coal."[73] This plan would limit transportation costs for both Russia and England and, hopefully, lead to lower costs for the global economy.

To push the point further, the report asserted Russia's historical role as the "natural" owner of Europe's oil; because Europe was dramatically increasing its use of the internal combustion engine and the diesel engine, it would need Russia's oil more than ever. "Russia, in the interests of the entire global economy, should export oil, replacing it at home with coal. This replacement will be beneficial for Russia because in giving 1 pood of oil she receives in exchange 2–3 times more per caloric value of coal."[74]

The entire world economy, Gosplan argued, was now dependent on oil, and if Europe wanted it to function, it would have to help Russia. Mechanical engineering was weakly developed in Soviet Russia, and it would need a significant amount of new technology in the energy sector to get the oil industry running reliably. Europe, it argued, had just as much of a stake in the transfer of this technology as Russia did.

Soviet delegates presented the case that Europe was dependent on Russia, and Gosplan echoed a similar line of reasoning. For Soviet Russia, the first priority was to reestablish agriculture to alleviate famine, then, in order of importance, was fuel, transport, and metals. The nature of the fuel sector, Gosplan argued, meant that it had to be developed at a pace outstripping the other sectors of industry. This was necessary because other sectors of the economy needed fuel to function and because the economy needed the benefits of export [currency and coal] that renewed production would bring.[75] The oil industry was singled out as the most important sector to target for recovery because costs, they believed, could be recovered quickly and export of oil products would bring in hard currency. The Donbas "was in second place," or more accurately, "almost equal to oil" in priority for recovery, particularly because of its transport connections with Moscow.[76]

Gosplan—through Strizhov's reports—formulated a worldview that asserted the interconnectedness of Russia's domestic recovery to the global energy market. In this view, Baku's oil was integral to Russia, Russia was integral to the reconstruction of Europe, and Russia relied on Europe as a market for Russian petroleum products. But Strizhov's reports to Gosplan went further than this and envisioned a strong centralized state that could harness the capacity of Azerbaijan's, now Russia's, oil in the name of establishing a rational, planned economy.

Objections from the Fields

There was also a concerted campaign from Azerbaijan to undermine granting foreign firms access to Baku's oil. Foremost among those resistant to Krasin and Lenin's concession policy were several influential Baku-based Bolsheviks—Sergei Kirov, Aleksandr Serebrovskii, and Orjonikidze. The Baku Bolsheviks were supported from Moscow by the prominent geologists Ivan Gubkin, and Strizhov.[77] Positing the argument that the oil sector was too important to entrust to foreign capitalists, they set out to prevent the realization of Krasin's plan for Baku. Inherent in this objection were also security concerns. Fear of British encroachment remained strong throughout the first half of the 1920s. The Bolsheviks in Baku sought to thwart Krasin by advocating to keep oil under Soviet control and by concluding an independent agreement with the American oil company the International Barnsdall Corporation. With an eye attentively focused on Europe and the United States, as well as on Shell and Standard, they sought to show the capitalist West, and the Soviet leadership, that Soviet engineers were just as capable as capitalist engineers.

Lenin was aware of the opposition to concessions from within the party and, alarmed, he did not let the issue pass. On April 2, 1921, on the heels of a major strike in the fields, Lenin sent Serebrovskii a letter instructing him to ensure full cooperation from Baku on the concessions policy: "It is extremely important that the Baku comrades grasp the *correct* (and approved by the Tenth Party Congress, that is, *mandatory* for members of the party) view on concessions" (emphases in original). That is, at least one quarter of Baku's oil fields would be leased through concessions. Ignoring the reality of the situation would only lead them to ruin. He continued,

> If in Baku you still have traces (even little ones) of the dangerous views and superstitions (among workers and among the intelligentsia), write me immediately: can you take care to break these prejudices completely and achieve loyal behavior according to the decision of the congress (on concessions) or do you need my help? ... There is nothing more dangerous and deadly to communism than a communist boasting "we can do it ourselves."[78]

Referencing the Tenth Party Congress and the ban on factions, Lenin insisted that Serebrovskii bring the Baku Bolsheviks into line, making it clear that disagreement over the concessions policy could lead to accusations of factionalism and would not be countenanced.[79] Despite the warning, Serebrovskii had the means to undermine Lenin's hard line on concessions through the Azneft's right to conclude contracts directly (also granted by Lenin to facilitate the industry's recovery). In October 1921, Serebrovskii, as head of Azneft, and the International Barnsdall Corporation, a US company, concluded an agreement whereby the American company would provide expertise and equipment to Azneft in Baku in exchange for oil and other petroleum products.[80] This is an important detail. The agreement was not signed by the Soviet government but by Serebrovskii and Azneft and brokered through the Main Oil Committee.

Antony Sutton's classic study on technology transfer argued that the Barnsdall agreement effectively reversed Baku's decline.[81] He chronicled an impressive turnaround in the early Soviet oil industry, showing the importance of new extraction technology, particularly rotary drilling and deep well pumps, to this revitalization. In his view, naïve Western businessmen were duped by Soviet disingenuousness into investing large amounts of capital only to be unceremoniously escorted out from the Soviet Union.[82] Russian historians offer a more measured assessment of the Barnsdall contract, noting that the agreement was significant but Soviet specialists still had to figure out how to manage the collapsing fields.[83]

According to Serebrovskii, the Barnsdall contract was an effort by himself, Kirov, and Gubkin to obstruct concessions as envisioned by Krasin. Instead of sweeping concessions, they pushed for limited technical assistance contracts. They hoped to show that the equipment and technical exchange would demonstrate that concessions were an unnecessary risk and keep control of Baku's oil in their hands.[84] Kirov was involved in the oil industry beginning with "his management of Caspian smuggling in the summer of 1919 to his battles to ensure adequate shipment of fuel to Leningrad in the early 1930s."[85] Lenin and the Politburo assigned Kirov to Baku in large part to assist Serebrovskii in the recovery of the fields.[86] Kirov, through extensive conversations with Serebrovskii and Gubkin, became convinced that concessions in Baku needed to be blocked.[87] He was one of the main sources of political clout behind the opposition while Gubkin and Strizhov provided the scientific grounding. When Kirov arrived in Baku in July 1921, he immersed himself in the details of the oil industry, spending significant time with Serebrovskii and Gubkin. He was a quick convert to the idea that rotary drilling and deep vacuums needed to be introduced in Baku (something that could only be done with foreign equipment), and Serebrovskii viewed his support of these innovations as equivalent to support for Azneft.[88]

The Barnsdall concession, initially signed in October 1921, was a contract for the exchange of knowledge and equipment for oil. The contract was strictly for technology transfer, drilling, and technical training. There were no rights of long-term land use, extraterritoriality, or other privileges often associated with concessions. The Soviets, however, called it as a concession, and it has thus retained the name in the secondary literature. According to this agreement, Barnsdall provided and installed equipment for rotary drilling and deep well pumping and then instructed Soviet oil experts and workers on their use.[89] The deal was made in some secrecy because there was speculation in the foreign press that the Barnsdall Corporation would be exploiting wells claimed by other companies. The claim was true.[90] This was particularly sensitive in the context of Genoa, where former owners were attentively following possible oil deals. In fact, Krasin was meeting the Barnsdall representative Mason Day during the conference, no doubt fostering rumors.[91]

At the Genoa Conference

As Barnsdall began drilling in Baku, the political and economic issues surrounding oil concessions were being debated and fought over in the international arena as thirty-four nations convened in Italy for the Genoa Conference from April 1 to May 19, 1922. The Bolsheviks desperately wanted a deal on concessions and had prepared extensive documentation on the hopes of concluding a deal. Despite the fact that Chicherin and the delegation sought "an acceptable middle line" between Russia's interests and those of the other European powers, he was preoccupied with trying to manage the terms of a possible break.[92] He knew that if Soviet Russia did not grant reparations for nationalized property, an agreement was unlikely, and therefore an early end to the conference was a probable outcome.[93] He emphasized that the Soviet delegation should do as much as possible to make it clear that they were willing to make a deal with the capitalist countries if such a break appeared to be imminent. That way they could salvage separate deals after the conference.

Just as during the preparatory phase, Chicherin was in regular contact with the Politburo and sent updates, concerns, and requests for clarification on policy positions. He also remained intent on managing Russia's image by managing what the Soviet press published. Controlling the flow of information was complicated by the distance between Genoa and Moscow, something Chicherin feared from the beginning. In mid-March, Chicherin sent a telegram to Molotov chastising him for an article published in *Pravda* that stated unequivocal Soviet positions on loan repayment and former owners. He noted, "If the article had been shown to us, in particular to comrade Ioffe, such a violation of orders would not have been tolerated."[94] He expressed his frustration that Central Committee directives were not being followed and asked Molotov to see to the situation.

Beyond wider political issues—such as diplomatic recognition and settling debts—there were more mundane problems preventing the Soviets from concluding successful negotiations at the conference, including internal divisions. The delegation was caught off guard by the informal style of negotiations, which were often in small groups, and could not agree on a counterstrategy. Rakovskii, the delegate from Ukraine, rejected absolutely the idea that Chicherin accept an invitation from Lloyd George (the British representative and architect of the conference) for a private meeting: "Personally, and as a delegate and member of the Central Committee I cannot agree to the most important questions being decided behind closed doors, face to face with Lloyd George."[95] Chicherin countered that this was "nonsense" and a refusal to participate would be grounds for the Western powers to call off the conference, and he attended the meetings regardless.[96]

The most significant obstacle for the Soviet delegation on a day-to-day level was that it had to wait for the Central Committee to send directives before it could proceed. Litvinov admitted that while the Soviets claimed they could not carry out negotiations on debts because the Western powers had not made their positions on Soviet counterclaims known, it was actually because they had not made up their minds on the details and did not have explicit instructions on how to proceed.[97]

Soviet Russia expended significant energy on Genoa, fearing that it faced economic collapse without outside assistance, and the delegation scrambled to appear professional and convince the Western powers to conclude an agreement with them. At the conference itself, they underestimated the reaction from the Western powers to Rapallo and overestimated their own ability to navigate the situation. Given the rapid changes after Genoa, they also overestimated the need for Western concessionaires to come in and fix their problems. The Soviets were not the only delegation intent on holding fast to positions that were sure to lead to a stalemate, however. There was no real agreement among the victors about how to proceed, and the sheer number of participants made the entire process unwieldy. Even states that wanted a peace settlement such as Britain and France remained at odds with one another over how to approach Russia and Germany, let alone the former territories of the Russian, Hapsburg, and Ottoman Empires. The smaller powers behaved in the same manner and sought alliances and pacts to counter the larger powers. Ultimately, "the course of the negotiations underlined the Allies' fundamental disunity, their lack of confidence, authority, and leadership, and their inability to give substance to Genoa's conciliatory facade."[98] The conference ended in a stalemate.

After Genoa

The Bolsheviks learned from the failure of Genoa that formal diplomatic recognition was not necessary to get the resources they needed from either businesses or governments. They could make business deals behind the scenes. For example, despite France's diplomatic animosity toward the Bolsheviks at Genoa, *Petrofina-Fransez*, the French subsidiary of the Belgian oil company *Petrofina*, concluded a marketing agreement to distribute Soviet oil in France.[99] *Petrofina-Fransez* and other French banks saw Soviet oil as a way to circumvent dependence on British and American owned oil majors. Soviet oil was also a way to recoup losses from prewar Russian debt.[100] Soviet and French interests found common ground in oil throughout the 1920s and expanded their ties in Iran.

The Barnsdall deal fell apart by January 1924. There were multiple complaints from Baku to Moscow about Barnsdall. Its American engineers did not arrive on time, machinery was improperly installed (leading to work stoppages and even strikes), and American workers brought goods into the country not permitted under the agreement. Barnsdall did not obey fire safety regulations, disregarded local customs by trying to force Muslim workers into the fields on Fridays—a day of rest in Islam. Barnsdall in turn complained to Azneft that it was not providing proper supplies, electricity, water, clay, lumber, cement, to carry out its contract.[101] The concession was terminated ahead of schedule because of poor planning on the part of both Azneft and Barnsdall.[102] Nonetheless, the Barnsdall agreement demonstrated that technology transfer—not a concession as envisioned by Krasin—was sufficient to transform the situation on the ground.

At the Genoa Conference, concessions policy was an economic policy designed to attract foreign capital to the Soviet republics. The idea of concessions was born out of economic desperation and fear of infrastructural collapse, but the policy evolved as shortages—in foodstuffs and material goods—became less acute and the transportation system resumed operation. By 1923, it was clear that Baku and Grozny had successfully rebuilt enough that concessions were no longer economically necessary and concessions policy transformed from an economic necessity to a political policy.[103] This marked a major shift. In June 1923, Maxim Litvinov, now acting head of Commissariat of Foreign Affairs, argued that the Soviet Union should not waste its time trying to cultivate relationships with Western oil companies or oppressed masses in the East. Instead, he argued, "Oil is our biggest trump card in our game with the global bourgeoisie." From now on, the Politburo must leverage oil to advance Soviet interests. Despite a willingness to negotiate with the oil majors, there was still strong anxiety about the vulnerability of the Caucasus to Western influence. Litvinov saw potential intrigue among foreign powers, of primary concern was its southern neighbor, Iran.

4

The Bolsheviks Go into the Oil Business, Kevir-Khurian, Ltd.

In November 1922, a few months after the Genoa conference, the Soviet Commissar of Foreign Trade, Leonid Krasin, was approached in Berlin by a wealthy former subject of the Russian Empire with a business proposition. Akakii Mefod'evich Khoshtariia, Georgian by birth, came to Germany with promises of a potentially lucrative oil concession in northern Iran. Khoshtariia's timing was impeccable and Krasin, as Khoshtariia surely knew, was open to doing business.

Establishing a Soviet presence in northern Iran was a vital security concern for the Bolsheviks. The Commissariats of Trade, Foreign Affairs and the Politburo feared that Baku's oil fields made the Caucasus vulnerable to attack. Moreover, European and American oil companies were looking to expand in the Middle East, and Iran offered the possibility of new oil concessions. The British maintained a strong presence in Iran, and the Bolsheviks were convinced that if oil was discovered in the north, they would encroach into the border region in the South Caucasus and threaten Soviet territorial integrity.

Krasin took a pessimistic view of Baku's future. He argued that if oil returns in northern Iran were significant, the British would seize "the whole of our Transcaucasia." In fact, if there was fear of new intervention anywhere on Soviet territory, Krasin asserted, "then that danger lies exactly in these oil and mining concessions which are now being procured by British and American capital in Persia."[1] Given the opportunity, he thought, the combined forces of British business interests and the British government would try to separate Transcaucasia from the USSR.

At the same time, it was precisely the lure of this oil, combined with the strategic location of the Baku-Batumi transit route from the Black to Caspian Seas, that could give the Bolsheviks leverage in the region. This chapter shows how the Bolsheviks used oil as a tool of state-building and foreign policy when they did not have the means to do so through formal state mechanisms. They relied on proxies and business deals to make connections and deter the British and other interests until they themselves were strong enough to conduct more traditional foreign policy through the Commissariat of Foreign Affairs. When the Bolsheviks seized power, a central tenant of their worldview had been that revolution would spread from Russia to Europe and across the globe. When the promised revolutions failed to materialize as Russia's Civil War drew to a close in late 1920 and early 1921, the Bolsheviks introduced a new course known as peaceful coexistence and sought diplomatic relations with other states. To that end, they shifted from spreading liberation movements to focus on economic recovery, state-building, and incorporating the Soviet Union into the world order. Oil was ideal for this new approach.

Around the time that Khoshtariia approached Krasin, the Soviet Union began using commercial firms such as the Amtorg Trading Company and All-Russian Co-operative Society, Ltd. (Arcos) as a proxy for diplomatic relations with the United States and Great Britain, respectively. The Bolsheviks also set up front companies, concealing the involvement of various commissariats and security organs behind business operations. One such company, explored by historian David Stone, was Wostwag, or the West-Osteuropäische Warenaustausch A. G., headquartered in Berlin. Established in 1923, Wostwag was initially an import-export business that, like any other Soviet foreign trade operation, exchanged Soviet agricultural goods for Western-European manufactured products. But by the late 1920s, Wostwag shifted from "trading chickens and bicycles" to funneling arms exports to Iran, Turkey, China, and Afghanistan and conducting intelligence work.[2]

For Krasin, the best way to make political inroads in Iran, protect the South Caucasus, and pursue the domestic economic imperative of the NEP was to pursue a coherent, systematic economic policy abroad.[3] Integrating the Soviet Union into the world economic system would guarantee Soviet power and ensure international investment in the Soviet state, which needed outside economic support to survive.[4] To pursue Soviet interests in Iran, the Bolsheviks set up a front company not unlike Wostwag in the form of an oil concession turned joint-stock company.[5] But while Wostwag was successful, the path of this company was bumpier.

On the one hand, oil gave the under-resourced Bolsheviks a tool to participate in both regional and international politics and pursue their more immediate goal of protecting Azerbaijan's border from the British. On the other hand, Soviet oil politics in Iran reflected the dynamic found in most Soviet policies of the time: a lack of official state capacity combined with a lack of political cohesion and the knowledge of how to achieve their goals. And while there was a clear imperative—secure the border, block the British—they frequently found themselves out of their depth. In the end, the anticapitalist Soviet Union embroiled itself in a capitalist competition for oil concessions in Iran with the far better equipped British and American business interests and managed to stake a claim for the Soviet state.

Finding a Way In

Soviet Russia and Iran signed the Russo-Persian Treaty of Friendship in February 1921. The treaty formalized diplomatic relations between the two countries and guaranteed noninterference in each other's domestic affairs. It renounced all claims between the two incurred prior to the Bolshevik Revolution of 1917. Key to this policy was Article 13, which stipulated that no third entity could establish concessions in northern Iran. In other words, no foreign company would be able to make a deal with Iran for the rights to either extract oil or set up an oil company in northern Iran. The article was directed at the British and served as a condemnation of imperial Russian politics, but it also put restraints on Soviet behavior.

Both the British and Russian Empires had long histories of interference in Iran. In the early twentieth century, the British presence was enhanced through a concession held by William Knox D'Arcy in southern Iran. Mozaffar ed-Din Shah granted a sixty-year concession to D'Arcy in 1901, allowing him to prospect for oil. Then, as part of the broader Great Power competition in the region, Britain and Russia concluded the 1907 Anglo-Russian Convention, formalizing spheres of influence in Iran, Afghanistan, and Tibet. In Iran, British interests were confined to the south and Russian interests to the north.[6] In 1908, D'Arcy hit a significant geyser in Masjid-i-Suleiman and subsequently formed the Anglo-Persian Oil Company (APOC), in which the British government eventually held significant interest.[7]

The 1907 treaty that divided Iran into northern and southern spheres was not a mere political distinction but had practical consequences.[8] The prewar economy of northern Iran was tightly bound to Russia, rather than integrated with the British-controlled south. The Russian government had helped its subjects, Khoshtariia among them, obtain concessions in Iran, building railroads, and setting up banking interests, textile factories, large fisheries, and timber operations. The Russian Ministry of Foreign Affairs had facilitated Khoshtariia's concessions for oil extraction and logging as well as for the construction of an (unrealized) rail link between Resht and Enzeli.[9] In addition to helping him secure his concession in 1916, the Russian government had provided him with a company of soldiers to guard it.[10]

But with the collapse of the Eastern Front in the First World War and the subsequent Russian Civil War, Britain had consolidated its hold over the whole of Iran, moving into the traditionally Russian dominated north. These incursions left foreign-held concessions such as Khostariia's in limbo. British troops then crossed the former border into Azerbaijani territory and occupied Baku in 1918, expressly to guard the oil fields, confirming by deed if not word that the spheres of influence no longer held. The brief occupation left the Bolsheviks with a lasting paranoia of British intentions in the South Caucasus, and the Soviet government sought a way to guarantee that British troops would not be located too close to the Soviet border.

In 1920, as the 11th Red Army invaded the South Caucasus, Khoshtariia gave up on the idea that the Bolsheviks would be ousted and sold his concession to the APOC. It was not even his to sell by 1920.[11] The Iranian parliament (hereafter: Majlis) had annulled the concession in 1918, and the Bolsheviks likewise renounced it in 1919 when the Soviet government gave up all claims to tsarist-era concession rights abroad. The APOC disputed the right of the Majlis to cancel the concession and asserted its ownership.[12] The dubious sale was enough to spark years of accusations and maneuvering among the Soviets, the APOC, and the Majlis as the British company continued to claim ownership.

After the abrogation of the APOC deal with Khoshtariia, Tehran invited foreign companies to compete for the former concession to counter Britain's significant influence. The possibility of obtaining a potentially lucrative oil concession attracted the attention of the Americans. Two American companies, Standard Oil of New Jersey (Standard), and the Sinclair Consolidated Oil Corporation (Sinclair), competed for rights to the northern provinces.[13] The Soviet government was anxious about what would happen in the event that large oil reserves were discovered, fearing that the foreign companies would want access to shipping routes through the Caspian or via land over Transcaucasia. The Bolsheviks were convinced that the lack of railroads and other transportation infrastructure connecting northern and southern Iran meant that any new, successful concession would have to use ports on the Caspian or go through Transcaucasia. The Soviet government watched closely, and nervously, as the British and Americans vied for influence so close to the new Soviet border.[14]

In 1920–1, the Bolsheviks had no inroads to the established trade and business networks in northern Iran. The prerevolutionary networks had been disrupted, and the Soviets did not have much to offer potential partners. Both the Iranian and Soviet governments were bound by Article 13 of the 1921 treaty. Iran could not turn to a third party to help it exploit its natural resources in the north and did not have the financial resources to develop the area independently. Not seeing an obvious way out of the situation, the Commissar of Foreign Affairs, Georgii Chicherin, decided to bide his time and protest formally if the concession was handed over to the Americans.[15]

In 1921, Iran, like its northern neighbors, was reeling from political and economic realignment and transition in the aftermath of the First World War. At the time, the Soviet representative in Tehran, Fedor Rotshtein, reported to Chicherin that the economic and political situation in Iran was dire. Schools were closing, and petty officials, police, and Cossacks were not getting their salaries; even the buffet at the Majlis had closed and representatives worked without food.[16] Rotshtein warned that a military rebellion was possible if the financial position of the Iranian government, and people, did not improve quickly. The Iranian government approached the APOC about an advance from the D'Arcy profits for the year to stabilize the situation in Tehran and was rejected.[17] The government then needed to look elsewhere.

Rotshtein argued that the British used the financial crisis to push the Iranians to approve other British ventures in railroads and concessions. Unaware that British resources in Iran were strained, Soviet representatives worked to convince officials in Iran that collaboration with the Soviet Union would be more profitable than continued dependence on the British.[18] Soviet representatives, like Chicherin and Krasin, believed that if they could not curb British influence, conflict was inevitable.

In early 1921, Reza Khan Pahlavi (from 1925, Reza Shah) indicated to Rotshtein that he would help prevent Britain from gaining concessions in the north and expanding its influence. He could only do this, he asserted, on the condition that he secure a loan that would allow him to hold off the British.[19] Although a loan was far beyond their capacity, Rotshtein told Reza Khan the Soviets would indeed be inclined to pursue a concession in the north if they were assured the effort would not run counter to Reza Khan's own plans. Reza Khan "reacted quite favorably to the idea that we pursue concessions."[20] Rotshtein was hesitant to take him at his word, however, noting that Iranian public opinion on the matter was unknown as were the positions of other elites in the area. Nonetheless, given enough time, he argued that the Iranian public, and Majlis, could be convinced to accept the Russians as concessionaires once again. Rotshtein assured Chicherin that the surest way to ingratiate the Bolsheviks with the Iranians was to offer tangible material or financial help. Rotshtein was actively wooing Iranian merchants as well as politicians, but in reality there was little he could offer.

To solve this problem, he advocated for the establishment of a Soviet financial institution as quickly as possible to secure the support of the merchants.[21] Rotshtein repeatedly suggested that the Soviet government find possible investors from either a Russian national or a German source as a way to gain a foothold in Iran. Capital from a third party, however, remained elusive until Khoshtariia approached Krasin with his proposal. Thus, when Khoshtariia visited Krasin in Berlin in November 1922 about a concession in northern Iran it appeared he was offering the opening the Bolsheviks had been seeking.

A Concession Abroad

Seizing the opportunity, Krasin instructed Khoshtariia to write out the details of his proposal to return the northern concession. While Khoshtariia laid out his plans to convince the Soviet government that he was their best option, Krasin secured the support of Chicherin and began to lobby Lenin.[22] Krasin sent the proposal to the Main Concession Committee in Moscow, the body responsible for representing the Soviet government to foreign governments to conclude concession agreements.[23] Khoshtariia laid out his proposal in a series of wide-ranging documents, which, in the archives, are titled Khoshtariia's Notes (*Zapiski Khoshtariia*).[24] He understood that the Soviet government occupied a weak position, and his overall argument was straightforward: he possessed the expertise and familiarity with northern Iran that the Bolsheviks needed, and he was willing to sell it to them. He appealed to the Soviet desire for recognition as a legitimate actor on the international stage by tying the concession to the contest with the British and to the prewar Russian government. He noted the success of the APOC in using oil interests to promote British influence in Iran; the prewar Russian government had pursued the same policy as the British, setting up private enterprises in Iran. He argued that he could do the same for the Soviets.[25] If the Soviet government wanted to expand its influence in northern Iran, then it needed to take advantage of "private initiatives," which would steer events in a direction profitable for the government.[26]

Khoshtariia's argument was one essentially of continuity. He encouraged the Bolsheviks to see him as a way to restore severed trade networks and offered a path for them to be players in Iran and restore some of Russia's lost position. This aligned with Krasin's views that the surest path to establishing a legitimate Soviet presence in Iran and supporting the economic imperative of reconstruction and the NEP at home was through a coherent, systematic economic policy abroad.[27] Krasin reported to Chicherin, Lenin, Stalin, and the Concessions Committee in Moscow that Khoshtariia would advocate for Soviet positions in Iran in return for assistance in getting the concession back. The Bolsheviks knew the ownership of the concession was contested, but Krasin pushed for Soviet participation because it offered a chance to stop the APOC. Echoing Khoshtariia, Krasin pointed out that the concession would give the Commissariat of Foreign Trade the opening to the Iranian market it was waiting for and would allow the Soviets to finally assert political influence.[28]

It seems that Krasin did not get the response he wanted because he repeatedly wrote Lenin to try to convince him to pursue a more aggressive and coherent policy in Iran. Krasin warned that if they failed to take advantage of economic opportunities in Iran, such as that offered by Khoshtariia, it would jeopardize Soviet security. He pressed that it was time for the Soviets to stop sitting on the sidelines and to take active steps to curb British influence. If they didn't, he believed, the Soviet Union would never have a secure hold on the border.[29]

As enthusiastic as Krasin and Chicherin were, even they wanted more information about Khoshtariia before they would commit to any kind of arrangement. The Concessions Committee sent requests for information on Khoshtariia to Georgian communists who were familiar with Iran and could speak to Khoshtariia's reliability. One of the people surveyed about Khoshtariia was Polikarp "Budu" Mdivani, the Georgian communist and member of the Iran Bureau of the Communist Party. Mdivani had worked with Khoshtariia in Iran during the Stolypin period when many radicals fled south to Iran.[30] A report on their relationship revealed that Mdivani acted as Khoshtariia's partner, lawyer, and general administrator prior to the Russian Revolution. In Enzeli and Resht, the two were so closely associated that "when Mdivani walked by people would say: 'there goes Khoshtariia.'"[31] Ultimately, Krasin was looking for a reason to cooperate with Khostariia, and Mdivani's endorsement of him and their prerevolutionary connections no doubt helped alleviate at least some of their hesitation. He had lived in Iran for years, knew the right people, and seemed to know how to do business there.

The Concessions Committee also wanted more information about the status of Soviet trade relations with Iran. In response to inquiries, the State Planning Committee of the RSFSR (later of the USSR, *Gosplan*), confirmed the dire Soviet economic position that Khoshtariia described in his notes. Trade with Iran had virtually halted in 1917, and the markets had been completely seized by the British. Further, the Discount and Loan Bank of Persia, the bank that the tsarist government had used to represent its interests in Iran, was no longer functioning.[32] The Soviet government essentially had to start from scratch.[33] The reports about Khosthariia himself were not encouraging, but Krasin was not deterred.[34] Instead, he continued to argue that the security of the Soviet border was at stake. He told Lenin that the situation in Iran was extremely threatening.[35]

Throughout Krasin's negotiations with Khoshtariia in late 1922, he argued to Moscow that as politically undesirable as Khoshtariia was, the Commissariat of Foreign Trade needed him. He was confident that they could find a way to ensure Khoshtariia's loyalty. Khoshtariia harbored great sympathy for Georgia, which worked in the Bolsheviks favor. Krasin also argued that cooperation with the Soviet Union was the only possibility left for Khoshtariia to get anything out of his concession. It was, he seems to have believed, a timely agreement that met the needs of both parties. Khoshtariia wanted his concession back, the Soviet Union wanted into Iran.[36]

Despite Krasin's sense of urgency, both the Concessions Committee and the Commissariat of Foreign Affairs rejected the proposal to cooperate on the northern concession. In January 1923, Khoshtariia presented his report to the Gosplan, acknowledging that the only chance of recovering the rights to the concession was with the help of the Soviet government. The members of the Gosplan, particularly Iurii Piatakov, argued that the whole proposal was too risky. The Soviets would be the only party with something to lose. Further, Piatakov dismissed Khoshtariia's claim that the concession was still legal—it was not—and decided against endorsing a Soviet attempt to secure the rights.[37]

The Commissariat of Foreign Affairs worried that an attempt to reclaim the concession would undermine the Russo-Persian Treaty of Friendship and reminded Krasin that the Soviet Union had already given up Russia's concessions. In the final instance, Piatakov told the State Bank that "Khoshtariia's industrial concessions are, at this moment, not of interest to us in and of themselves, only as a means to block the English in northern Persia."[38]

The Soviets, then, would not pursue the northern concession but Khoshtariia had a second proposal. There was another oil concession available outside of the

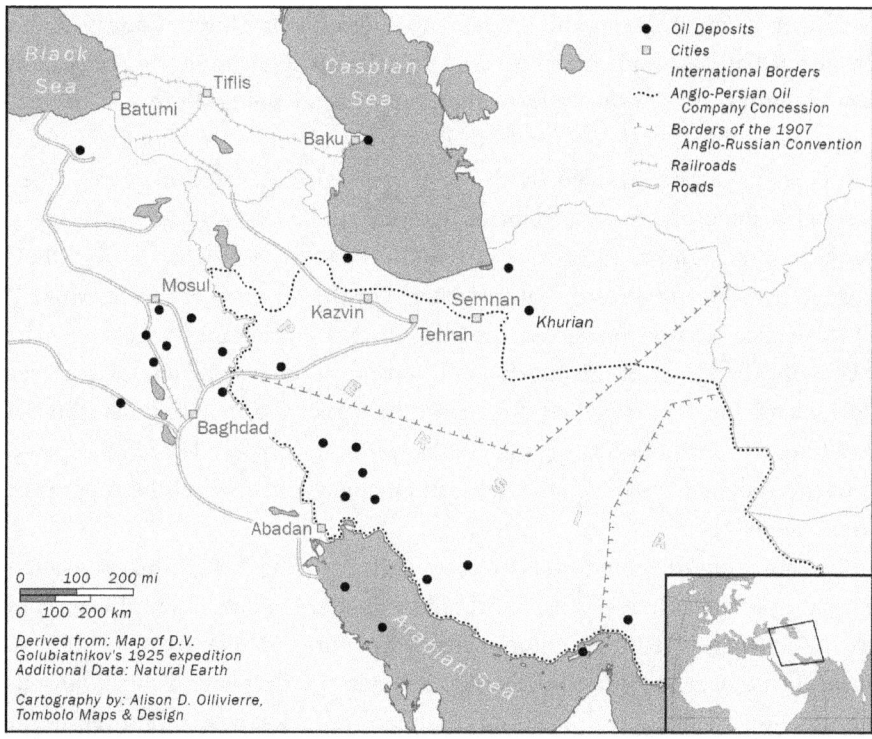

Map 4.1 Map of Soviet oil expedition, 1925

five northern provinces, located in the two regions of Semnan and Demgan, east of Tehran. The Semnan fields (Dasht-i Kavir-i Khurian) lay in a salt desert 13.26 miles from the city of Semnan in north-central Iran. This concession was located closer to the British dominated territories, in a tract of land that became known as the Semnan concession.[39] Free from the conflicts that marred the original proposition, the Soviet commissariats approved Khoshtariia's second proposal and agreed to help him secure the Semnan concession.[40] Whether there was any oil to be had in Semnan was unknown. The pursuit of the concession was, at least, at first, a political project that offered the Bolsheviks a way in. If the fields yielded returns, all the better (see Map 4.1 here).

Concession Strategy

Soviet policy now had three objectives: promote a strong Iran, find a way to keep the British from obtaining the northern concession, and pursue the rights to the Semnan concession. Each of these was tied to the larger policy of protecting the

Bolshevik Revolution at home, securing the border in the South Caucasus, and ensuring that Baku's oil remained in Soviet hands. Obtaining the concession would not just be a business transaction but a deeply political process. In Iran, concessions that allowed the right to land use and the exploitation of natural resources were only granted by the Shah through a *firman*, or decree. They were also subject to the oversight of the Majlis. The decrees for the northern provinces and Semnan already existed and needed to be purchased from their current owners, and then officially registered by the Ministry of Public Works.[41] Once the decrees were registered, the Majlis had to approve the concessions. The Majlis also had the right to attach conditions to proposals and abrogate earlier agreements much as they had done with the earlier deal between Khoshtariia and the APOC. To block the British in the north, the Soviets decided to try and influence policy in favor of an American company and also get the support of local merchants.

The situation in Semnan was more complicated. The Soviets did not want a formal concession that the Majlis would be able to regulate. They also wanted to avoid the connotations of imperialism that pursuing a concession implied. Instead, the plan was for Khoshtariia to obtain the decree and set up an oil-prospecting company with local merchants or notables, who would register it as an Iranian company. This would bypass parliamentary oversight. The Soviets would run the company behind the scenes and share the profits with whomever they could get to invest in the company. Khoshtariia's role as an intermediary would distance the Bolsheviks from Semnan and let them claim compliance with Article 13 of the 1921 treaty. To add a further layer of concealment, the Soviets would set up a bank to finance and manage the concession/company. The bank would also be set up by a private company. Participation in the company through a bank would, in theory, protect the Bolsheviks from accusations of imperialism by the British government and the Iranian public.[42]

While using Khoshtariia could have been, on the face of it, a savvy way to enter the market, it was impossible to completely disconnect the pursuit of the decrees for Semnan from the larger political situation in Iran or the northern concession. Despite the convoluted business arrangements, the Soviet role in Semnan did not remain as secret as they had hoped. Already in early 1923 a representative from the Concessions Committee wrote that rumors were spreading in Tehran about Soviet negotiations with Khoshtariia. Soviet sympathizers complained that entering into a deal with Khoshtariia was ill-advised because of his earlier involvement with the British and the APOC. The Iranian press was reportedly hostile to the proposed collaboration. In light of these and other negative reports, the Concessions Committee announced it would not work with Khoshtariia until it received direct orders from the Commissariat of Foreign Affairs instructing it to do so.⁴³ The State Bank also demanded Khoshtariia sign an additional secret agreement.⁴⁴

For their part, members of the Majlis feared that a deal with Khoshtariia would block the American oil companies from bringing badly needed resources to the Iranian market.⁴⁵ Boris Zakharovich Shumiatskii, now the Soviet representative in Iran, defended the collaboration with Khoshtariia to Moscow, arguing that his

> appearance [is] also the first serious entry of Soviet Russia in the Persian economic market. If Khoshtariia begins his work in Persia with those undertakings we gave him, in the form we stipulated, and does not compromise us politically, that is, if we frame the question in terms of using Khoshtariia as a businessman and an organizer acting *according to our plans*, and use the capital standing behind him, then, naturally, the situation changes and cooperation with Khoshtariia will be achieved.⁴⁶

Both Krasin and Shumiatskii were intent on moving forward with Khoshtariia. Once again, pushing through objections, and most likely with Krasin's intervention, Khoshtariia signed the additional agreement, and the Concessions Committee was instructed to move forward.⁴⁷

The Northern Concession

Having decided to forgo the pursuit of the five provinces in the northern concession, the Soviets turned their attention to the competition between Standard and Sinclair. Both American companies lobbied factions in the Majlis to support their claims to the north. The Anglophile faction of the Majlis supported Standard because it was known to cooperate with the APOC. The National Bloc, which was established and coordinated by Shumiatskii, sought a "neutral" American company and supported Sinclair over Standard.⁴⁸

In June 1923, the Majlis approved a bill to allow two "independent and creditworthy" American companies, Standard and Sinclair, to compete for the northern concession.⁴⁹ The bill also stipulated that the company awarded the northern concession would be required to give the Iranian government a loan of $10 million.⁵⁰ At this juncture, both Sinclair and the Soviets began funneling money and promises to the National Bloc.⁵¹

Chicherin and Shumiatskii believed there was a possibility that the Soviets could have some leverage over Sinclair as the smaller and less established US company. Shumiatskii emphasized that Sinclair may ultimately be able to secure the concession because it could bring something to the table that Standard never could: Soviet participation. Talks with Sinclair about using Soviet territory for transit, specifically to construct a pipeline, were already in progress, and Sinclair had sent a representative to Moscow to negotiate. Chicherin stressed that Soviet involvement should remain secret until Sinclair officially obtained the concession and a final agreement on the pipeline was signed.[52] If all else failed, and a deal went forward without Soviet involvement, they could demand compensation for allowing a third power to obtain a concession in the north.

A further provision approved by the Majlis stipulated that one of the five northern provinces that made up the concession—either Gilan or Mazandaran—would have to be given to an Iranian company. An Iranian-owned concession, as Chicherin saw it, presented many of the same difficulties as an American concession, that is, choosing the lesser of two evils. With the American, the choice was between Standard and Sinclair, but the stakes with an Iranian owner would be very different. In the case of an Iranian-controlled province, the Soviets would pursue a policy that would strengthen the "national Persian bourgeoisie" and attempt to form an alliance. That way, according to the logic of the Commissariat of Foreign Affairs, the Iranian owner of the concession would pursue the Soviet policy of strengthening Tehran. It soon became clear that the wealthy and influential Iranian and member of the Majlis, Todzhar Busheri (Mu'in al-Tujjar Bushiri or Hadji Moin ot-Todjar Busheri), was the most likely person to receive the concession. Busheri had connections to the British government and had purchased mining rights from them in the Persian Gulf.[53] Additionally, any new concession would require equipment and expertise, and Standard had already approached Busheri in case the other provinces went to Sinclair.

Despite Busheri's connections to the British, Chicherin argued that the Soviets could convince him to work with them and turn the Iranian province into a base of Soviet activity. Chicherin sought to play into the Iranian desire to rid their territory of British influence, and Shumiatskii lobbied members of the National Bloc to grant one of the provinces to an Iranian and prevent the American concession from having complete control of the border region.[54] The Majlis indeed granted Busheri a concession in Gilan where he worked with the Soviets.[55] From the Soviet point of view, they succeeded in sabotaging the Anglo-American plans by ensuring that an Iranian had the rights to one of the northern provinces but also succeeded in advancing their own position. A Busheri-controlled concession would act as a site of Soviet influence and a lever they could use to expand ties with the Iranian national bourgeoisie.[56]

The rest of the northern concession, outside of Gilan, was awarded to Sinclair. The company signed an agreement with Reza Khan on December 20, 1923, for a fifty-year concession for rights in Astarabad, Azerbaijan, Khorasan, and Mazandaran. After all of this maneuvering, the deal did not ultimately go through, first, because "borrowing the APOC's tactics, Standard challenged Sinclair's contract on the grounds that the Khoshtariia concession—split 50/50 between Standard and the APOC—was still valid."[57] And second, Sinclair was embroiled in a scandal in the United States where a Senate investigation revealed that it had received the rights to an oil lease in Wyoming by bribing officials at the Department of Interior. The Teapot Dome scandal, as it was known, threw Sinclair's reliability into doubt, and it was unable to pay the Iranian government the $10 million loan. Further allegations of bribery, this time coming from Iran's Minister of Finance, emerged and the public turned against the American companies.[58] The ongoing struggle for influence in the Majlis between the National Bloc, the Anglophiles, and others resulted in complete inaction.

The Semnan Concession

As the deal for the northern concession stalemated, Boris Shumiatskii set about pursuing the rights to the Semnan decree on Khoshtariia's behalf.[59] The Commissariats of Foreign Affairs and Trade claimed to follow the letter of the law in the pursuit of the decrees, but in fact foreigners were not allowed mining rights in Iran. This made the legitimacy of the company open to pressure if the Soviet role became public. They decided to hedge their bets.

In 1924, the Iranian government declared a review of all decrees related to mineral concessions, "Apparently, twenty-three *farmāns* dealing with oil concession[s] were presented for registration, all were rejected as illegal except the 1880 *farmān*, which was then registered by the Ministry of Public Works on 8 July 1924 … It seemed that the then Minister of Public Works, Alī-Akbar Dāvar, obtained the original *farmān* and sold it to Khushtārīā."[60] In other words, all decrees, except for the Semnan decrees, were ruled invalid. The British discovered that Khoshtariia had the decree, and the APOC immediately protested and claimed the Semnan region belonged to the D'Arcy concession. The Iranian government disagreed.[61] Khoshtariia moved forward and registered the four decrees with the Ministry of Public Works in September 1924, giving him the right to the exploitation of the lands, including Semnan, for 70 years.[62] And "after a series of ... Sharia rituals," the decrees were handed over to the Soviets, and Shumiatskii reported that they were "now a little 'Sinclair.'"[63]

Given the outcome of the audit, it is very likely that the Bolsheviks were behind it. This appears even more likely considering that a year later the Supreme Soviet of the Economy authorized large bribes for influential Iranians both in the form of shares in the company as well as cash payments. Khoshtariia arranged for the Minister of Social Work Ali-Akbar Davar, Abdolhossein Teymourtash (soon to be Minister of Court), and several other notables to receive shares in the future company and direct payments. Soviet archives also note that the Shah had already received "a bedroom in the style of Ludwig XIV and Italian marble at the cost of 50,000 tuman and the right to receive 250,000 tuman in shares."[64]

Less than a month after these payments were authorized, on November 5, 1925, the owners signed an agreement to form a company, Kevir-Khurian, Ltd. The company was registered in Tehran with the stated goal of "the extraction of oil at Kevir-Khurian in the Semnan viliayet," and in December, the Iranian government confirmed the company's charter.[65] Differing somewhat from the Supreme Soviet of the Economy documentation, a copy of the final agreement was listed as shareholders: Ruspersbank (the Soviet Union) with 65 percent of the stocks and Khoshtariia with 20 percent. The remaining 15 percent went to other influential Iranians, including Reza Shah and Teymourtash.[66]

In the political push to obtain the decrees, a Soviet geologist had not even surveyed Semnan and Demgan. Despite this rather significant oversight, there was some hope that the success of the APOC in the south could be replicated in the north. In summer 1925, the geologist Dmitrii Vasil'evich Golubiatnikov, who had overseen various geological surveys of the Absheron peninsula in the tsarist period, assembled a team and headed to Iran on a surveying expedition. He was conscious of the political role the Soviets wanted the concession to play. He emphasized the growing importance of oil to all cultured nations and highlighted the Soviet Union's difficulty in obtaining lands for new drilling and exploration at home. He directly linked the concession in Semnan to the fact that the Baku fields were old, and it was unclear how many reserves would still be recoverable. It was this difficulty, as far as he was concerned, that saw the Soviet Union prospecting for oil in neighboring Iran.

The expedition drilled twenty-three wells, two of which yielded oil, and one yielded gas. Golubiatnikov's conclusion was cautionary. The hope that the northern desert was composed of the same gypsum and salt tier as the south was dashed. The oil in the south was a light-weight variety, and what he found was not encouraging. He noted that the difference in quality between the two oils was "dramatic" (*rezkaia*). Semnan oil could not be refined into products important for export and could not produce gasoline at industrial capacity. Being careful not to take a firm position, he warned against making a final judgment until deep-drilling exploration was carried out.[67]

A Soviet Sinclair

By the time Kevir-Khurian, Ltd. was registered, no one quite knew what to do with it. It had largely been the project of Krasin and Shumiatskii. Krasin was now the Soviet ambassador to France, and Shumiatskii was transferred to Leningrad, leaving the company without an advocate. None of the agencies involved in setting it up wanted to pay for it.[68] The Soviet of Labor and Defense issued a decree charging the Supreme Soviet of the Economy with administering it and told it not to commit more than 60,000 rubles to the task. It simply passed responsibility onto the Azneft in Baku.[69]

To gain a better understanding of the situation, Iakov Vasilevich Lavrentev, a representative of the economic Soviet and a member of Azneft's board in Baku, traveled to Kevir-Khurian's offices in Tehran. He was a representative of both the economic Soviet and a member of the Azneft administration and requested a meeting to discuss the status and goals of Semnan. He confided that he did not know much about the company and all that he was able to gather was that Azneft was supposed to be in charge of Semnan and that they were given 60,000 rubles to carry out their work. Because of the paltry sum assigned to Kevir-Khurian, Ltd., Azneft "presumed that for the USSR Semnan was of 90% political interest and only 10% economic."[70] After spending time in Iran, however, he was convinced that the attention the concession was drawing from the local merchants and the scrutiny and expectations attached to Soviet success meant that the Soviet Union should view it more as "50/50." He would report back to Moscow that the company needed more attention.

Kevir-Khurian was attracting a great deal of scrutiny in Tehran. The company was registered in accordance with Iranian law, but, as anticipated, the rights were subject to outside pressure. Even if the exact ownership structure of the company remained secret, Soviet involvement clearly was not. Even pro-Soviet members within the Majlis began to insist that the Soviets sign a supplemental agreement unrelated to the decrees. In mid-1927, factions within the Majlis insisted that the company be formally converted into a concession given the obvious Soviet participation. The company's detractors argued that allowing the Soviets to function through an Iranian company implied that Kevir-Khurian, Ltd. would have the right to unlimited exploitation of oil in Semnan and that the Soviet presence could not be regulated. This was, of course, intentional. The Soviets wanted a company rather than a concession precisely to avoid the scrutiny of the Majlis and because the effort to get it through the legislative body would detract from resources aimed at keeping American and British oil interests in check. A public debate would cause "if not a scandal and complete failure, then at the very least would create such conditions under which the Company, although formally registered and not annulled, could not practically function."[71]

The prospect of major oil profits, however remote, was appealing enough that the Shah and Minister of Court continued to offer their support behind the scenes. But the political situation was uncertain enough that support would collapse in the face of a social scandal.[72] The Soviets had to tread lightly and respect, as far as possible, the boundaries established by Iranian politics. This was precisely the reason the Soviets decided to work through Khoshtariia to begin with. At best, this gave them a technical out, but it was not convincing. The insistence on an additional agreement stalled work at Kevir-Khurian. The Iranian government conveyed to the Soviets that signing an additional agreement would solve the problem and avoid a scandal in the Majlis. The Soviets relented and began drafting terms for a new agreement (essentially the $10 million loan that fell through with Sinclair), although they did not concede to a formal concession and made little progress.[73]

Neutral Foreign Capital

The political stalemate helped mask the Soviet Union's inability to finance the company. The Majlis now stipulated that the Soviet Union accept the participation of a third party, so-called neutral foreign capital, in Kevir-Khurian. The push to bring in another party has been attributed to the Anglophile bloc as well as the Minister of Court, Teymourtash, who pushed for French participation. In fact, the Soviets had their own reasons for wanting to bring in foreign, and specifically, French or German capital.[74] They needed financing. And it was increasingly clear that they needed out of the deal with Khoshtariia.

As early as January 1926, the Commissariat of Foreign Affairs and the Supreme Soviet of the Economy admitted that they had made major mistakes with

Khoshtariia. They had invested substantial resources and money into getting the decrees and knew they were unlikely to turn a profit. What's more, Khoshtariia had registered the company before all of the details with the Soviets were finalized, trapping them in the arrangement. They had hoped to form a partnership with Khoshtariia and use him as sort of a middleman. A representative of the bank set up to finance Kevir-Khurian stressed that Khoshtariia was absolutely not a middleman; he was the owner of the company and if they forgot that they could get into trouble.[75] What's more, they had already given the shares to Reza Shah and could not take them back.[76] The Commissariat of Foreign Affairs insisted that "*we cannot, for political reasons, refuse*" to continue the relationship with him because it would amount to ceding northern Iran to the British.[77]

Despite Lavrentev's earlier trip to Tehran, Azneft was still largely disconnected from what was happening on the ground. Azneft ran its offices in Iran through Persia Azneft, or PersAzneft, located in Tehran. PersAzneft's Commissioner of the Board, Lantsov, arrived in Baku at some point in late 1927 or early 1928 to update the main office. Once in Baku, he refused to return to Tehran, informing Azneft and Moscow of the dismal political situation surrounding Kevir-Khurian.[78] He reported to Azneft that

> I am never going there again because I do not have the slightest desire to struggle with Khoshtariia's clique; and in the end they will break their own necks because the way things are right now, anyone who touches this business—and tries to curb the voracious appetite of Khoshtariia—will have to crawl out of there like out of a cesspit.[79]

Lavrentev corroborated the accusations that the "Soviet citizen" Khoshtariia was robbing them blind [*grabiashchego nas napravo i nalevo*].[80]

While PersAzneft was technically subordinate to Azneft, the trust had little way of monitoring the day-to-day functioning of the branches. Azneft's inability to oversee the Tehran branch exacerbated the operation of Kevir-Khurian. Two members of Kevir-Khurian's board were instructed to follow-up and audit the relationship between Kevir-Khurian, Azneft, and its various branch offices. On their arrival in Tehran, one of the primary questions they were supposed to answer was whether PersAzneft was indebted to Azneft, a straightforward question that, it increasingly became clear, did not have a straightforward answer.[81]

They reported that the relationship with PersAzneft was "complicated." Not only were Kevir-Khurian's accounting records themselves incomplete, PersAzneft's were a mess, making a budget difficult to formulate. Their investigation revealed that between November 1926 and February 1928 PersAzneft had extended credit to Kevir-Khurian and its employees in the form of money, goods, and oil products without prior approval. It extended credit throughout Iran, and possibly even to Baku.[82]

The expense calculations for workers sent from Baku to Kevir-Khurian encountered a more significant problem. Three members of the board, including Khoshtariia, refused to carry out directives and "follow a different policy and do not consider themselves subject to Soviet laws, referring to the fact that the Joint Stock Company was affirmed and acts on the basis of Persian laws."[83] Further, the accountant in charge at Kevir-Khurian never once visited the work sites and only corresponded by mail with the accounting clerk on site. The accounting books had no clear system of organization. Thus, "there are not complete financial statements [from the fields] which cover the whole period of Kevir-Khurian's operation."[84]

The books made it clear: Khoshtariia was using Kevir-Khurian to rob the Soviet government, confirming the worst rumors making their way to Moscow. He made constant demands, including for an additional salary. Although the proposal to give him even more money was blocked, the bank backed him "because for that sum—800 tuman a month—there is no reason to bring a scandal on ourselves."[85] The biggest obstacle to Soviet control of the Kevir-Khurian was the structure of both the company's board and the revisory committee, that is, the financial side of the company and the administrative side of the company. Although the Soviet government was technically in control of 65 percent of the shares of the company, Khoshtariia was actually in control of both the board and the revisory committee.[86] Additionally, Khoshtariia used the frequent absence of Soviet representatives on trips to Semnan and Baku as opportunities to pursue his own course; he demanded additional payment from the company before he would approve budgets and attempted to undermine elections to the board.[87]

Khoshtariia refused to sell his shares to a third party, making it impossible to remove him from the company or get other financing. He was in complete control of Kevir-Khurian.[88] In an effort to mitigate the problems on site, members of Kevir-Khurian's administration requested a permanent accountant, an engineer, a foreman, and a bookkeeper in the fields. "All of the people should be, first and foremost, loyal and absolutely soviet people, and moreover modest (preferably bachelors). We are under a microscope here [*my zdes' na vidu*] and our staff need to be selective and qualified."[89]

The troubles in Tehran were compounded by complications on site in Semnan. Kevir-Khurian went ahead with the construction of two drilling towers, but the engineers were not comfortable working without a final agreement with the Iranian government. The head of exploration for Kevir-Khurian, Ali Aga Babaev, reported to Azneft that they were spending too much money and that he was against proceeding. However, Teymourtash, the Minister of Court, warned Babaev that Azneft needed to undertake serious exploratory work, "otherwise the English will use agitation in the press and propaganda among the local population to try to create such unpleasant circumstances for our work that we will be deprived of the opportunity to undertake exploration."[90] Babaev continued that only removing Khoshtariia and his "negative influence" would allow them to move forward.[91] He cautioned against a large changeover in personnel, either on the board of Kevir-Khurian in Tehran or on site in Semnan, however, "because that would be taken into account among Persian circles and construed as our wavering and uncertainty in such a serious matter."[92]

Kevir-Khurian now posed a significant reputational threat to the Soviets and, if exposed, would damage the image of Soviet competency, reveal the fact that the Iranian leadership was invested in the company, and "lead to a scandal."[93] Knowing that they did not have the funds to undertake serious work, the need to project "an illusion of work" was critical.

Pivoting Abroad

The Supreme Soviet of the Economy, the Commissariats of Foreign Affairs and Trade, and the Concessions Committee all acknowledged the need to wrest control of Kevir-Khurian from Khoshtariia. Even in the case of a unanimous decision, the Soviet bureaucracy was too chaotic to move forward. The Commissariat of Finance approved the money needed to buy out Khoshtariia but they could not figure out where the money should come from and the effort once again stalled out.[94]

The development that triggered the audit into PersAzneft and Kevir-Khurian to begin with was something the Soviets desperately wanted: a deal with the French. In early 1928, Iurii Piatakov, now the Soviet trade representative in France, concluded a preliminary agreement with the French subsidiary of the Belgian company, *Petrofina-Fransez*. With French diplomatic recognition of the Soviet Union in late 1924, the Soviets signed a deal with *Petrofina-Fransez* for the exclusive right to import Soviet gasoline and oil to France.[95] The French agreed to finance the purchase of Khoshtariia's shares, but the Soviets could not convince him to sell. Moreover, the agreement would not go into effect until the Soviet Union and the Iranian government came to a final agreement on the status of Kevir-Khurian, either by converting it into a concession or some other arrangement.[96] At this time, the deal-maker and middle man Calouste Gulbenkian, well-known for his role in facilitating a similar deal in Mesopotamia (Iraq) through the Turkish Petroleum Company, offered to resolve the issue with Khoshtariia through the creation of a new Soviet-Franco-Iranian company. This offer was not pursued although Gulbenkian did enter into other arrangements with the Soviets.[97]

As the Soviets sought to extirpate themselves from the spectacularly bad deal with Khoshtariia, the working situation in Tehran became impossible. The Iranian members of the board and their staff kept constant watch over the Soviet representatives and would not let them work. "We literally have to speak to each other in stealth during business hours, and nonetheless, we are the only ones doing any work, we are required to be there during business hours and a lot of time is wasted. We end up doing actual work during the second half of the day and part of the night."[98] In spite of the hostile situation, they could not relocate the offices because the Bolsheviks were negotiating with the Iranian government over new terms to the agreement, and they did not want to jeopardize their position by admitting how untenable the situation actually was.

Beyond the fact that the deal with *Petrofina-Fransez* was based on as-yet-unattained stocks, it was on precarious ground from the beginning.[99] Ultimately, the Iranian government agreed to buy Khoshtariia's shares, with financing from the French subsidiary. In April 1929, during negotiations in Paris, the Bolsheviks had presented a new geological survey conducted by Golubiatnikov from Semnan and reported that exploratory work in two of the three regions within the concession were promising.[100] The French conducted their own survey, telling the Soviets the region was likely productive and telling the Iranians the opposite. They then approached the Iranians directly about setting up a concession without the Soviets. The Soviets discovered the double-dealing and refused to move forward with a deal of any sort.[101]

As Kevir-Khurian, Ltd. stalled in a bureaucratic quagmire, Stalin pushed the Soviet Union headlong into rapid industrialization and five-year plans. Hopes of turning Kevir-Khurian, Ltd. into the Soviet Sinclair became irrelevant as events at home rapidly outpaced developments in the salt desert of Semnan. The Soviets no longer pursued a policy of peaceful coexistence. With Stalin's ascent to power, he had introduced Socialism in One Country, and the Soviet Union increasingly turned inward, no longer seeking close ties abroad. But in Tehran, the political climate also shifted dramatically. In 1932, amidst plummeting global oil prices and political scandal, Reza Shah turned on Teymourtash, having him arrested and "several of the enterprises with which he had been connected were disapproved of by Riẓa Shah, and the Kavīr-i Khūrīān was one of them."[102] The Soviet Union did not give up its claims on Kevir-Khurian, Ltd., but the company ceased to function.[103]

As Krasin had articulated in somewhat different circumstances, at some point, one must acknowledge that "in terms of managing production, outstanding revolutionaries and eminent experts and theoreticians of communism turned out to be somewhat unfit masters."[104] These words apply just as well to the Bolshevik foray into the oil business. The reliance on Khoshtariia proved costly, and the company never got off the ground. Nonetheless, in Kevir-Khurian, Ltd., Krasin had crafted a policy that helped the Soviets gain a political foothold in Iran and create a buffer zone in the northern provinces to block the British. Given how few resources the Soviets possessed at the time, the decision to use oil politics as a foreign policy proxy and partner with Khoshtariia was a clever one, even if the results did not measure up to the vision.

5

A Contribution to the History of the Revolution in the Periphery

At noon on March 23, 1925, the bells of the Kremlin tower rang out over Red Square to mark the funeral procession of Nariman Narimanov. Amid crowds and fanfare, members of the Presidium of the Soviet Communist Party paid their respects to the prominent Muslim political leader, playwright, doctor, educator, and "leader of the revolution in the East." After this public display of grief, Narimanov was interred in the Kremlin wall, an honor limited to a select few.[1] His interment in the brick necropolis marked his transformation into a symbol of the success of Soviet power in the periphery.

This public memorial was in stark contrast to the internal battle within the party that had raged around Narimanov throughout 1923–4. In June 1923, less than two years before his death, the Central Control Commission of the Communist Party accused him of undermining Soviet policy in the Caucasus and subsequently forbade him from returning to either Azerbaijan or the South Caucasus.[2] There was no press coverage of the internal investigation and no public denunciation of Narimanov. His banishment was suppressed from the public, hidden until the Soviet Union's last days.[3]

Narimanov held several high positions in the party and Soviet state. In 1920, Vladimir Lenin appointed Narimanov chairman of Azerbaijan's Soviet of People's Commissars, the head of the Soviet government in Baku. In return, Narimanov had promised to provide the political and social stability necessary to maintain Soviet power and ensure Russia's access to Baku's oil. With the creation of the Transcaucasian Republic in March 1922, he was appointed co-chairman of the new republic and transferred to the federation's administrative center in Tiflis. After the creation of the Soviet Union in December 1922, he was appointed co-chair of the Executive Committee of the USSR, the highest governing body in the Soviet Union. In January 1923, he moved to Moscow to take up his new post.[4] The appointment was prestigious on its face, but he understood the intent was to exile him from Azerbaijan.[5]

Not long after, in early summer 1923, Narimanov submitted a wide-ranging antiparty manifesto, A History of Our Revolution in the Periphery (*K istorii nashei revoliutsii v okrainakh*), to Iosif Stalin at the Russian Central Committee.[6] He wrote his history to inform Moscow of the internecine rifts that he thought were derailing the revolution in Azerbaijan and the Caucasus. The formal establishment of the Soviet Union did not create consensus in Baku, Tiflis, or Moscow about what constituted independence, sovereignty, or autonomy. Narimanov thought Moscow was pushing revolutionary change too fast in the South Caucasus, and he resented his loss of authority over Azerbaijan. The Azerbaijan Communist Party had split into factions. Narimanov advocated for local discretion in implementing policies and slower integration of Azerbaijan into Moscow's fold while his rivals sought centralization and rapid revolutionary change. His history was as an instructional corrective, one that he thought could keep the center from making further policy mistakes in the East. As had long been said in the lands of the former Russian Empire, God, after all, was high above and the tsar was far away.

Stalin, whom Narimanov saw as a sympathetic ally from the South Caucasus, had encouraged him to submit his forty-seven-page manifesto to the Central Committee. Shortly thereafter, the presidium of the Central Control Commission (hereafter: Control Commission) of the Russian Communist Party, the Central Committee's disciplinary body, summoned Narimanov for an inquiry, suggesting that Stalin orchestrated the investigation.[7] This chapter examines two issues: first, the polemics of the Control Commission's investigation into Narimanov and the conflicts that fractured the party in Azerbaijan; second, it argues that the Baku organization helped Stalin consolidate control over the party apparatus in Azerbaijan in 1923 and remove Narimanov from a position of influence, which ultimately aided Stalin's takeover of the party in the South Caucasus.

The circumstances that Narimanov leveraged in his rise through the party—his personal connection to Lenin, Baku's oil, Azerbaijan's strategic location, and his influence with nonparty Muslims—were now vulnerabilities. With the economy recovering and the creation of the USSR, Moscow needed to ensure that Azerbaijan would not be a source of instability. There was anxiety in Moscow about the security of Azerbaijan's border with Iran and the precarious peace within Transcaucasia, which made Narimanov's potential opposition a liability, not merely a nuisance. More than just concern about national politics, Narimanov's history alarmed the Control Commission because it carried foreign policy implications.

Lenin had been the arbiter of Soviet policy and had consistently backed Narimanov in Azerbaijan, viewing him as a strong leader who would foster support for Soviet power among nonparty members and mitigate the worst tendencies of the Bolsheviks. But the Azerbaijan Communist Party was fractious, and Narimanov failed to align its members under his leadership. By 1923, Lenin was too ill to dictate the minutia of party disputes, and Narimanov was increasingly unable to rely on his patronage to block moves against his power. In Baku, right and left factions were trying to cement their personal power by filling political posts with cadres loyal to them. Broadly, Narimanov was part of an accommodationist right faction that wanted to introduce Bolshevik policies slowly while the left faction was more militant and pushed for strong centralized power. The Control Commission's investigation into Narimanov illustrates a wider political shift in the Soviet Union that marked the removal of Lenin's supporters and, in the non-Russian regions, the end of a politics that tolerated decentralized local control. Consolidation of Soviet power over the borderlands was increasingly important as the Soviet Union adopted the policy of Socialism in One Country, which turned away from international revolution to build socialism at home. The shift was part of the struggle for control over the party between Stalin and Trotsky.

Centralization and consolidation were not merely about following Moscow's orders. They were about ensuring that the party apparatus, through bodies like the Control Commission, directed policy and appointments. From 1923 to 1924, the core of Iosif Stalin's power base—Sergo Orjonikidze, Anastas Mikoyan, and Sergei Kirov—allied with Azerbaijani, Armenian, and Georgian communists in the South Caucasus, including major figures in the Azerbaijan Communist Party, such as Mirza Davud Huseynov and Ruhulla Akhundov, and effectively eliminated Narimanov's influence and took over the party apparatus in Azerbaijan. This strategy of shifting alliances, behind the scenes maneuvering, and the factionalism it engendered, was how Stalin ultimately took control of the Party apparatus not only of Transcaucasia, but the Soviet Union by the late 1920s.

National Deviation and the Central Control Commission

In spring and summer 1923, two major policy shifts shaped the future of Azerbaijan. In April 1923, the Twelfth Party Congress met in Moscow and introduced a new approach toward the non-Russian nationalities in the Soviet Union—the policy of *korenizatsiia*, or indigenization. This policy sought actively to train and promote non-Russians for party work.[8] It also supported a plethora of native-language schools and publications in the national republics. In principle, indigenization was a policy directly in line with Narimanov's views. But the party congress was dominated by a recent scandal in Georgia, known as the Georgian Affair, the roots of which lay in the formation of the Transcaucasian Republic and its subsequent incorporation into the Soviet Union on December 30, 1922.[9]

The leaders of the Georgian Central Executive Committee, notably Budu Mdivani and Filipp Makharadze, opposed the creation of the Transcaucasian Republic and had wanted Georgia to join the Soviet Union on an equal footing with Russia, not as part of a regional republic. Sergo Orjonikidze, the head of the Caucasus Bureau, and Stalin pushed hard for unification and the debate escalated, culminating in an alcohol-fueled confrontation where Orjonikidze punched a fellow communist after a dinner party. Like Narimanov, the group around Mdivani petitioned Lenin, who interceded on their behalf from his sick bed. Lenin denounced Stalin and Orjonikdze's behavior as demonstration of Great Russian chauvinism—that is, of a stronger nation imposing its will on a weaker one—and demanded an investigation into the matter. Lenin was too ill to intervene more forcefully, and the Politburo ultimately backed Stalin and Orjonikidze, relatively unconcerned with nationalities policy. Against this backdrop, the Twelfth Party Congress convened, and the dispute between the Georgian party and Stalin and Orjonikidze took center stage.

Following on the heels of the Twelfth Party Congress, in June 1923, the Fourth Conference of the Central Committee of the Russian Communist Party met in Moscow with representatives from the national republics and non-Russian regions. During the conference, Stalin unleashed an attack on the prominent Tatar and National Communist Mirsaid Sultan-Galiev and marked the beginning of a campaign by Moscow against so-called national deviation. National deviation was a blanket charge against non-Russians accused of promoting national identity at the expense of communism. A flexible concept, national deviation could accommodate an array of accusations depending on the circumstances. Muslim Communists across the former Russian Empire had coupled the Bolshevik Revolution to the national anticolonial struggle, Narimanov included.[10] Stalin, in particular, increasingly viewed these local movements as a threat to the Soviet project. While there were theoretical and policy dimensions to the charge of national deviation, in practice it was used as a campaign to remove opposition to Bolshevik power, or more precisely opposition to Stalin's power, at a local level across the Soviet Union.

The Bolsheviks thus introduced a policy to promote the interests of national minorities (indigenization) at the same time that they introduced a mechanism to suppress those interests (national deviation) when it suited them. For Azerbaijan, the attack on Sultan-Galiev was a warning to Narimanov and his policies of local accommodation. It was in the context of these two formative events, the creation and incorporation of the Transcaucasian Republic into the Soviet Union and the campaign against national deviation, that Narimanov wrote A History of Our Revolution in the Periphery.

The Control Commission's investigation into Narimanov was timed to coincide with the Fourth Conference of the Central Committee because representatives from the republics were in Moscow. The commission held the first of a series of explosive meetings on June 13. According to the meeting chair Emelian Iaroslavskii, the Control Commission called the meeting "to clarify whether Narimanov's *zaiavlenia* has any merit [*osnovanie*]."[11] Iaroslavskii claimed it was his duty to find out if there was truth to Narimanov's claims and if there was "to take urgent measures to eliminate unhealthy phenomena in the organization."[12] He warned that, after the Twelfth Party Congress, "even the smallest mistakes in these [border] republics can lead to adverse results."[13] Although Iaroslavskii claimed to believe there was little in common between Narimanov and Sultan-Guliev, the matter had to be investigated to make sure "that there are no roots of Sultan-Galiev's ideas in Narimanov's report."[14] Iaroslavskii also connected the investigation into Narimanov to potential Azerbaijani chauvinism and pointed to Georgia as an example of the type of "local chauvinism" they were concerned about.[15] Regardless of what Iaroslavskii believed, the Control Commission and the Politburo were alarmed because Narimanov had clandestinely distributed his history within party circles and, significantly for the investigators, they found a copy with Sultan-Galiev when he was arrested.[16]

Narimanov was embittered by the course that Soviet power had taken in Azerbaijan, but, importantly, he argued that the errors were policy mistakes. He did not advocate for an independent Azerbaijan. He advocated for a better communist Azerbaijan, and he had not given up on the dream of spreading revolution throughout the Muslim world. He did not reject the Bolshevik vision of reshaping Muslim life in the South Caucasus, but he strongly objected to the way they were doing it. In the text of his history, he accused almost the entire party leadership in Azerbaijan of advocating one position in Baku and another in Moscow. He accused Russians and Armenians of plotting against Muslims and fostering factions.[17] Around every corner he saw conspiracy and personal plots. From his point of view, far from having resolved economic and political conflicts, the unification of Armenia, Azerbaijan, and Georgia into the Transcaucasian Republic exacerbated nearly every dispute.

Many of those singled out in Narimanov's history, including Orjonikidze, Sergei Kirov, Ruhulla Akhundov, Mirza Davud Huseynov, and Anastas Mikoyan, attended the June meetings. Narimanov was told to repeat the charges outlined in his history and then the accused responded. It was a format designed for confrontation. Narimanov's reply to Iaroslavskii was unapologetic. He had not submitted his history to the Control Commission but to the Central Committee. He explained, "I am writing a history of the revolution in the periphery of the republic and I considered it necessary to bring to light those facts that I considered indispensable."[18] Iaroslavskii responded that it was irrelevant to whom the petition was submitted, it was the business of the Control Commission. The Control Commission, he noted, paid special attention to Narimanov's claims because of his own position within the party and because he accused three members of the Central Committee (Kirov, Orjonikidze, Mikoyan) of wrongdoing. Finally, and most importantly, "because correct party policy in the A.S.S.R. [Azerbaijan SSR] has major [*gromadnoe*] influence on the laboring masses of the entire Muslim east."[19]

Narimanov was under the impression that the Control Commission's role was restricted to expelling people from the party. He had not realized that his history could lead to an investigation.[20] It is difficult to believe that Narimanov thought his account would remain a secret, or even that he wanted it to be, given that he had been distributing it; but the commission's report indicated that he was shocked that it had a copy.[21] That policy disputes were a cause for censure, and not debate, seems to have taken him aback. It is difficult to gauge how seriously Narimanov took the commission's investigation at first, but it quickly became apparent that it would have personal consequences for him, and would determine who would be enforcing Soviet policy in Azerbaijan.

Having successfully petitioned Moscow in the past, Narimanov likely expected support from the Control Commission. This time, however, the outcome was very different. While Stalin may have forwarded Narimanov's manifesto to the commission, there was no shortage of opposition against him in Baku. Narimanov's former deputy, Beybut Shahtakhtinski, had denounced him to the commission, now attacking his once friend and ally. He wrote that Narimanov aspired to be "the idol of nationalists, the leader and god of Azerbaijani communists, the king of Azerbaijan" and the leader of the east.[22]

From the beginning of the Moscow meetings, Narimanov asserted that the investigation was a pretense whose outcome was predetermined and designed to remove him from a position of influence.²³ This was certainly true. The investigation was personal but the language of policy—of factions and deviations—was used to remove him. It is clear that Narimanov did not fully understand either the stakes of the investigation or who was behind it until after it was concluded.

Oil and the National Question

The first person to address Narimanov's allegations at the June 13 Control Commission meeting was Orjonikidze. The two immediately clashed, with each accusing the other of slander. In his history, Narimanov claimed that the fundamental source of conflict between himself and Orjonikidze was the nature and degree of Azerbaijan's autonomy from Soviet Russia. In contrast, Orjonikidze claimed that Narimanov was misstating the nature of their disagreement. Their dispute was not about sovereignty but about oil. The question was whether Azerbaijan or Russia would enter the foreign market "as the owners of Azerbaijani oil." Orjonikidze explained, "The principle disagreement was about Azerbaijani oil. Comrade Narimanov, and also at that time comrade Guseinov [Huseynov, the Azerbaijan Commissar of Finance], were both against Soviet Russia, rather than Azerbaijan, going on the foreign market as the owners of Azerbaijani oil." If Russia was the owner, Narimanov argued, Azerbaijan would lose credibility in the Muslim East and, by association, any chance of carrying out revolution there. Orjonikidze then mitigated his accusation and added, "I think it is important to point out that comrade Narimanov never objected to the release of oil to Russia for internal use."²⁴

Despite Orjonikidze's claim, oil was tightly connected to autonomy. The deal between Lenin and Narimanov tied the two inextricably together. For Narimanov, the distinction between internal and external ownership of Baku's oil remained vital as the prospect of unifying Azerbaijan to its neighbors became more likely. He supported the shipment of Baku's oil through Astrakhan to Russia proper and had advocated among the Muslim population to ensure limited opposition to the policy, even going so far as to argue that Azerbaijan's oil was Armenia's oil, a position with which he was never comfortable.²⁵ He was well aware that this looked like colonialism but decided it was worth the gamble. The lines between what constituted domestic use and foreign consumption may have been clear to Narimanov, but as Transcaucasia was unified and then incorporated into the USSR, those definitions changed.

In 1920, Narimanov insisted that Soviet Azerbaijan, and the Revolution, were safer under the umbrella of Soviet Russia. He had supported Russian ownership of Azerbaijan's oil only as long as Russia pursued policies he agreed with, and inasmuch as he felt he had a say over the direction of the Revolution. As policy shifted with the consolidation of Soviet power in the early 1920s, his personal influence waned and alongside this his view of Azerbaijan's relationship to Russia shifted.

In the idiom of the Twelfth Party Congress, Narimanov now linked the oil question to the national question. He argued that oil and the national question were different expressions of the same problem: Moscow's exploitation of Azerbaijan. Narimanov, like many non-Russians, believed Soviet power had become hostile and was a proxy for Russian colonialism. The distinction between how Narimanov viewed national deviation and the official party line reflects the deep and widening chasm in power relations among Soviet nationalities.

He located Moscow's shift in Eastern policy, away from spreading revolution and toward diplomatic and trade ties, with the imperative to secure Baku's oil. He insisted in his history that "it would have been so easy [to create a model Azerbaijan] if there had not been Mikoyan and Sultan-Zade's communist revolution in Iran, if I had not been surrounded by small souls who only thought about today's situation, if the Center trusted me."[26] But Moscow, the center, trusted only Orjonikidze. He continued, "Soviet Azerbaijan voluntarily declared that oil belongs to the laborers of Soviet Russia … every worker and peasant has had it explained to them what oil means for Soviet Russia. In the first year, Azerbaijan gave not only oil but also paid from its own state treasury the salaries of [oil] workers. That is what creates national deviation."[27]

National deviation was rooted in material inequalities, both actual and perceived, as much as ideology. As far as he was concerned, the Azeri people had upheld their end of the arrangement—they had sent oil north to Russia and let the Red Army into their country. In return, Narimanov had expected the profits and prosperity of the oil industry to lift Azerbaijan out of chaos. Instead, he argued, they were given a monarchy under the dominion of Aleksander Pavlovich Serebrovskii and the Azneft.[28] He insisted, correctly, that Azerbaijan had been twice stripped of its autonomy, first in its subordination within the Transcaucasian Republic and then again with the incorporation of the Transcaucasian Republic into the USSR. In oil, Narimanov saw not only Azerbaijan's literal loss of control over its natural wealth but the increasingly marginalized exercise of political and cultural sovereignty. This also coincided with his own marginalization.

Narimanov had warned that the distribution of Azerbaijan's oil to its recent adversaries—particularly Armenians—would sow resentment if not handled delicately. When he wrote his history, peasants in Azerbaijan continued to burn kindling rather than kerosene, which was both expensive and difficult to obtain. Moreover, kerosene was more expensive in the Azerbaijani city of Ganja than the Georgian city of Tiflis. This stark material reality would, and did, lead to accusations of colonialism from the countryside.[29] He saw clear reasons for these disparities. He claimed that the oil committee and the Baku Soviet were filled with Russians, Armenians, and Jews, insinuating that they simply did not care about Muslims. He blamed Serebrovskii for withholding oil products from Azerbaijan. Narimanov was correct that the oil committee, and later oil trust, did not represent the interests of Azerbaijan. It was not designed to. It was an all-union enterprise and directed to provide for the Soviet Union.

Azneft was subordinate to Moscow. But it was also responsible to the Baku Soviet, the city council, and the Azerbaijan Soviet of People's Commissars by virtue of geography and had to continually negotiate its relationship to the city and the city's administration.[30] In October 1921, the Soviet of People's Commissars and Azneft concluded an agreement to establish an oil fund (*neftefond*) that would provide Azerbaijan with a share of Baku's oil: 15 percent of Azneft's output per year.[31] This negotiation took place during wider negotiations delineating the allocation and control of resources in the lead up to the creation of the Transcaucasian Republic.

The oil fund was earmarked for the recovery of Azerbaijan's industry and economy, and the council had discretion over its distribution. According to the initial agreement, signed by Serebrovskii and Narimanov, Azneft's products would be used as fuel, distributed to Azerbaijan state enterprises, used as barter, as well as distributed to the population.[32] But Serebrovskii consistently found reasons not to release the products. The deputy chair of the Azerbaijan Soviet wrote to Moscow that "Serebrovskii's refusal is significantly harming the material basis of the ASSR's [Azerbaijan SSR] budget and is making our difficult financial situation even worse. Serebrovskii's behavior makes it impossible to continue to work with him."[33]

Further exacerbating Azerbaijan's budget, Azneft paid virtually no taxes to the city, and the Baku Soviet complained that since late 1921, the oil trust had "paid less than any Baku restaurant."[34] The Baku Soviet did not blame Azneft, however, but Moscow. As a trust, Azneft was expected to fend for itself. The only way it could cover costs was to sell oil products. Moscow expected Azneft to provide oil and oil products to numerous organizations and state bodies free of charge in the name of solidarity and reconstruction. Those organizations felt no obligation to pay Azneft, and the result was harming the recovery of Azerbaijan's economy.[35]

Regardless of whether peasants in the countryside were going without kerosene because of bureaucratic confusion caused by the federal structure, because the leadership of Azerbaijan did a poor job, or because Serebrovskii was a tyrant, the result was the same. Peasants suffered. This mattered because it undermined popular support for the Soviet government. Oil was a political problem as much as an economic problem, and Narimanov understood this. If the Transcaucasian Republic was going to be successful, the oil question needed to be addressed.

Origin of Factions in the Party

Narimanov's influence with the Bolsheviks was based primarily on his close relationship with Lenin.[36] The main opposition to Narimanov and his policies came from other Muslim communists, members of the prerevolutionary *Hummet* party who now held high positions in the Azerbaijan Soviet Government, and the Azerbaijan Communist Party. They viewed him as far too lenient in his dealings with merchants and mullahs. They resented that he had pushed for the *Hummet* to be incorporated into the Bolshevik Party in 1919, effectively ending their independence. They did not agree that his mandate from Lenin made him the obvious leader of Azerbaijan and did not like the way that Narimanov repeatedly petitioned Lenin to intervene in Baku's affairs, or his insistence that his ties to Lenin put him above party discipline.[37]

The conflict in the Azerbaijan Communist Party centered around a group of men loyal to Narimanov and a coterie of more militant, and much younger, Bolsheviks. Narimanov's right faction included Sultan Majid Afandiyev, Dadash Buniatzade, Mir Bashir Qasimov, Teymur Aliev, Qazanfar Musabekov, Ali Heydar Shirvani (Şirvani-Mustafabəyov), and Movsum (Israfilbekov) Kadyrli. They believed that for the Revolution to succeed, Bolshevik policies had to adapt to local circumstances and could not rely on violence to impose Soviet power on an unwilling population. The left faction was led by Mirza Davud Huseynov, Ruhulla Akhundov, and Ali Heydar Qarayev, and they were backed by Sergo Orjonikidze, Sergei Kirov, and Anastas Mikoyan.[38] Huseynov, a member of the *Hummet* from 1919, was elected chairman of the Central Committee of the Azerbaijan Communist Party in 1920 and served as both the Commissar of Finance and Foreign Affairs, first of the Azerbaijan SSR and later of the Transcaucasian Republic. Akhundov was a left Social Revolutionary after the 1917 Revolutions and joined the Communist Party in 1919, at Mikoyan's urging. He took various posts after 1920, including the secretary of the Baku Committee, secretary of the Azerbaijan SSR Central Committee, Commissar of Enlightenment, and editor of the newspaper *Revolution and Nationality*. Qarayev was a member of the Azerbaijan Central Committee (hereafter: Azerbaijan CC) and served as Commissar of Labor of the Azerbaijan SSR, Commissar of Justice, and numerous other party positions. This left faction sought centralization of control and power through the party apparatus.[39] This faction of the Azerbaijan Communist Party helped Stalin consolidate control over the party in Azerbaijan.

Narimanov's critics objected to the way he positioned himself as the leader of all Muslims of the Soviet republics and a dictator of the East writ large, which alienated Muslim and non-Muslim Bolsheviks alike.[40] Many chose not to follow his orders. The Azerbaijan Communist Party was completely factionalized: "The Turkic [Azeri] communists were opposed to the Armenians and Russians, the Baku committee of the party would not subordinate themselves to the orders of the Presidium, the Presidium overturned the decisions of the Baku committee, the young *hummetists* were ignored by the older ones, and the careerists worked against whatever Bolshevik was in office."[41]

In his petitions to Moscow and in his later history, Narimanov depicted himself as an innocent victim of aggressive Bolshevik policies, but the situation was far messier. He did not have a monopoly on how Muslim communists viewed the Revolution, and what he presented as an impassioned plea to liberate Azerbaijan was to his more militant comrades accommodationist and nationalist. From the view of the left wing of the party, his policies were counterrevolutionary. His conflict with his fellow Muslim communists also had distinctly personal and familial dimensions. It was the intertwinement of these dimensions—political, personal, and strategic—that led to his removal from the South Caucasus.

Parsing who carried what kind of influence when in the South Caucasus is overshadowed by Stalin's later rise to dictatorial power. This is doubly difficult in Azerbaijan because the Communist Party there was an extension of Stalin's patronage network from the early Soviet period. He was from the South Caucasus and had cut his teeth on party work in Baku.[42] Many of the actors involved in establishing Soviet power in Azerbaijan—Orjonikidze, Kirov, and Mikoyan—were part of Stalin's inner circle. But Stalin also had strong allies in the prominent Azeri Bolsheviks Huseynov and Akhundov. He did not take over the party so much as they facilitated his control and were key to his consolidation of power in the South Caucasus. The ultimate success of this patronage network did not come down to his machinations alone. Orjonikidze carried the weight of enforcing policy on the ground and creating coalitions necessary for the Stalin-aligned faction to succeed.[43] And those coalitions had their own agendas.

As early as summer 1920, the divergence between the right and left positions was already clear. The party organized an extraordinary food commission, which went into Baku's city center and requisitioned sugar, food, and any manufactured goods it could locate. Groups of armed men entered people's homes and violated numerous local customs. The commission then redistributed the seized foodstuffs to oil workers, which led to a surge of anti-Soviet sentiment and general unrest in the city. Aleksandr Serebrovskii, head of the Azerbaijan Oil Committee, noted that after this episode the commissariat in charge of food supply was forced to adopt new methods and was no longer carrying out requisitions, in an effort to prevent unrest.[44] Such a policy would have elicited not only fear and frustration—not to mention revealing the emptiness of Soviet claims to respect the population—but memories of similar requisitions during the Baku Commune.[45] Significantly, Narimanov blamed Qarayev and Huseynov for perpetuating violence, not Serebrovskii, Orjonikidze, or Moscow.[46]

In late August 1921, a series of plenary meetings of the Azerbaijan CC addressed the existence of "different lines of thinking" in the party. The reports were careful to avoid calling the divisions "factions"—that would be a clear breach of party discipline and a violation of Lenin's recent ban of factions at the Tenth Party Congress in March 1921. The controversies, in part, involved Narimanov, who attempted to resign from his post as head of the Azerbaijan Soviet of People's Commissars.

Kirov, the Moscow-appointed head of the Azerbaijan Communist Party, rejected Narimanov's resignation request because, Kirov noted, Lenin and the Russian Central Committee had sent Narimanov to Azerbaijan from Moscow with specific directives to establish Soviet power in Azerbaijan. Kirov would not approve Narimanov's request because his assignment was not complete. Narimanov argued that the members of the Azerbaijan CC were impossible to work with and that they refused to follow his directives.[47] According to Afendiyev, Narimanov had some local support but was viewed primarily as Moscow's man—a view demonstrating the challenge, or perhaps impossibility, of being both Moscow's voice and the voice of the people. Others sympathized with Narimanov, noting that the Azerbaijan CC often ignored Moscow's directives, making Narimanov's role as enforcer an unenviable one. Party discipline was erratic, inconsistent, and virtually unenforceable throughout 1920.

Narimanov defended his attempt to resign when the Central Committee invited him to a plenum to explain his position.[48] He took issue with the recently appointed Azerbaijan Politburo because it was undermining his agreement with Lenin. Narimanov reiterated his argument that the Azerbaijani countryside had to be integrated with Baku and reminded his fellow Bolsheviks that they owed him a debt because he had arranged matters "so that Soviet Russia could live quietly and use the oil and oil products" from Baku.[49] Narimanov further claimed that he had achieved the goal of integrating Baku with the rest of Azerbaijan and he blamed the other members of the Politburo for making his work more difficult.[50] In return, he had expected to have a greater say in the course of Bolshevik policies in Azerbaijan. This part of his deal with Lenin was not being honored. Of course, the countryside had not by any stretch of the imagination been integrated into the rest of Azerbaijan. At best, there was an absence of active warfare and even that was a dubious claim.

Narimanov had not anticipated resistance to his power from his fellow Muslim Bolsheviks. He, it seems, believed that his mandate from Lenin was enough to guarantee obedience. While he wielded a certain amount of authority among the wider population and among prewar revolutionaries, years of war had radicalized the Bolsheviks and Narimanov's propensity to compromise was not viewed as a valuable asset in Soviet Azerbaijan. Afandiyev grasped the heart of the problem more clearly than did Narimanov, observing that "Russia is moving forward but Baku is remaining behind. We haven't reconciled ourselves to the new influence of Soviet Russia. The Baku organization has always been a revolutionary one, even in times of peace. We continue to be revolutionary even now when the rest of the country is working in harmony for the interests of the workers. It is a survival from the old revolutionary Baku organization."[51] He concluded that it was time for the Baku Bolsheviks to accept that they could no longer act however they pleased. They needed to throw off the past when they made their own decisions and to align their policies with the other Soviet republics. The long process of negotiation from a revolutionary party to a ruling party, the negotiation between centralization and local control, was already fully evident.

Disagreements around the unification of Azerbaijan, Armenia, and Georgia and control over policy mounted over the course of 1921, and Narimanov repeatedly petitioned Lenin to remove his opponents from Azerbaijan. According to Orjonikidze, he was the one who ended up having to push Narimanov's transfers through the party, which notably included Mikoyan, and Levon Mirzoyan, future first secretary of the Azerbaijan Communist Party.[52]

In October 1921, Narimanov sought an audience with Lenin. They met in Moscow, and Lenin reaffirmed his support for Narimanov's approach of toleration and accommodation for the implementation of cultural policies in Azerbaijan. On October 17, 1921, the Politburo instructed Stalin to detail its policy toward Azerbaijan, this time in writing. The result, "Directives from the Central Committee of the Russian Communist Party (b) to the workers of Azerbaijan" was a temporary vindication of Narimanov's policies.[53] The directive instructed the party to consider carefully the "national and religious" features of the Muslim population before pursuing policies or hasty actions that could "cause discord among the working class and undermine the unity between workers and peasants."[54] This was also, of course, Lenin's view of nationality policy.

Lenin then summoned Huseynov and Akhundov to Moscow to clarify Moscow's policy in Azerbaijan—that is, Narimanov's position.[55] Despite this, just days after these discussions, Orjonikidze sent Lenin and Stalin a telegram warning them that Huseynov and Akhundov could not be trusted as their ultimate goal was to remove Narimanov from power. If Lenin wanted to keep Narimanov, he would have to transfer Akhundov and Huseynov from the Caucasus.[56] This is what happened. In December 1921, Akhundov and Huseynov were both transferred to Moscow, where Huseynov worked under Stalin as the Deputy Commissar for Nationalities.[57]

These transfers did not stabilize the situation. In January 1922, Narimanov was chosen to attend the forthcoming Genoa Conference, and in April he was sent to Italy, although he did not to take part in the negotiations at the conference. He was sent to Genoa so that the Transcaucasian Regional Committee, which replaced the Caucasus Bureau and was in charge of party policy, could remove his supporters in his absence. Kirov and Mirzoyan transferred Narimanov's allies from Baku and elevated his rivals while he was away, for example, by appointing Aiub Khanbudagov secretary of the Central Committee of the Azerbaijan Communist Party. On his return, Narimanov was himself transferred to Tiflis as part of the presidium for the newly formed Transcaucasian Republic, ostensibly a higher position but removed from Azerbaijan's center of power.[58]

Allegations and Accusations: Eastern Policy

Narimanov's opening sentence in his history was that Georgii Chicherin, the Commissar of Foreign Affairs, did not understand Eastern policy.[59] The core of this claim centered around the Soviet abandonment of revolution first in Iran and then throughout the Muslim East over the course of 1921. Moscow had shifted to a noninterventionist foreign policy that aimed to strengthen Bolshevik power by ensuring that bordering states were not at risk of being invaded by Britain, rather than export revolution. Narimanov rejected the turn toward support for national and bourgeois democratic governments and insisted it was still possible to spread revolution.

Narimanov had welcomed the Bolsheviks, and the Red Army, into Baku in no small part because he wanted to bring revolution to Muslims across the Near East (Iran, Turkey, Afghanistan). He hoped to establish Bolshevik power in Iran and argued that the Soviet trade agreement with England throttled any hope of spreading communism to Iran. In his view, it also consigned the Muslims of the Near East to backwardness and exploitation at the hands of the imperialist powers. In his history, he took aim at the much-vaunted Congress of the Peoples of the East, held in Baku in September 1920. The whole congress was, he insinuated, a display of exoticism. A few photographs of intimidating men of the East "holding unsheathed daggers, revolvers, bombs, and knives, threatening European capital."[60] A nice show to intimidate England with the prospect of stirring up the Muslims. Instead of debating the content of the policy, which had long been resolved in their view, the commission was concerned with Narimanov's personal attacks on members of the Central Committee.

Despite the commission's disinclination to discuss Eastern policy, Narimanov's comrades from Baku took serious issue with his views. Kirov in particular expressed frustration with Narimanov's position and asked him what exactly he was trying to achieve. Kirov pointed out that Narimanov tried to have everyone who did not support his ideas about exporting revolution to Iran removed from Baku. He continued, "Com[rade] Narimanov believes that all of eastern policy is mistaken: no one else understands it, com[rade] Chicherin doesn't understand, the Central Committee of the party approaches it incorrectly—only Narimanov and Narimanov alone can formulate eastern policy and only he can make this claim."[61] This was exactly what Narimanov had argued, that he should be in charge of formulating Eastern policy.

In fact, he never had authority over Azerbaijan's foreign policy, not even when it was ostensibly independent. As Narimanov had traveled from Moscow to Baku in spring 1920 and the 11th Red Army approached the South Caucasus, Stalin and Orjonikidze intervened with Lenin to ensure that Narimanov's authority as head of Soviet Azerbaijan would not extend beyond the Caucasus.[62] From the beginning, Narimanov's position in the Bolshevik Party was conditional, at least as far as Stalin and Orjonikidze were concerned. Moscow did not want Baku to have too much of an influence over foreign policy. Curtailing Narimanov's power was a way to hedge against local initiative and potential cross-border agendas. It was a security measure. It is not clear how much Narimanov was aware of any of this.

The commission also solicited Chicherin's view on whether the Commissariat of Foreign Affairs' policy ever deviated from the Central Party line during 1920–1 period when the Soviet government sponsored the Gilan Soviet Republic in Iran. Chicherin, predictably, defended the Commissariat of Foreign Affairs' policies in Iran, Turkey, and Afghanistan. Narimanov, Chicherin reported, not only openly refused to abide by Central Committee orders but supported an array of dubious actors. People Narimanov called the "revolutionary movement," Chicherin denounced as fanatics, bandits, careerists, monarchists, rich landowners, and opium addicts. Narimanov's continued support of "these elements" led to a rift with the Central Committee. Chicherin told the commission that Narimanov was not the only Bolshevik in Gilan who had to be corrected, all of the comrades from the Caucasus had needed reminding. At present, however, none of the leadership, except Narimanov, doubted that the Gilan fiasco was "deeply harmful to the communist movement and the international position of the Soviet republics."[63]

The problem was that Narimanov did not fall in line after an official policy change. The most troubling aspect about him for his comrades and the investigators was not that he had pursued his own line in Gilan and in Iran over the course of 1920–1. Orjonikidze had done the same and had gone so far as planning a march on Tehran. The other comrades involved in Gilan, especially Orjonikidze and Mikoyan, understood that the situation had changed and that there was a new policy. They obeyed the Central Committee's orders, especially on foreign policy. As much as Orjonikidze could be a rogue actor, it is clear from the stenographic reports that the commission considered him reliable. The commission did not trust Narimanov. What Narimanov did not seem to grasp yet was that they were also part of a stronger patronage network coalescing around Orjonikidze in Transcaucasia.[64]

Unification, Independence

Narimanov's dispute with Orjonikidze did not end with oil. Narimanov accused Orjonikidze of working to isolate him politically, while Orjonikidze countered that he had acted as a buffer between Narimanov and his opponents, namely the younger generation of Baku Bolsheviks led by Huseynov and Akhundov.[65] Orjonikidze reminded the commission that he had shielded Narimanov not because he liked him but because he understood that Narimanov was an important public figure in Baku and because Moscow (Lenin) wished it.[66]

Orjonikidze cited Lenin's removal and transfer, at Narimanov's request, of Huseynov and Akhundov, as well as Lominadze, Mikoyan, Sarkis, and others from the Baku Committee. Nearly all of them were Armenian, Russian, and Georgian and, he accused, Narimanov was fiercely Armenophobic. Orjonikidze also noted that he supported Narimanov's request to block the expulsion of several of Narimanov's close friends during the 1921 party purge for stealing because "then we would not have a single Muslim left in the Narkom [Soviet of People's Commissars] and we would have a major scandal on our hands."[67] Narimanov's continual requests to transfer his opponents likely demonstrated for the commission that he was in fact pursuing his own agenda.

In his history, Narimanov claimed that Orjonikidze's power was based on bluster and coercion, that Soviet power in Azerbaijan was propped up at the barrel of a gun [*na shtykakh*—literally, by bayonet]. Orjonikidze responded,

> Comrade Narimanov says that everything I do is built on browbeating [*mordobitiie*]. It's a blatant lie! Let Narimanov prove even one case when I used browbeating, except one case when I hit that one comrade in the face in Tiflis, also a Georgian, and it's a well-known fact to all of the comrades here and it was discussed in the CC [Control Commission]. Let Narimanov prove to me that my work is based on browbeating!"[68]

Orjonikidze absolutely relied on violence and intimidation to implement his policies as everyone there was well aware.[69] Narimanov was not against using unsavory methods himself, and the charge was not likely convincing.[70]

But that was not really the point for the commission. Orjonikidze detailed his understanding of the situation and wove an alternate history. Narimanov saw himself under siege as Azerbaijan slipped further and further away from the future he had envisioned for it. Orjonikidze saw in Narimanov a power-hungry manipulator using his influence with Lenin to push out his competition and consolidate his control over the Baku Soviet of People's Commissars.[71] This was obviously overstating Narimanov's influence. But it was not untrue, either. Narimanov did appear to want sole authority over Azerbaijan, despite the Transcaucasian Republic and his high position within it. Much as Orjonikidze wanted control over Transcaucasia.

In Azerbaijan, the disputes between Narimanov and the left faction had as much to do with experience in the underground as age. There was a sharp division between those who stayed in Baku during the Baku Commune, under the Musavat, and through the occupations of 1918–20 and those who fled to safety or served behind the lines. Narimanov was recalled to Astrakhan before the collapse of the Baku Commune and then to Moscow. Legitimacy was increasingly associated with actions during wartime. Narratives of Civil War experience became vital to political legitimacy throughout the Soviet Union, and this held true in Azerbaijan as well.[72]

During the commission's sessions, Narimanov's opponents focused on his absence from the underground and denounced him as a coward for capitalizing on their sacrifices. Orjonikidze, Mikoyan, Akhundov, and Huseynov all made their disdain for him clear. These experiences in the underground had become bound up with the debates on the unification of Transcaucasia, specifically the nature of Azerbaijan's relationship to Russia. Whether Azerbaijan would remain independent, unify with Russia, or maintain some form of autonomy in a federation with Russia had all been possible. The left faction pointed out that the decision to organize around an independent Azerbaijan had been made on the ground in 1919.[73] Mikoyan explicitly connected the two. After the collapse of the Baku Commune in July 1919, he joined the underground in Baku, but no one went with him, least of all Narimanov "an old man [*starik*]." Mikoyan countered,

> I alone stayed in Baku during the savagery of the Turks, the English, and all the rest. I worked in that difficult time among the Muslim workers, I hid with them, in the Muslims regions. We broke Shauiman out of jail and at that difficult time com[rades] AKHUNDOV and GUSEINOV started working with us. I was the one who first came up with the slogan: 'Long live Soviet Azerbaijan!' I raised the question about the necessity of attracting Muslim workers at a time when Narimanov wasn't in the Caucasus."[74]

Mikoyan, Akhundov, and Huseynov all worked to organize an Azerbaijani party on the ground between 1918 and 20. Narimanov, meanwhile, pursued the formal incorporation of the *Hummet* Party into the Bolshevik Party. This was approved in July 1919 by the Politburo and created an autonomous Muslim wing of the Bolshevik Party and then the creation of an Azerbaijan Communist Party.[75] Despite Mikoyan's confidence that his slogan was the origin of an independent Azerbaijan and Narimanov's certainty that he was the true representative and leader of Azerbaijan, the status of both Azerbaijan and Muslim communists remained deeply fraught. What role the Transcaucasian Republic would play within the Soviet Union and how federalism would actually function in Transcaucasia was still being worked out in all three of the republics. It mattered who proposed what when because legitimacy in the Bolshevik Party depended on being in the right faction at the right time. Party culture was increasingly insistent that there was one correct way to build communism and past mistakes either needed to be accounted for or punished.

Narimanov rehashed many of these controversies: that Huseynov changed his position on the economic unification of Transcaucasia, defending it in Baku and denouncing it in Moscow; Orjonikidze took credit for Lenin's position on unification (the process was in fact initiated by Orjonikidze); and Akhundov was against unification altogether.[76] He also accused Kirov and Orjonikidze of lying to Moscow and claimed they covered up the Red Army's assault of worshipers on the day of Ashura, a day commemorating the martyrdom of Imam Huseyn among Shiia Muslims. He saw a pattern of misrepresentation that was also played out in the Georgian Affair. There was no local nationalism in Georgia, Narimanov claimed. The only fault of the former Georgian Central Committee was that it directly confronted Orjonikidze and Kirov about lying to the center. He warned that unification was proceeding too quickly. He viewed attacks on Muslim religious practices as akin to attacks on Georgian national institutions.

Narimanov had supported the unification of Transcaucasia, but the impetus for unification had largely come from two sources: the Azerbaijan Communist Party and Orjonikidze.[77] There were lengthy debates but no consensus emerged in the Azerbaijan party over unification. Despite initial support, by summer it was clear that many of the Muslim communists were against unification. Even Narimanov had serious reservations about whether unification would benefit Azerbaijan and had pushed for the administrative center to be located in Baku, not Tiflis. This would balance the center of power away from Georgia. In summer 1921, neither political nor economic unification was popular in Azerbaijan. In August, Huseynov, then Commissar of Finance and Akhundov, a member of the Azerbaijan CC, went so far as to petition Lenin to try to stop the formal unification of Transcaucasia.[78] Framing unification as an obligation to end ethnic conflict, Orjonikidze and Kirov forced the issue, and the Azerbaijan party ultimately approved unification.[79]

The conflicts between Narimanov and the left faction were about political allegiances, not just unification. They had largely agreed that unification would not benefit Azerbaijan, but all of them endorsed the proposal in the end. By 1923, the factions had more or less switched positions. It was now Huseynov and Akhundov who were firmly in Orjonikidze's, and Stalin's, corner.

Early Bolshevik rule in Azerbaijan was shaped by war and marked by expropriations, violence, and the suppression of political and class enemies. Red Army soldiers and the secret police ran amok in Baku and in the provinces. In the outskirts of the city, workers in the oil fields continued to suffer severe shortages, and in the countryside, villages resisted Soviet rule, hid livestock, and refused to cooperate. Narimanov argued that Muslims suffered disproportionately and sought, unsuccessfully, to intervene.[80] He no longer argued that Moscow could shield Baku.

Narimanov did not build coalitions within the party and instead petitioned Lenin. He was still attempting to leverage his position within the Bolshevik Party to pursue his own course in Azerbaijan, and the distance between his line and party practice was growing, especially in light of the new policies on national deviation. Huseynov and Akhundov were more embedded in the party apparatus. They pursued Narimanov's removal, much as he did theirs, but they built a much more effective faction, and once Orjonikidze and Stalin stopped shielding him, he rapidly lost authority. Huseynov and Akhundov demonstrated their loyalty to the Bolshevik cause even if this meant supporting positions with which they personally disagreed. Narimanov was now unwilling to do so. These divisions became increasingly untenable both politically and within the new federal structure of the Transcaucasian Republic.

The Azerbaijan Cheka

The commission was suspicious of Narimanov's ongoing links with Iran and with religion. His lax treatment of worshippers commemorating the Shiia holy day of Ashura, which marks the martyrdom of Imam Huseyn, also drew the commission's ire. The events show the sharp divergence between the centralizing left faction and accommodationist right faction. On the Day of Ashura, a procession, called the *Shakhsei-Vakhsei* in Russian, made its way through the streets of Baku as participants cut and beat themselves in a show of mourning and commemoration.[81] Many members of the Azerbaijan CC wanted to ban the procession which they viewed as religious fanaticism. Narimanov insisted that the party should not antagonize the participants. His position prevailed in 1920 and 1921 when he was in Baku, but while he was attending the Genoa Conference in 1922, Kirov and Levon Mirzoyan proposed a ban on the procession, and Red Army soldiers fired on participants. It was precisely these kinds of actions that Lenin's appointment of Narimanov had been intended to curb, and such episodes further discredited Soviet power in the eyes of the Muslim population.[82]

The commission's report presented a completely opposing view. They believed Narimanov was against any kind of prohibition or restrictions on the procession and on religion in general. This position did not align with the current party line and antireligious campaign being conducted elsewhere in the Soviet Union. This could not have been surprising. Iaroslavskii, the commission's chair, was a staunch atheist who led the Anti-Religious Commission (later, the League of the Militant Godless), evangelizing for the destruction of religion.[83] According to the investigation, Comrade Qarayev and other influential leaders worked with the mullahs to explain to the people that they would not be allowed to march, that this type of display was no longer permissible. They claimed they did not shoot into the procession unprovoked. The crowd attacked the soldiers, the report insisted, and that is what led to the altercation. Particularly damning for the commission was not Narimanov's refusal to ban the procession but the fact that he distributed sugar to the participants at earlier processions. The commission argued that, in effect, Narimanov publicly participated in a religious ritual. Moreover, he distributed sugar to "religious fanatics" when workers were not receiving sugar because of food shortages.[84] The commission stated clearly that "it believes that in a Soviet state such religious propaganda as patronizing fanatical processions" cannot be tolerated.[85] Narimanov wanted the population to support him, and, through him, the Soviet government. The commission on the other hand expected him to abide by party policy and figure out how to bring Muslim peasants and religious adherents into the fold. His role was not to make policy but to carry it out.

Throughout 1923, the secret police, the Azerbaijan Extraordinary Commission for the Struggle Against Counterrevolution and Sabotage, or Cheka (hereafter: AzCheka), had been following Narimanov and reporting on his activities.[86] The commission did not believe that he had given up fomenting revolution in the East. These reports, called *svodki*, were included in the Central Control Commission's investigation to support its case that Narimanov and his allies were acting against Soviet power and posed a security threat. These *svodki* reported on public gatherings, the content of speeches, rumors, and the movements of members of the Azerbaijan communists. The reports found spies everywhere. Much of their suspicion of Narimanov centered around his support for his former personal secretary, Ali Heydar Shirvani, and another expelled party member.[87] Kirov repeatedly named Shirvani a "bad character" and recalled that Shirvani explicitly disobeyed directives against active work in Iran. He had printed proclamations on behalf of Ekhsanulla Khan, the former Jangali who had relocated to the Soviet Union after Kuchuk's collapse.[88]

Several of the *svodki* relayed that Narimanov's supporters, including Ekhsanulla Khan and Shirvani, were trying to turn Persian workers against Soviet power and of receiving major funding from Tehran.[89] Another accused Shirvani of organizing an underground organization against Soviet power in Black City, the predominately Muslim oil-worker region. The group supposedly agitated among Muslim workers against communists and claimed the Soviets worked only on behalf of Russia and ignored the needs of Iranian subjects.[90] The AzCheka was clearly suspicious of the Persian Charitable Society, which it saw as a front for disgruntled Iranians who had been kicked out of the Communist Party.[91] They viewed Narimanov's continued association with the Iranian groups with deep alarm. It is clear that informants understood Narimanov's standing with the AzCheka even if he did not. One such report warned that a worker, Mashadi Huseyn, should not be trusted because he was working "hand in hand with Narimanov."[92] Even working with him was deemed reason enough for suspicion.

The question loomed, was Narimanov helping to sow discontent with Soviet policies in another country? This would be a dangerous position indeed. The *svodki* began in January 1923 at the height of the conflict over the Transcaucasian Republic and the increasing suspicion of national communists. This mattered, but the local context was more consequential to Narimanov's fate. Until February 1921, the AzCheka had been led by Aiub Khanbudagov, whom Narimanov had appointed to the position to help him target his opponents, Mirzoyan, Akhundov, and Huseynov. The Azerbaijan Orgburo and Politburo removed Khanbudagov from that post after numerous improprieties. In his place, they installed Mir Jafar Baghirov, the future leader of Azerbaijan who brutally oversaw Stalin's purges of the 1930s. Initially, he was a far more effective operative against Narimanov's opponents. For example, Baghirov obtained compromising material on Akhundov in mid-1921 and used it to block his appointment as permanent secretary of the Central Committee of the Azerbaijan Communist Party. At some point after this, Khanbudagov appears to have passed information critical of Narimanov onto Mirzoyan, Akhundov, and Huseynov. This was quite possibly done in exchange for that same position under Kirov as secretary of the Central Committee of the Azerbaijan Communist Party in March 1922.[93] By the time of the Control Commission investigation, Baghirov had also joined the group against Narimanov, and given the content of the *svodki*, he had already done so by January of that year. Perhaps they were better than Narimanov at understanding who was increasingly in control.

The Commission's Judgment

The commission compiled its findings and recommendations together with supporting evidence some five months after the Moscow meetings in a report dated November 12, 1923.[94] The commission recommended the "complete noninterference of Narimanov in the Azerbaijan organization," and it reached four concrete conclusions: (1) Narimanov knowingly reported false information to the Central Committee about the situation in Azerbaijan; (2) he leveled a number of slanderous, shameful, and unconfirmed accusations at Central Committee members Orjonikidze, Kirov, and Mikoyan; (3) his entire report was imbued with the completely uncommunist spirit of nationalism, Armenophobia, and Judeophobia; and (4) he leveled slanderous accusations at comrades and leaders of the Azerbaijan organization.[95] Further, it recommended a "severe reprimand" for Narimanov's behavior toward his comrades and the party, especially because he was himself a candidate member of the Central Committee. At the same time, the commission did not find his comrades blameless. It found that the Azerbaijan CC and the Baku Committee did not work energetically enough to reach the peasantry and allowed it to continue to languish under kulaks.[96] There were serious obstacles in distributing oil products to peasants in Azerbaijan. They laid the blame at the local level. The commission demanded more vigorous action. The Politburo concurred and passed a resolution barring Narimanov from Azerbaijan, but no severe reprimand was handed down.[97]

An Addendum and Other Letters

Narimanov wrote an addendum to his history in December 1923 and a postscript in 1924, and he doubled down on his accusations. The addendum's tone was more urgent than his original history and filled with warnings about Azerbaijan's future. He still sought to position himself as the rightful leader of Soviet Azerbaijan. He recounted that the commission told him his history would lead the party to delusion; that Stalin told him he should have focused on policies and not have called people out by name. Narimanov was defiant and insisted that people be named.[98]

It was at this point that Narimanov's perception of Orjonikidze dramatically shifted. He had considered his disputes with Orjonikidze a local matter related to Transcaucasia, Iran, and their interpersonal history. That Orjonikidze was a Baku Bolshevik. It was now clear, he wrote, that Sergo was a representative of the center (although Orjonikidze did not yet view himself in this light).⁹⁹ Further, he realized that Stalin supported, and had always supported, Orjonikidze and his policies in Transcaucasia.¹⁰⁰

A year after the initial investigation, he once again warned that catastrophe was on the horizon. This time his tone was not just alarmed but desperate. He denounced Armenian and Russian chauvinism but reserved his ire for the faction within the Azerbaijan party, referring to himself in the third person throughout: Sergo needed Narimanov out of the Caucasus, Narimanov's promotion to Moscow was a pretense to install Mirzoyan, no one dares say the name Narimanov in Azerbaijan.¹⁰¹ Absent from his earlier history, in these letters he took aim at the secretary of the Central Committee in Azerbaijan, his former ally, Khanbudagov, and recounted new factions, new alignments.¹⁰² He repeatedly blamed Orjonikidze and Stalin for the course the revolution had taken in Azerbaijan but also for moves against him personally.¹⁰³

Narimanov's Exile in Moscow

After Lenin's death in January 1924, the Politburo built a cult of personality around Narimanov, referring to him, rather cynically, as the "Lenin of the East." In February 1925 they organized a celebration of Narimanov's literary works, staged his plays in Moscow, and had them translated into Russian.¹⁰⁴ The Moscow Institute of Oriental Studies bore his name. He died, reportedly of a heart attack, on March 15, 1925, not far from the Kremlin. Within hours, the Politburo had decided to stage a large funeral on Red Square.¹⁰⁵ And like Lenin, they refused to send his body home for burial. Instead, it was displayed for twenty-four hours as mourners filed past, bells rang out, and his comrades extolled his virtues.

The Politburo suppressed the entire episode because it feared that publicly condemning Narimanov could undermine the legitimacy of Soviet policies in the Near East and policies of indigenization at home.¹⁰⁶ He was removed because he was a political liability and a security risk. He failed to consolidate the Azerbaijan Communist Party around his leadership, he espoused a brand of national communism unpalatable to the emerging consensus that was potentially resonant with the population, and he was the nominal head of a strategically important border republic with large oil deposits and a Muslim population resistant to Soviet power.

Most consequential, he had completely misunderstood the power structure. He, of course, had no way of knowing the roles that Stalin, Orjonikidze, Kirov, and Mikoyan would play in the future of the Soviet Union. But in his insistence that he could bring educational enlightenment through Bolshevism, he seriously misjudged his capacity to steer the course of the revolution, even as his comrades helped Stalin secure his hold over the party in Azerbaijan.

Despite the fanfare of Narimanov's funeral, he became persona non grata in the 1930s, and his name became synonymous with national deviation.[107] He was rehabilitated during the thaw under Khrushchev, but the Control Commission investigation remained secret. His warnings about the chaos in the party were prescient. He was right to see intrigue and double-dealing, in part because he also engaged in it. His removal may have solved the immediate concern around national deviation and neutralized a potential foreign policy and image problem, but by no means did it resolve the conflicts in the Azerbaijan party. The strong patronage networks that had coalesced around Orjonikidze, Kirov, and Serebrovskii failed to hold when all three of them were moved to other posts by the mid-to-late 1920s. The success of the Transcaucasian Republic, like the cohesion of the Azerbaijan party and the success of the oil industry, had been dependent on the force of these personalities and patronage networks.[108] The new head of the Azerbaijan party, Levon Mirzoyan, did no better than Narimanov in balancing the factions, and by 1929 Stalin intervened and overturned the leadership in Azerbaijan once again.[109]

The Transcaucasian Federation had been designed as a political unit to mitigate and channel national sentiment through a federal structure and secure Soviet power.[110] It is not surprising that this was fraught with conflict. The factionalism in Azerbaijan worked to Orjonikidze and Stalin's favor as they bolstered their supporters. The consolidation of the Transcaucasian Federation completed the binding of the South Caucasus to Soviet Russia that Narimanov had hoped to achieve through his position in Azerbaijan. He had pictured himself as the mediator of Soviet power. Instead, Orjonikidze played this role. The creation of the Transcaucasian Federation allowed Orjonikidze the leeway to resolve regional conflicts without directly involving Moscow.[111] The deal for power, originally predicated on oil and autonomy, had been renegotiated, and Narimanov was no longer part of it.

Conclusion

That Azerbaijan's lot was to feed the Bolshevik Revolution with its oil was an idea that needed to be explained. Whatever his reservations about the method and timing, Nariman Narimanov clearly articulated this reality in summer 1921 when he argued that "a great historical role fell to the lot of small Azerbaijan: it feeds Russian industry, and it must."[1] This book traced the material and political connections fostered by the imperative to possess Baku's oil and illustrated that the energy scarcity of the early 1920s was pivotal in shaping Soviet power in the South Caucasus. The Bolshevik leadership, in Baku as much as in Moscow, was keenly aware that oil was valuable as much for the potential alliances it wrought as for the hard currency it could procure. Numerous factions, none of which neatly reflected national, ethnic, or linguistic boundaries, battled over the unification of the economy and railroads, the allocation of oil products, foreign concessions, and control of the Party in Azerbaijan. These debates were simultaneously about center-periphery relations and who would be able to leverage resources to enforce their vision of Soviet power in the periphery.

In 1920, the prerevolutionary world was in tatters and Azerbaijan and Russia had embarked on divergent social and political trajectories. The economic and political ties between the two had been severed and would need to be bound back together in a deliberate project to set them back on the same path. Part of this project was the reconstruction of the oil industry and the rebinding of Azerbaijan to Russia. The political and propaganda effort was led by the Caucasus Bureau and Sergo Orjonikidze who worked to ensure the primacy of the Bolshevik Party throughout the South Caucasus. In tandem with this effort, in Party speeches, newspaper columns, at mosques, and innumerable meetings, Narimanov linked the fate of Azerbaijan and Muslims to Soviet Russia and promised liberation from imperialism. He argued that unification with Russia, and more reluctantly with Armenia and Georgia, was the path to a better future.

And the price for entry was Baku's oil. He set about trying to convince the population of Azerbaijan, and at times himself, that the price was worth paying.

While Narimanov did what he could to compel his vision of the future into reality, Aleksandr Serebrovskii faced the ruin of Baku's fields. Throughout 1920–1, Serebrovskii argued that without a functioning oil industry—and everything it enabled from industry to heating and trade—the Revolution was doomed. Moscow needed more than just Baku's oil, however. It needed stability in the South Caucasus to take advantage of the oil industry's potential and the infrastructure networks to ship it. After the folly of trying to set up a Soviet republic in Gilan, Moscow needed the Bolsheviks who had been forged in Baku—Orjonikidze, Anastas Mikoyan, and Narimanov, foremost among them—to fall in line.

After taking Azerbaijan, Armenia, and Georgia, the Bolsheviks needed to shift to state-building, diplomacy, and business deals to recover from the economic ruin of war. The Bolsheviks approached the oil industry strategically, as potential leverage. With the failure to reach an agreement at the Genoa Conference, and in retaliation for the Soviet refusal to grant compensation for nationalized property, the oil majors announced a boycott of Soviet oil products. The boycott was short-lived, and the Bolsheviks negotiated, often behind the scenes, a series of technology transfers, business deals, and marketing agreements. This strategy—combined with a tremendous domestic effort to save the fields—catalyzed the recovery of Baku's crude production. The campaign to rebuild the industry was successful. Year-on-year oil production grew both in Baku and Grozny, along with exports. By 1923, production outpaced demand and accounted for 23.6 percent of industrial exports.[2] By 1928, export levels were three times greater than they had been on the eve of the First World War, and in the first five-year plan oil exports were the largest source of foreign exchange earnings.

The Soviet Union exported higher value-refined products and used heavier fuels at home. In 1929–30, 100 percent of fuel oil production and 70 percent of kerosene production was reserved for internal use. In contrast, all solar oil and 80 percent of gasoline were exported, even as they made up larger shares of production.[3] However, with Stalin's Great Break and the frenzy of rapid industrialization, the recovery in Baku's fields was largely squandered and production was redirected to the domestic market. The pressure to drill wells to exhaustion once again damaged the industry and harmed production. In 1932, oil exports accounted for 28.6 percent of production, and in 1939 exports accounted for only 1.65 percent.[4] This legacy, the absence of Soviet oil on the international market in the 1930s, has obscured the success of the industry's recovery in the 1920s.

Initial attempts by Narimanov to ensure that the Azerbaijan SSR directly benefited from Baku's oil largely failed. In the negotiations for the creation of the Transcaucasian Republic, he signed an agreement with Azneft to create an oil fund for the reconstruction of Azerbaijan. The oil fund would be used as fuel, bartered, distributed to industry in Azerbaijan, and given to peasant households. This dream did not come to fruition. By 1930, central planning for Azneft was completely uncoupled from planning for Transcaucasia, let alone Azerbaijan. Chemical plants, hydro stations, and mining did not coordinate with Azneft, the largest oil trust in the Soviet Union.[5] Did industries that were run from Moscow but located in the periphery amount to extractive colonialism or some other dynamic that mirrored the reconstruction process more generally? For Azerbaijan it was clear that Baku's oil belonged to Moscow, not the Azerbaijan SSR or even the Transcaucasian Republic.

The harsh centralization of the Party and the consequences of Stalinism still distort our view of the 1920s, particularly in the non-Russian regions. This book showed that the Commissariat of Nationalities served as a way station for Stalin's allies from the South Caucasus who were exiled from Azerbaijan. It is unlikely that Ruhulla Akhundov and Mirza Davud Huseynov were the only so-called National Bolsheviks Stalin had transferred to far-away cities because they disagreed with the accommodationist policies of the Lenin era. Once the political climate was more favorable, he sent them back. The question of the Commissariat of Nationalities, and its relationship to Stalin's patronage networks in the periphery, may be more significant than historians have recognized. It was not just that Stalin took over the Party apparatus. Local communists, for their own reasons, helped him to do so. In Azerbaijan, a left faction of Azeri Bolsheviks sought to take over the Party for themselves and eliminate their rival and succeeded in doing so by siding with Orjonikidze and Stalin.

The dictates of Stalin demanded the erasure of important figures from the 1920s along with the projects they undertook to construct the Soviet Union. Excised from newspaper accounts, scrubbed from pictures, removed from their posts, and purged from official histories, we still do not know much about Nariman Narimanov, Aleksandr Serebrovskii, Ruhulla Akhundov, Leonid Krasin, or even Sergo Orjonikidze. After their metaphorical erasure from Soviet histories, many of the people in this book, including Serebrovskii, Akhundov, Huseynov, and Qarayev, virtually the entire Azerbaijan Communist Party, met the same fate as hundreds of thousands of others and were executed in the Great Purges of 1937 and 1938.[6] The purges targeted Party members, cultural and intellectual elites, and then spread across broader population. Orjonikidze went on to lead the People's Commissariat of Heavy Industry and oversaw the implementation of five-year plans and the industrialization of the Soviet Union. He died in 1937, mostly likely by suicide, after attempting to resist Stalin's persecution of the Commissariat of Heavy Industry. Only Narimanov and Krasin passed away in the mid-1920s before the mass violence of the late 1930s cannibalized the Communist Party. Despite the attempt to write them out of history, the archives are full of the lively debates, arguments, and sketches of these old Bolsheviks and the visions they hoped to manifest into reality.

Notes

Introduction

1 Vladimir Genis, *Krasnaia Persiia: Bol'sheviki v Giliana 1920–1921: Dokumental'naia khronika* (Moscow: Tsentr strategicheskikh i politicheskikh issledovanii; MNPI, 2000), 385–6.
2 Timothy Edward O'Conner, *The Engineer of Revolution. L. B. Krasin and the Bolsheviks, 1870–1926* (Boulder, CO: Westview Press, 1992), 40–6.
3 For an overview of the Caucasus and its relationships with its neighbors, see: Galina M. Yemelianova and Laurence Broers, eds. *Routledge Handbook of the Caucasus* (New York: Routledge, Taylor & Francis Group, 2020).
4 The question of whether the Soviet Union was an empire and what analytical tools should be used to analyze it has been a source of debate for more than two decades. The historiography of the early Soviet Union broadly posits competing frameworks for understanding this question—either that the Soviet Union was a modernizing state or it was an empire similar to the British or French empires. Some major works that address these questions include, Terry Martin, *The Affirmative Action Empire: Nations and Nationalism in the Soviet Union, 1923–1939* (Wilder House Series in Politics, History, and Culture. Ithaca: Cornell University Press, 2001); Douglas Northrop, *Veiled Empire: Gender and Power in Stalinist Central Asia* (Ithaca: Cornell University Press, 2004); Francine Hirsch, *Empire of Nations Ethnographic Knowledge and the Making of the Soviet Union* (Ithaca: Cornell University Press, 2005); Adeeb Khalid, *Making Uzbekistan: Nation, Empire, and Revolution in the Early USSR* (Ithaca: Cornell University Press, 2015). More recent literature argues that the Soviet Union had multiple overlapping systems of nation and empire that operated at the same time. For example, Krista Goff, *Nested Nationalisms. Making and Unmaking Nations in the Soviet Caucasus* (Ithaca: Cornell University Press, 2020); Claire Kaiser, *Georgian and Soviet. Entitled Nationhood and the Spector of Stalin in the Caucasus* (Ithaca: Cornell University Press, 2023). This literature has shown that the Soviet Union fostered nations with the active participation of local elites, who often took advantage of the Soviet system for their own ends. This book argues that this was also the case outside of nation-building.
5 This approach was inspired, in part, by the work of Timothy Mitchell, *Carbon Democracy. Political Power in the Age of Oil* (New York: Verso, 2011).
6 See Goff's discussion of layered inequalities in the Soviet Union. She writes,

> Indeed, in many post-Soviet states like Azerbaijan the Soviet experience has been inscribed in a framework that highlights how Moscow and Russians, as the proxy nation of Soviet power in the periphery, marginalized and discriminated against non-Russian peoples and republics, rendering all non-Russians equally innocent and equally disenfranchised from the power structure in which they lived. This narrative is blatantly untrue. The Soviet system was committed to national equality in some very real ways, but also fostered structures of inequality. (Goff, 2020: 5)

7 The English-language scholarship on the early Soviet Union has almost completely neglected oil and energy as serious topics of investigation, with a few exceptions. Daniel Yergin's expansive narrative addresses the international context around the early Soviet oil industry. Daniel Yergin, *The Prize. The Epic Quest for Oil, Money, and Power* (New York: Free Press, [1991] 2009). There are increasingly domestic accounts. See, for example, Christina E. Crawford, *Spatial Revolution. Architecture and Planning in the Early Soviet Union* (Ithaca: Cornell University Press, 2022). For two recent dissertations, see Rebecca Hastings, "Oil Capital: Industry and Society in Baku, Azerbaijan, 1870-present" (PhD dissertation, University of Oregon, 2020) and Jonathan H. Sicotte, "Baku: Violence, Identity, and Oil, 1905–1927" (PhD dissertation, Georgetown University, 2017).

There is a robust Russian-language scholarship, which includes Azerbaijani scholars. Some of these works have reevaluated previous Soviet-era studies but remain Moscow-centric while others favor an Azerbaijani national line or provide a high-level overview of international politics. For example, for Moscow-centric studies, see A. A. Igolkin, *Otechestvennaia neftianaia promyshlennost' v 1917–1920 godakh* (Moscow: Rossiiskii gosudarstvennyi gumanitarnyi universitet: 1999); A. A. Igolkin, *Sovetskaia neftianaia promyshlennost' v 1921–1928 godakh* (Moscow: Rossiiskii gosudarstvennyi gumanitarnyi universitet, 1999); V. N. Kostornichenko, *Inostrannyi kapital v sovetskoi neftianoi promyshlennosti (1918–1932)* (Volgograd: Volgograd State University: 2000); A. K. Sokolov, "Sovetskii 'Neftesindikat' na vnutrennem i mezhdunarodnykh rynkakh v 1920-e gg.," *Ekonomicheskaia istoriia. Obozrenie*, 10 (Moscow: 2005) 101–31. For an Azerbaijani national view, see Farhad Jabbarov, *Bakinskaia neft' v politike sovetskoi Rossii (1917–1922 gg.)* (Baku: Azerbaijan National Academy of Sciences, 2009), and for an overview of international politics and Azerbaijani oil, see El'mira Muradalieva, *Krov' zemnaia- neft' Azerbaidzhana i istoriia* (Baku: "Mutardzhim," 2005).

8 The export of refined oil products grew steadily throughout the 1920s. By 1926, it had reached almost twice the production levels of 1913, and by 1928 three times. In the first five-year plan it was the largest source of foreign currency in 1932 and accounted for nearly 19 percent of all exports from the USSR, by far the largest share. A. A. Igolkin, "Neftianoi faktor vo vneshne ekonomicheskikh sviaziakh

Rossii za poslednie 100 let," *Ekonomicheskii vestnik Rostovskogo gosudarstvennogo universiteta* 6, 1 (2008), 88.

9 The Soviet Union concluded numerous trade deals in 1921, followed by diplomatic recognition a few years later in 1924 with most of the Allied powers. The United States withheld recognition until 1933.

10 The Persian Empire ceded what is today contemporary Azerbaijan, Armenia, and parts of the north Caucasus to Russia after a series of wars in the early nineteenth century in the Treaty of Gulistan in 1813 and the Treaty of Turkmenchai in 1828. The annexation of Georgia began earlier in 1801. Despite the political change, the peoples of both empires remained connected by deep cultural, linguistic, religious, and familial ties. There is also a large Azeri/Turkic-speaking population in northern Iran, and successive Azeri political movements have advocated for the political unification of what they call northern and southern Azerbaijan.

Prelude: A Historical Sketch

1 From 1850 to 1872, St. Petersburg had given preferential rights to Armenian drillers, while Azeris opened small refineries. Ronald Grigor Suny, *Baku Commune, 1917–1918. Class and Nationality in the Russian Revolution* (Princeton: Princeton University Press, 1972), 4–5. On the wider impact of the 1872 land auctions, see Nicholas Lund, "At the Center of the Periphery. Oil, Land, and Power in Baku 1905–1917" (PhD dissertation, Stanford University, 2013), 29–35.
2 Tatar was a general term for Muslims in the Russian Empire and did not distinguish among the many ethno-linguistic or confessional groups.
3 Suny, *Baku Commune*, 5.
4 For a refutation of the monopoly thesis, see Lund, "At the Center of the Periphery," 4–5.
5 V. N. Kostornichenko, "K voprosu o natsionalizatsii otechestvennoi neftianoi promyshlennosti v 1918 g.," *Ekonomicheskaia istoriia*, 10 (Moscow 2005), 82.
6 See Yergin, *The Prize*, 42–7.
7 Yergin, *The Prize*, 43–5; Igolkin, *Otechestvennaia*, 23.
8 Guseinov, I. A., A. S. Sumbatzade, A. N. Guliev, I. A. Tokarzhevskinin, eds. *Istoriia Azerbaidzhana*, volume 2 (Baku: Izdatel'svto Akademii Nauk Azerbaidzhansoi SSR, 1960), 212.
9 Lund, "At the Center of the Periphery," 7.
10 Igolkin, *Otechestvennaia*, 43–5.
11 Ibid., 17.
12 Mitchell, *Carbon Democracy*, 35; Igolkin, *Otechestvennaia*, 17. The interplay between the coal and oil industries in both Russia and the Soviet Union is

complicated. The imperial Russian government and the Soviet government, for many of the same reasons, believed that coal was a more reliable fuel source. For a variety of political reasons, some of which are explored in Chapter 3, coal had pride of place.

13 Firouzeh Mostashari, "Development of Caspian Oil in Historical Perspective," in *The Caspian Region at a Crossroad. Challenges of a New Frontier of Energy and Development*, ed. Hooshang Amirahmadi (New York: St. Martin's Press, 2000), 98.
14 Lund, "At the Center of the Periphery," 11.
15 Suny, *Baku Commune*, 13; Audrey Altstadt-Mirhadi, "Baku. Transformation of a Muslim Town," in *The City in Late Imperial Russia*, ed. Michael Hamm (Bloomington: Indiana University Press, 1986), 290–2.
16 Suny, *Baku Commune*, 28–68; Audrey Altstadt-Mirhadi, "Baku," 305.
17 Altstadt-Mirhadi, "Baku," 288–9.
18 Ibid., 294.
19 Suny, *Baku Commune*, 7.
20 Leslie Sargent, "The 'Armeno-Tatar War' in the South Caucasus, 1905–1906: Multiple Causes, Interpreted Meanings," *Ab Imperio* 4 (2010): 183; Hastings, "Oil Capital," 70; Lund, "At the Center of the Periphery," 145.
21 Igolkin, *Otechestvennaia*, 22–3.
22 Ibid., 23; Yergin, *The Prize*, 117.
23 Suny, *Baku Commune*, 45–7.
24 Yergin, *The Prize*, 116–17.
25 Kostornichenko, "K voprosu o natsionalizatsii," 83.
26 Audrey L. Altstadt, *The Azerbaijani Turks: Power and Identity under Russian Rule* (Stanford: Hoover Institution Press, 1992), 46.
27 Kostornichenko, "K voprosu o natsionalizatsii," 83.
28 The Nobel Brothers represented about 25 percent of Baku's production in 1916. See Sicotte, "Baku," 106.
29 Starting in 1912 the tsarist government restricted oil exports and during the war banned them completely. S. S. Aliiarov, *Neftianye monopolii v Azerbaidzhane v period pervoi mirovoi voiny* (Baku: Izdanie AGY, 1974), 21–2.
30 Igolkin, *Otechestvenaia*, 46–9.
31 Ibid., 47–68.
32 Sicotte, "Baku," 97.
33 See the collection Ronald Grigor Suny, Fatma Muge Gocek, and Norman Naimark, eds., *A Question of Genocide: Armenians and Turks at the End of the Ottoman Empire* (New York: Oxford University Press, 2011).
34 Tadeusz Sweitochowski, *Russian Azerbaijan, 1905–1920: The Shaping of National Identity in a Muslim Community* (Cambridge: Cambridge University Press, 1985), 105–28.

35 For a helpful overview, see Arsène Saparaov, "Between the Russian Empire and the USSR. The Independence of Transcaucasia as a Socio-Political Transformation," in *Routledge Handbook of the Caucasus*, ed. Galina M. Yemelianova and Laurence Broers, 123–5.
36 For a detailed examination of these topics, see Michael A. Reynolds, *Shattering Empires: The Clash and Collapse of the Ottoman and Russian Empires 1908–1918* (Cambridge: Cambridge University Press, 2011), 167–218.
37 There are many works on the ADR. For brief overviews, see Sweitochowski, *Russian Azerbaijan*, 129–64; Kelsey Rice, "Forging the Progressive Path: Literary Assemblies and Enlightenment Societies in Azerbaijan, 1850–1928" (PhD dissertation, University of Pennsylvania, 2018), 231–8. For a monograph with a diplomatic focus, see Dzhamil' Gasanly, *Vneshniaia politika Azerbaidzhanskoi Demokraticheskoi Respubliki (1918–1920)*, volume 1 (Moscow: Flint, 2010). On nation-building and its place in the ADR, see Aidyn Balaev, *Azerbaidzhanskaia natsiia: osnovnye etapy stanovleniia na rubezhe XIX-XX vv* (Moscow: OOO "TiRu," 2012).
38 In October 1917, the local city council, dominated by left Social Democrats, voted to assume governing power of Baku and agreed to hold elections. The elections were held on October 22 and the Musavat was the clear victor, but the Bolsheviks refused to recognize the election results and it was called off. Suny, *Baku Commune*, 154–6; for a wider view, see Jörg Baberowski, *Vrag est' vezde: Stalinizm na Kavkaze*, trans. V. T. Altukhova (Moscow: ROSSPEN, 2010), 112–18.
39 Suny, *Baku Commune*, 231–2; Sweitochowski, *Russian Azerbaijan*, 118–19, 136.
40 On the March Days, see Sweitochowski, *Russian Azerbaijan*, 112–19; Michael G. Smith, "Power and Violence in the Russian Revolution. The March Events and Baku Commune of 1918," *Russian History* 41 (2014): 197–210. For competing historiographies on the March Days in Russian-, English- and Turkish-language sources, see footnote 48 in Michael Smith, "The Russian Revolution as a National Revolution: Tragic Deaths and Rituals of Remembrance in Muslim Azerbaijan (1907–1920)," *Jahrbücher für Geschichte Osteuropas* 49, 3 (2001): 377.
41 Smith, "The Russian Revolution," 377.
42 Suny, *Baku Commune*, 224.
43 Richard Pipes, *Formation of the Soviet Union: Communism and Nationalism 1917–1923* (Cambridge: Harvard University Press, 1964), 200.
44 On the violence and desperation in the contested regions, including Nagorno-Karabakh, Zangezuer, and Nakhchivan (among others), see Baberowski, *Vrag est' vezde*, 160–78.
45 Saparaov, "Between the Russian Empire and the USSR," 125.
46 Sweitochowski, *Russian Azerbaijan*, 140–57.

1 The Soviet Invasion of Baku and the Reconstruction of the Oil Industry

1 A. Igolkin and Iu. Gorzhaltsan, eds., *Russkaia neft' o kotoroi my tak malo znaem* (Moscow: "Olimp-Biznes," 2003), 164.
2 Igolkin, *Russkaia neft'*, 168–9.
3 Rossiiskii Gosudarstvennyi Arkhiv Ekonomiki (RGAE), f. 270, op. 1, d. 8, l. 27.
4 In 1921–2 Transcaucasia was the front line of a debate about how the Soviet Union should draw its internal borders, based on ethnicity or economic expediency. Hirsch, *Empire of Nations*, 62–98. I think the unification of Transcaucasia was driven as much by the economic paradigm, based on the structure and exploitation of the oil industry, as it was by the ethnographic paradigm. The two systems operated simultaneously.
5 RGAE, f. 270, op. 1, d. 8, l. 53b–54. The archival quote is from I. Peshkin, *Leninskaia komandirovka* "Stanitsy minuvshego" October no. 11, 1966, 155–70.
6 RGAE, f. 270, op. 1, d. 2, l. 1. The dates on his biographical sheets do not always match.
7 RGAE, f. 270, op. 1, d. 8, l. 54.
8 RGAE, f. 270, op. 1, d. 2, l. 1–6.
9 Ibid., l. 4–6. By 1920, Serebrovskii was a member of the Central Committee of the Azerbaijan Communist Party, by 1922 a member of the All-Russian Central Executive Committee, and candidate of the Central Committee of the All-Union Communist Party in 1925. He held posts in the Supreme Soviet of the Economy, including Deputy Chairman of the RSFSR in 1921; he also headed the oil industry and later the gold industry. Reference Guide to the Communist Party of the Soviet Union, 1917–91, http://www.knowbysight.info/SSS/05532.asp (accessed October 12, 2020).
10 RGAE, f. 270, op. 1, d. 8, l. 53ob.
11 RGAE, f. 270, op. 1, d. 7, l., 17.
12 Ibid.
13 Control over the industry fell under Serebrovskii's mandate, first in the Azerbaijan Oil Committee and later as the restructured and renamed Azerbaijan Central Oil Administration (Azneft).
14 Sergei Mironovich Kostrikov, better known as Sergei Kirov, was an old Bolshevik whose assassination in 1934 was used by Stalin as a pretense to spark the Great Purges. He held a variety of Party posts throughout the civil war, including Soviet representative in independent Georgia in 1920, representative to Poland, member of the Caucasus Bureau, and from July 1921 to January 1921 first secretary of the Central Committee of the Communist Party of Azerbaijan.

15 On the Caucasus Bureau, see Stephen Blank, "Bolshevik Organizational Development in Early Soviet Transcaucasia: Autonomy vs. Centralization, 1918–1924," in *Transcaucasia, Nationalism and Social Change: Essays in the History of Armenia, Azerbaijan, and Georgia*, ed. Ronald G. Suny (Ann Arbor: University of Michigan Press, 1983), 307–40.
16 RGAE, f. 270, op. 1, d. 8, l. 27–8.
17 Ibid., l. 54.
18 In total, Baku had 310 million poods* (37,214,886 barrels), Grozny had 43 million (5,162,064 barrels), and Ebma 14 million pood (1,680,672 barrels) of oil. In contrast, in 1919 Soviet Russia's total consumption of oil products stood at 26 million pood (3,121,249 barrels), of which 13 million pood (1,560,624 barrels) went to the railroads. By May 6, half a million pood (300,012 barrels) were shipped to Astrakhan and sent up the Volga. By the end of the month, more than 16 million pood (1,920,768 barrels) had been shipped. See RGAE, f. 270, op. 1, d. 8, l. 54, and Igolkin, *Otechestvennaia*, 112–13. Although the majority of oil went to fuel the railroads, it consisted of only 6.7 percent of the fuel they used; coal stood at 5.1 percent—the other 66.1 percent of fuel used by the railroads in 1919 was lumber.
*8.33 poods = 1 barrel (42 gallons US).
19 Igolkin, *Otechestvennaia*, 115.
20 Rossiiskii Gosudarstvennyi Arkhiv Sotsial'no-politicheskoi Istorii (RGASPI) f. 85, op. 5, d. 46, l. 1.
21 Igolkin, *Otechestvennaia*, 115.
22 Ibid., 112–31.
23 I. A. Guseinov, M. A. Dadashzade, and A. S. Sumbatzade, eds., *Istoriia Azerbaidzhana, chast' pervaia*, volume 3 (Baku: Izdatel'svto Akademii Nauk Azerbaidzhanskoi SSR, 1963), 247–9.
24 Azərbaycan Respublikası Dövlət Arxivi (ARDA), f. 1610, op. 16, d. 3, l. 1–2.
25 ARDA, f. 1610, op. 16, d. 3, l. 2ob.
26 Ibid., l. 1–2.
27 ARDA, f. 1610, op. 13, d. 246, l. 17–18.
28 Ibid., l. 28.
29 Ibid., l. 19–23.
30 Ibid., l. 26.
31 Ibid., l. 26.
32 Ibid. l. 27–8.
33 ARDA, f. 1114, op. 1, d. 6639, l. 2ob. In the first quarter after nationalization extraction dropped to 28.3 percent.
34 ARDA, f. 2548, op. 1, d. 4, l. 11.
35 Ibid., l. 12.
36 Ibid., l. 19.

37 ARDA, f. 1114, op. 1, d. 6639, l. 3ob.
38 Ibid., l. 3ob-4.
39 Ibid., l. 6.
40 Ibid., l. 10.
41 ARDA, f. 1610, op. 16, d. 3, l. 2.
42 ARDA, f. 2548, op. 1, d. 4, l. 2.
43 Ibid., l. 11.
44 Ibid., l. 17. The decision to mobilize workers from across the region quickly ran into problems. A month after the resolution, groups of workers arrived in Baku but there were no available apartments, and they essentially became refugees. Moreover, to attract workers from Iran, Azneft paid the bailers in Iranian currency, ARDA, f. 1114, op. 1, d. 6639, l. 30ob.
45 Igolkin, *Otechestvenaia*, 118–19.
46 These requests continued until the final invasions. For example, A. V. Kvashonkin, O. V. Khlevniuk, L. P. Koshelev, and L. A. Pogovaia, eds., *Bol'shevistskoe rukovodstvo: Perepiska, 1912-1927* (Moscow: ROSSPEN, 1996), 174–5.
47 RGASPI, f. 64, op. 1, d. 90, l. 53; RGASPI f. 85, op. 5, d. 52, l. 35–9. Also, Genis, *Krasnaia Persiia*, 77.
48 RGASPI, f. 85, op. 13, d. 34.
49 Ibid., l. 2-3.
50 RGASPI, f. 85, op.13, d. 26, l. 1.
51 Baberowski, *Vrag est' vezde*, 259.
52 RGASPI, f. 85, op. 13, d. 27, l. 6.
53 Baberowski, *Vrag est' vezde*, 259. Disarming Azeri peasants: RGASPI, f. 85, op. 13, d. 33; disarming Armenians: RGASPI, f. 85, op. 13, d. 34, l. 3.
54 RGASPI, f. 85, op. 13, d. 35, l. 3. Likely referring to Nikifor Nesterovskii.
55 "Provokatsiia Musavata i Dashnakov" May 31, 1920, in Nariman Narimanov, *Izbrannye proizvediniia*, volume 2. *1918-1921* (Baku: Azerbaidzhanskoe gosudarstvennoe izdatel'stvo, 1989), 286–9. The Dashnaktsutyun was (also known as the Dashnak–Armenian Revolutionary Federation), the party in charge of independent Armenia.
56 In exchange, Soviet Russia agreed that Nakhchivan, the territory disputed by Armenia and Azerbaijan, would belong to Soviet Azerbaijan and the province of Kars would be returned to Turkey. This treaty, known as the Treaty of Moscow, was negotiated with the as-yet unrecognized Turkish Republic under the leadership of Kemal Ataturk. It was reaffirmed in October 1921 with the Treaty of Kars.
57 ARDA, f. 1114, op. 1, d., 6639, l. 30ob.
58 RGASPI, f. 85, op. 5, d. 46, l. 6, 9. There was an Azerbaijani foreign trade commissariat as well as Armenian, Russian (Rossiiskii) and Georgian foreign trade commissariats, all of which were competing with one another and perpetuating

the existence of the speculators in the market. In addition, they were conscious of looking incompetent to European observers.
59 RGASPI, f. 85, op. 5, d. 46, l. 1–2. There was also extreme inflation because they were indiscriminately printing money.
60 RGASPI, f. 85, op. 5, d. 46, l. 1.
61 Transcaucasia was central to a larger debate on regionalization, or how the Soviet Union should draw its internal borders. One commissariat proposed that the Soviet Union be organized along ethnographic lines, divided by ethnicity and nationality, into separate republics. A competing paradigm from the State Planning Committee (Gosplan) argued that the new state be organized along economic lines. The economic model was explicitly based on European colonial models of economic exploitation and wanted to divide the Soviet Union into production zones. Hirsch, *Empire of Nations*, 64, 72. The economic paradigm had already taken shape in the South Caucasus, even while Gosplan outlined its border proposal. Gosplan established its commission on economic regionalization in spring and summer of 1921, during and after the events described further on. In other words, Gosplan was arguing for a model that already existed in South Caucasus and it took shape in Baku.
62 S. V. Kharmandarian, *Lenin i stanovlenie zakavkazskoi federatsii* (Yerevan: Izadatel'stvo "Aiastan," 1969), 96–7, 127.
63 Avtandil Mikhailovich Menteshashvili, *Bol'shevistskaia pressa Zakavkaz'ia v bor'be za obrazovanie zakavkazskoi federatsii i Soiuza SSR (1921–1922 gg.)* (Tbilisi: Izdatel'stvo Tbiliskogo Universiteta, 1972), 22. There is a large literature on the unification, for example, Kharmandarian, *Lenin i stanovlenie*. For an overview, see Blank, "Bolshevik Organizational Development in Early Soviet Transcaucasia," 305–38.
64 Kharmandarian, *Lenin i stanovlenie*, 127.
65 Menteshashvili, *Bol'shevistskaia pressa*, 21.
66 RGASPI, f. 85, op. 5, d. 46, l. 1–31.
67 Also, Kharmandarian, *Lenin i stanovlenie*, 124–5. Quoting Lenin: "The conversation is about the unification of the Caucasian republics in one economic center: Georgian, Azerbaijani, and Armenian. Azerbaijan produces oil, it is necessary to transport it through Batum through Georgian territory, so it will be a one economic center."
68 For example, Altstadt, *The Azerbaijani Turks*, 109.
69 On this episode, and the important role that Orjonikidze played in Transcaucasia, see, Jeremy Smith, "The Georgian Affair of 1922—Policy Failure, Personality Clash or Power Struggle?" *Europe-Asia Studies* 50: 519–44.
70 Despite this early support, by August 1921 both Huseynov and Ruhulla Akhundov, a member of the Azerbaijan CC, petitioned Lenin to stop the formal unification of Transcaucasia. Sergei Kirov, the head of the Azerbaijan Communist Party,

and Stalin overrode these objections at an Azerbaijan party meeting in February 1922 and forced their position in favor of unification. Baberowski, *Vrag est' vezde*, 248. These internal disputes only worsened over time, eventually leading several opponents of unification, including Huseynov and Ruhulla Akhundov, to ally with Orjonikidze and remove Narimanov from power. This is discussed in Chapter 5.

71 In May 1919, the Caucasian Regional Committee decided the economies should unify; Kharmandarian, *Lenin i stanovlenie*, 30–1. During the invasion of Azerbaijan, on May 4, 1920, Orjonikidze and Kirov sent Lenin a telegram stating: "We will carry out military-economic unification with Soviet Russia. Experience requires us to supply the Sovnarkom with authority over all of Caucasia and further … Don't give Narimanov that kind of authority." RGASPI, f. 85, op. 13, d. 12, l. 10.

72 Baberowski, *Vrag est' vezde*, 234.
73 RGASPI, f. 85, op. 5, d. 46, l. 1.
74 Ibid., l. 9.
75 Ibid., l. 2.
76 Ibid.
77 Igolkin, *Otechestvennaia*, 130.
78 RGAPSI, f. 85, op. 5, d. 46, l. 28.
79 Refineries were located both in Baku and Batumi. It was cheaper to ship crude oil to Batumi and have it processed there.
80 RGASPI, f. 85, op. 5, d. 46, l. 28.
81 Ibid., l. 15.
82 Ibid., l. 13.
83 Baberowski, *Vrag est' vezde*, 247–8.
84 Narimanov, *Izbrannye*, 489.
85 RGASPI, f. 64, op. 1, d. 13, l. 223. This formal independence did not mean independence in practice. The Georgian and Transcaucasian Republics were still expected to maintain complete subordination to the Central Committee.
86 RGASPI, f. 64, op. 1, d. 1, l. 230.
87 The Caucasus Bureau received multiple complaints about Serebrovskii's behavior and he responded that "the oil industry depends on the proper functioning of the UNIFIED FOREIGN TRADE COMMISSARIAT." In other words, if it did its job properly, he would not have to use other means. RGASPI, f. 64, op. 1, d. 75, l. 145.
88 Dzh. B. Guliev and Kh. G. Vezirov, eds., *V. I. Lenin ob Azerbaidzhane* (Baku: Azerbaidzhan gosudarstvennoe izadtel'stvo, 1970), 308–9, fn 115; Serebrovskii was asking Lenin to make official his telegram from April 2, reprinted in ibid., 211–12.
89 Azneft could initiate and conclude deals but they had to be approved by the Commissariat of Foreign Trade; Azneft still have to get personal approval from Lenin before it could make the exchanges, RGAE, f. 270, op. 1, d. 8, l. 55ob–56.

90 RGEA, f. 270, op. 1, d. 8, l. 56. Paraphrase from Peshkin's account. More details on the *Sosifross* agreement in Jabbarov, *Bakinskaia*, 176; A. P. Serebrovskii, *Rukovodstvo V.I. Lenina vosstanovleniem neftianoi promyshlennosti* (Moscow: Gospolitizdat, 1958), 13–15.
91 RGASPI, f. 64, op. 1, d. 28, l. 11–18.
92 The decree on profit earning only became an officially mandated goal on April 10, 1923. Before then, they were expected to make enough money to fund their own operations (something that did not happen), which amounted to the same thing. On trust reform, see Sokolov, "Sovetskii," 104–5; on *khozrazchet* and *glavki*, see Ivar Smilga, *Vosstanovitel'nyi protsess: Piat' let novoi ekonomicheskoi politiki (mart 1921 g.-mart 1926 g.) Stat'i i rechi* (Moscow: Izdatel'stvo "Planovoe khoziaistvoe," 1927), 9–15, 36–7, 40.
93 Sokolov, "Sovetskii," 105; Igolkin, *Sovetskaia*, 25–6.
94 A. A. Igolkin, "Sovetskii neftianoi eksport v gody predvoennykh piatiletok," *Neftianoe khoziastvo* 9 (2006), 139; Igolkin, *Sovetskaia*, 26, 29.
95 Igolkin *Sovetskaia*, 33.
96 Ibid., 35–6.
97 Guliev and Vezirov, *Lenin*, 239, 240, 312 fn 133.
98 Ibid., 313 fn 141; 252.
99 ARDA, f. 411, op. 1, d. 26, l. 1; Guliev, *Lenin*, 313 fn 141; also see Jabbarov, *Bakinskaia*, 176–8.
100 RGASPI, f. 64, op. 1, d. 66, l. 8.
101 Ibid., l. 4.
102 Ibid., 4–4ob.
103 Ibid.
104 Ibid.
105 Ibid., l. 4ob.
106 RGASPI, f. 64, op. 1, d. 66, l. 3; He was also accused of circumventing the Commissariat of Foreign Trade at Batumi by interfering with the distribution of goods at the port warehouses, RGASPI, f. 64, op. 1, d. 75, l. 241.
107 RGASPI, f. 64, op. 1, d. 66, l. 1–2.
108 RGASPI, f. 64, op. 1, d. 75, l. 145–6.

2 Revolution in the Muslim East: The Bolsheviks and a Soviet Republic in Iran

1 Narimanov frequently referenced this arrangement with Lenin, Rossiiskii Gosudarstvennyi Arkhiv Sotsial'no-poliotichekoi Istorii (RGASPI), f. 64, op.1, d. 90, l. 19–20; Baberowski, *Vrag est' vezde*, 230–1, 264–5.

2 RGASPI, f. 64, op.1, d. 90, l. 19–20.
3 Gasanly, *Vneshiaia politika*, 13; I disagree that Narimanov was mere window dressing for the Bolsheviks.
4 For the reformist movement in Central Asia, see Adeeb Khalid, *The Politics of Muslim Cultural Reform: Jadidism in Central Asia* (Berkeley: University of California Press, 1998) and Khalid, *Making Uzbekistan*. Also see Alexander Morrison's review essay "Muslims and Modernity in the Russian Empire," *The Slavonic and East European Review* 94, 4 (October 2016): 715–24.
5 For his argument that the Bolsheviks should focus on the East, particularly Iran, not Europe, see Nariman Narimanov, *Izbrannye proizvedeniia. Volume 2* (Baku: Azerbaidzhanskoe gosudarstvennoe izdatel'stvo, 1989), 234–41.
6 The classic work on this is Suny, *Baku Commune*. Also see Smith, "The Russian Revolution," 363–88; Michael G. Smith, "Anatomy of a Rumour: Murder Scandal, the Musavat Party and Narratives of the Russian Revolution in Baku, 1917–1920," *Journal of Contemporary History* 36 (April 2001): 211–40.
7 The March Days happened in the wider context of the First World War and the collapse of the Caucasus front. Soldiers from the Russian imperial army abandoned their posts and as the front disintegrated numerous groups started arming themselves and disarming potential rivals. Armenian troops, rightly, feared the Ottomans would push north and Muslims in the Caucasus, who were not allowed to serve in the tsarist army, were largely unarmed and sought to find weapons wherever possible out of fear they would be attacked. This led to a series of skirmishes and attacks in the South Caucasus and along the borders of both Iran and the Ottoman Empire. For a brief overview of this situation, see Baberowski, *Vrag est' vezde*, 122–9; Swietochowski, *Russian Azerbaijan*, 105–19.
8 Michael G. Smith, "Stalin's Martyrs: The Tragic Romance of the Russian Revolution," *Totalitarian Movements and Political Religions* 4, 1 (2003): 95–126.
9 Narimanov, *Izbrannye*, 185.
10 The relationship between the *Hummet* and the Bolsheviks was ambiguous. Because the *Hummet* was technically part of the Baku Committee of the Russian Social Democratic Workers Party (RSDWP), and they often worked together, most Soviet-era sources say that Narimanov was a member of the RSDWP from 1905, or even 1904. The parties only merged in 1919, however.
11 Also RGASPI, f. 588. op.2 d. 177, l. 244.
12 Pezhmann Dailami, "The First Congress of the Peoples of the East and the Iranian Soviet Republic of Gilan, 1920–21," in *Reformers and Revolutionaries in Modern Iran*, ed. Stephanie Cronin (New York: Routledge, 2004), 89.
13 For more on the Azerbaijan Soviet Socialist Republic (and the contemporary Republic of Azerbaijan) and Iranian Azerbaijan, made up of the provinces of East Azerbaijan and West Azerbaijan, see Kelsey Rice, "The Caucasus and Iran," in

Routledge Handbook of the Caucasus, ed. Galina M. Yemelianova and Laurence Broers (New York: Routledge, Taylor & Francis Group, 2020), 347–58.

14 For an overview of Narimanov's biography and the Bolshevik Party in Azerbaijan up to 1920, see Baberowski, *Vrag est vezde*, 219–34.

15 Narimanov, *Izbrannye*, 185–96; Ibid., 176–815, "S kakim lozungom my idem na kavkaz."

16 Narimanov, *Izbrannye*, 189.

17 Richard K. Debo, *Survival and Consolidation: The Foreign Policy of Soviet Russia, 1918-1921* (Montreal: McGill-Queens University Press, 1992), 179–80.

18 This was reiterated by Orjonikidze, RGASPI, f. 64, op. 1, d. 25, l. 1.

19 Baberowski, *Vrag est' vezde*, 229. Narimanov lobbied consistently for Moscow to pursue an active policy in Iran. See Narimanov, *Izbrannye*, 239, 253–6. For more on this, see Swietochowski, *Russian Azerbaijan*, 168–72; Dailami, "The First Congress," 91–4.

20 He initially argued for an independent Soviet Azerbaijan after the collapse of the commune, Swietochowski, *Russian Azerbaijan*, 169; he then advocated for Azerbaijan to become part of the RSFSR but was overruled and seems to have changed his mind later. Baberowski, *Vrag est' vezde*, 229–30.

21 Ibid., 232–3.

22 Narimanov, *Izbrannye*, 269. For more on how he viewed his role see, ibid., 253, 255, 257.

23 For the various posts, see A. A. Pashaev and M. I. Naidel, eds., *Dekrety Azrevkoma, 1920-21: Sbornik dokumentov* (Baku: Azerbaidzhanskoe gosudarstvennoe izdatel'stvo: 1988), 13–14.

24 RGASPI, f. 588, op. 2, d. 176, l. 28–9.

25 RGASPI, f. 85, op. 13, d. 12, l. 101.

26 Genis, *Krasnaia*, 77–8.

27 Ibid.

28 Ibid.

29 On connections between Russia and Iran, see Houri Berberian, *Armenians and the Connected Revolutions in the Russian, Iranian, and Ottoman Worlds* (Oakland: University of California Press, 2019) and Stephanie Cronin, ed., *Iranian-Russian Encounters. Empires and revolutions since 1800* (New York: Routledge, 2013).

30 Pezhmann Dailami, "The Bolsheviks and the Jangali Movement," *Cahiers du Monde russe et sovietique* 31, 1 (January–March, 1990): 44. Russian Azerbaijan and Iranian Azerbaijan are also known as Northern and Southern Azerbaijan, respectively.

31 Tadeusz Swietochowski, "The Himmet Party. Socialism and the National Question in Russian Azerbaijan 1904–1920," *Cahiers du Monde russe et sovietique* 19, 1/2 (January–June, 1978): 122.

32 Baberowski, *Vrag est' vsede*, 222.
33 Dailami, "The Bolsheviks and the Jangali Movement," 44.
34 Ibid., 45; Genis, *Krasnaia*, 148-9. The Soviet concessionary agreement with Khoshtariia is the subject of Chapter 5.
35 Moriz Deutschmann, "Cultures of Statehood, Cultures of Revolution: Caucasian Revolutionaries in the Iranian Constitutional Movement, 1906-1911," *Ab Imperio* 2 (2013): 178.
36 Dailami, "The Bolsheviks and the Jangali Movement," 45.
37 On these meetings, see Cosroe Chaqueri, *The Soviet Socialist Republic of Iran, 1920-1921. Birth of Trauma* (Pittsburgh, PA: University of Pittsburgh Press, 1995), 169-71.
38 Vladimir Genis, *Bolsheviki v Giliane: provozglashenie Persidskoi sovestskoi respubliki, Voprosy istorii*, 1 (1999): 64. Also see Debo, *Consolidation*, 184-7.
39 Ottoman, Russian, and British troops had all occupied Iran during the war, undermining the government.
40 Raskolnikov, F. F., *Tales of Sub-Lieutenant Ilyin*, trans. Brian Pearce (New York: New Park Publications), 124.
41 Debo, *Consolidation*, 184.
42 See Oliver Bast, "Duping the English and outwitting the Russians? Iran's foreign policy, the 'Bolshevik threat', and the genesis of the Soviet-Iranian Treaty of 1921," in *Iranian-Russian Encounters. Empires and revolutions since 1800*, ed. Stephanie Cronin (New York: Routledge, 2013).
43 Raskolnikov, *Tales of Sub-Lieutenant*, 132.
44 Genis, *Bolsheviki*, 66.
45 Ibid., 67.
46 Bast, "Duping the English," 275.
47 Chaqueri, *The Soviet Socialist Republic*, 183.
48 RGASPI, f. 159, op. 2, d. 51, l. 12.
49 Genis, *Krasnaia*, 82.
50 Ibid., 87.
51 The *Adalat*, under the leadership of Sultanzade, argued that Iran had already passed through a bourgeoisie revolution in 1909 and was therefore ready for a socialist revolution on the order of the October Revolution.
52 RGASPI, f. 85, op. 5, d. 52, l. 44.
53 Genis, *Krasniia*, 80.
54 Afandiyev was a member of the RSDWP since 1904, a member of the failed Baku Commune, and a member of *Hummet*.
55 Chaqueri, *The Soviet Socialist Republic*, 153-5. The *Adalat* allied with the Baku Commune in 1918. Sweithocowski, *Russian Azerbaijan*, 170-1.

56 Chaqueri, *The Soviet Socialist Republic*, 158. A report submitted to the Caucasus Bureau noted that the *Adalat* congress held in June marked the "liquidation" of the *Adalat* and its merger with the Russian Communist Party, RGASPI, f. 64, op. 1, d. 20, l. 19; The ICP elected Lenin and Nariman Narimanov honorary chairmen but it was divided by factions from the outset. Two Bolsheviks from the Caucasus, Abukov and Naneishvili (also a member of the Caucasus Bureau and thus subordinate to Orjonikidze), headed the so-called national-revolutionary faction which argued that Iran was not ready for a socialist revolution and should cooperate with the bourgeoisie. This was the line that the Commissariat of Foreign Affairs was to adopt in short order. The more radical left faction was "purely communist," and it was to this wing that Sultanzade and Agaev belonged.

57 Genis, *Krasniia*, 151; The Iran Bureau stated that (1) the national liberation movement of Persia may rely on the petty-bourgeois but not the landowners, (2) military goals include chasing out the British and overturning the Shah in Tehran as well as a peasant revolution and land reform, (3) all propaganda must follow these lines, (4) with the goal of supporting anti-British elements the Party will support the leader of the Iranian movement [Kuchuk] for its own ends, (5) the Iranian revolution will only be assisted through Communist organizations [Iran Bureau], and (6) in addition to the goals of ousting the British and strengthening communism the Iran Bureau must organize troops, RGASPI, f. 64, op. 1, d. 20, l. 19–21.

58 The initial agreement was concluded with Raskolnikov, Orjonikidze, members of the *Adalat* leadership, unnamed Turkestani Communists, and the Jangali delegation. Chaqueri, *The Soviet Socialist Republic*, 180–3, 191–2.

59 RGASPI, f. 159, op. 2, d. 51, l. 4

60 Ibid.

61 Ibid., also Chaqueri, *The Soviet Socialist Republic*, 237–9.

62 RGASPI, f. 85, op. 5, d.52, l. 42.

63 Sultanzade, an Iranian born Armenian revolutionary, was the founder of the Communist Party of Iran and leader of the *Adalat*. See Genis, *Krasnaia*, 112–27.

64 To do something *po-bakinskii* [in a Baku-manner] was a euphemism that Ordjonikidze used in his early correspondence when he referred to the use of violence to achieve a policy directive or goal. RGASPI, f. 85, op. 5, d. 52.

65 RGASPI, f. 85, op. 5, d. 52, l. 44–5.

66 The archival sources often used the term "Baku comrades" [*bakinskie tovarishchi*]. I am using Baku Bolsheviks to capture the wider coalition of actors and to emphasize that they were often acting on their own initiative.

67 Genis, *Krasnaia*, 253; RGASPI, f. 64, op. 1, d. 20, l. 58.

68 On Narimanov's role, see Genis, *Krasnaia*, 435–9. Haider Khan was never approved by Moscow; his appointment came from the Azerbaijan government, Chaqueri,

The Soviet Socialist Republic, 332–3. The meeting of the Iran Bureau opened with a fistfight, Genis, *Krasnaia*, 434.
69 Genis, *Krasnaia*, 438.
70 RGASPI, f. 159, op. 2, d. 51, l. 127.
71 Louis Fischer, *The Soviets in World Affairs. A History of the Relations between the Soviet Union and the Rest of the World*, Volume 1 (Princeton: Princeton University Press, 1951), 289.
72 E. H. Carr, *The Bolshevik Revolution 1917–1923*, Volume 3 (New York: Macmillan Company, [1953] 1961), 293–4.
73 Fisheries concessions were not annulled. Miron Rezun, *The Soviet Union and Iran. Soviet Policy from the Beginnings of the Pahlavi Dynasty until the Soviet Invasion in 1941* (Geneve: Sijthoff & Noordhoff International Publishers, 1981), 18.
74 Rezun, "*The Soviet Union and Iran*," 369. In 1941, however, the treaty would be used as a justification for the joint Soviet-British occupation of Iran, which was intended to counter German moves in the country and secure oil transport routes.
75 RGASPI, f. 159, op. 2, d. 27, l. 91–2, 96–8, 100–4.
76 Ibid., l. 100.
77 In his report to the Central Committee, he wrote, "I, finally, thought that as the leader I would be able to fix all of the mistakes of our Eastern foreign policy that the Commissariat of Foreign Affairs and Baku Soviet allowed, and those mistakes need to be noticed." Narimanov, *Izbrannye*, 239; also see 253–6.
78 He made this argument frequently. For another example, see Narimanov, *Izbrannye*, 243.
79 Narimanov, *Izbrannye*, 240. Narimanov's frustration with the institutional dismissal of Muslim voices was exacerbated by what he felt was an interpersonal chauvinism from his non-Muslim comrades. In a report submitted to the Central Committee on the history of *Hummet*, he addressed the accusation of his fellow Baku Bolsheviks that *Hummet* did nothing to further the revolution. Their mistake, he pointed out, was in confusing Baku for all of the Caucasus. Narimanov, *Izbrannye*, 243.
80 Genis, *Krasniia*, 83.
81 Ibid.
82 RGAPSI, f. 64, op. 1, d. 25, l. 1.
83 Chaqueri, *The Soviet Socialist Republic*, 286–7. This view was expressed outright by Lenin and Trotsky. However, it was not based on the desire to abandon revolution as much as it was to maintain Soviet power.
84 Sokolov, "Diplomaticheskaia deiatel'nost' akademika F.A. Rotshteina 20-e gody XX veka." *Novaia noveishaia istoriia* 2 (2007): 158–60.
85 Sokolov, "Diplomaticheskaia deiatel'nost," 160–1; Chaqueri, *The Soviet Socialist Republic*, 330–1.
86 RGASPI, f. 64, op. 1, d. 206, l. 116.

87 Ibid., l. 120.
88 Genis, *Krasnaia*, 376–7.
89 Ibid., 377.
90 This account, which is quoted from Chicherin's letter, comes from Genis, *Krasnaia*, 378. For a full account of the evacuation, see 373–87.
91 For various alliances see Chaqueri. Political crisis in Tehran, and Reza's coup there, meant the Soviets delayed evacuation of "Azerbaijani" troops, 340–1.
92 The account that follows is based on a report found in RGASPI f. 159, op. 2, d. 51, 43–54.
93 RGASPI, f. 159, op. 2, d. 51, l. 43. Report from the Soviet representative in Iran Khavin to Chicherin. Also see, Chaqueri, *The Soviet Socialist Republic*, 360–1.
94 RGASPI, f. 159, op. 2, d. 51, l. 43–9.
95 Ibid., l. 45.
96 Ibid., l. 43–9.
97 Genis, *Krasnaia*, 468–9; Chaqueri, *The Soviet Socialist Republic*, 362–3.
98 RGASPI, f. 159, op. 2, d. 51, l. 53–4. The exact offenders are often not named, instead the terms "*predstavitelei Azerbaidzhana*" or more sarcastically "*upomianutye azerbaidzhanskie gosti*" are used.
99 RGASPI, f. 159, op. 2, d. 51, l. 135; this is echoed in Chicherin's correspondence with Rotshtein as well, V. V. Sokolov, "Diplomaticheskaia deiatel'nost'," 164; RGASPI, f. 159, op. 2, d. 51, l. 53.
100 RGASPI, f. 159, op. 2, d. 51, l. 80.
101 Ibid., l. 55.
102 Ibid., l. 56.
103 Ibid.
104 Ibid., l. 77–8.
105 Ibid., 80.
106 Ibid., 134.
107 Ibid., 133.
108 Ibid., 134.

3 Bolsheviks on the World Stage: Soviet Concessions Policy and the Oil Question

1 Anna Louise Strong, *The First Time in History. Two Years of Russia's New Life (August 1921 to December 1923)*, New York: Boni and Liveright, 1925. http://www.marxists.org/reference/archive/strong-anna-louise/1925/first_time/ch05.htm (accessed November 20, 2020).

2 "Oil Lease Talk Stirs Genoa Delegates; Russians Deny They Will Give Monopoly," *New York Times*, May 5, 1922, ProQuest Historical Newspapers.
3 Timothy O'Conner, *Diplomacy and Revolution* (Ames: Iowa State University Press, 1988), 81.
4 After the treaty, there was widespread consensus that the Allied powers would not reach a general agreement with Soviet Russia or Germany, Carr, *The Bolshevik Revolution*, 376.
5 Edwin J. James, "Germans Reject French Peace Terms unless Allies Are to Act in Concert; Oil excitement Spreads at Conference," May 5, 1922, ProQuest Historical Newspapers; "British Deny Shell Deal," *New York Times*, May 4, 1922, ProQuest Historical Newspapers.
6 Carr, *The Bolshevik Revolution*, 378-9; Louis Fischer, *Oil Imperialism. The International Struggle for Petroleum* (Westport, CT: Hyperion Press, 1926), 50-60.
7 Carole Fink, *The Genoa Conference. European Diplomacy, 1921-1922* (Chapel Hill: University of North Carolina Press, 1993); Carole Fink, Axel Frohn, and Jurgen Heideking, eds., *Genoa, Rapallo, and European Reconstruction in 1922* (New York: Cambridge University Press, 1991). See the chapter by A. A. Fursenko, "The Oil Problem and Soviet American Relations at the Genoa Conference of 1922."
8 Antony C. Sutton, *Western Technology and Soviet Economic Development 1917 to 1930* (Stanford, CA: Stanford University Press, 1968), 6-9. Sutton calls these Type I, Type II, and Type II concessions. The Soviet Union entered into all three types in the 1920s. For more on Soviet concession, see A. A. Igolkin, *Sovetskaia neftianaia promyshlennost' v 1921-1928 godakh* (Moscow: Rossiiskii gosudarstvennyi gumanitarnyi universitet, 1999); Kostornichenko, *Inostrannyi*.
9 For the competition between Standard and Sinclair, see Michael Rubin, "Stumbling through the 'Open Door': The US in Persia and the Standard-Sinclair Oil Dispute, 1920-1925." *Iranian Studies*, 28, 3/4 (Summer-Autumn, 1995): 203-29; Yergin, *The Prize* (New York: Free Press, [1991] 2009), 178-80.
10 On backroom alliances and oil deals, see Gregory P. Nowell, *Mercantile States and the World Oil Cartel, 1900-1939* (Ithaca: Cornell University Press, 1994), 154-5.
11 Igolkin, *Sovetskaia*, 96-9; Fischer, *Oil Imperialism*, 43.
12 This was previously a German share, but it was given to France after the Versailles Treaty. Yergin, *The Prize*, 173.
13 Fischer, *Oil Imperialism*, 39. The competition between these companies in northern Iran is the subject of Chapter 4. On the American reaction, see Yergin, *The Prize*, 179.
14 Rossiiskii Gosudarstvennyi Arkhiv Ekonomiki (RGAE) f. 4372, op. 5, d. 34, l. 3-4.
15 RGAE, f. 4372, op. 5, d. 34, l. 4-4ob. Gosplan believed that the US was likely to use all of its reserves leaving Soviet Russia with a monopoly, RGAE, f. 4372, op. 5, d. 34, l. 4-5.

16 RGAE, f. 4372, op. 5, d. 34, l. 4. While the prewar Russian petroleum industry mainly produced kerosene for the domestic market, there was an assumption that Soviet Russia would produce heavy fuels for exportation.
17 RGAE, f. 4372, op. 5, d. 34, l. 5.
18 Ibid., l. 5ob.
19 Serebrovskii, *Rukovodstvo*, 4. Serebrovskii believed they would gladly cooperate to prevent a Soviet recovery.
20 Igolkin, *Sovetskaia*, 100.
21 A. A. Igolkin, "The High Price of Soviet Oil," *Oil of Russia: Lukoil International Magazine*, 1, 2005. www.oilru.com/or/22/359/ (accessed September 5, 2022).
22 From 1925, it was the Political Bureau of the Central Committee of the Communist Party.
23 Rossiiskii Gosudarstvennyi Arkhiv Sotsial'no-polioticheskoi Istorii (RGASPI), f. 159, op. 2, d. 15, ll. 3–5.
24 RGASPI, f. 159, op. 2, d. 15, l. 5.
25 Ibid., l. 11.
26 Ibid., l. 4. They were also being pushed by other countries to clarify the relationship between the republics, Ibid., l. 11.
27 It was renamed the Transcaucasian Federative Soviet Socialist Republic.
28 RGASPI, f. 159, op. 2, d. 15, l. 7.
29 Ibid., l. 118.
30 Ibid., l. 16.
31 Ibid., l. 68–9.
32 Ibid., l. 66.
33 Ibid., 71. Others argued that they cultivate disagreement among the Western powers and lay the groundwork for bilateral agreements later. This is much closer to the actual result. RGASPI, f. 159, op. 2, d. 16, l. 187–9.
34 RGASPI, f. 159, op. 2, d. 15, l. 67.
35 Azneft. *Obzor Azerbaidzhanskoi Neftianoi Promyshlennosti: Za piat' let natstionalizatsii 1920–1925* (Baku: Gosudarstvennoe Ob"edinenie Neftianoi Promyshlennosti, 1925), 12.
36 Ibid., 12–13.
37 RGASPI, f. 159, op. 2, d. 15, l. 108. The report, with some commentary, is on pages 107 to 115 and serves as the basis for the following discussion.
38 See Lund, 'At the Center of the Periphery', 2013.
39 RGASPI, f. 159, op. 2, d.16, l. 286.
40 Nowell, *Mercantile States*, 151.
41 RGASPI, f. 159, op. 2, d. 15, l. 110.
42 Ibid.

43 Ibid. He recommended a trade-off and gave a nominal example, "Assume that the country uses 350 million poods of oil. Of that amount maybe no more than 150 million poods are specific to oil consumption/for special oil furnaces, for the chemical industry etc./ the remaining 200 million poods are simple caloric fuel which, with corresponding alteration of the furnaces, can be replaced with coal." There are 8.33 pood in 1 barrel of oil.
44 On coal and oil in the Soviet Union, see Igolkin, *Sovetskaia,* 6–13, 43–57.
45 Igolkin, *Sovetskaia,* 45.
46 Ibid., 46.
47 RGASPI, f. 159, op. 2, d. 16, l. 287.
48 RGASPI, f. 159, op. 2, d. 15, l. 113.
49 Ibid., l. 113–14.
50 Ibid., l. 115.
51 Ibid., l. 109.
52 Ibid., l. 107.
53 Ibid., l. 66.
54 Ibid., l. 66–71, 77, 127.
55 Gosudarstvennyi Arkhiv Rossiiskoi Federatsii (GARF), f. 8350, op. 1, d. 51, l. 17–20.
56 GARF, f. 8350, op. 1, d. 51, l. 17.
57 Ibid., l. 19.
58 Ibid.
59 Ibid., l. 19–20.
60 K. S. Basinev, ed, *Professor Ivan Nikolaevich Strizhov 1872–1953* (Moscow: Izdatel'stvo "Neft i Gaz" RGU nefti i gaza im. I.M. Gubkina, 2005), 8–9, 21, 23.
61 RGAE, f. 4372, op. 5, d. 34, l. 67–74. *Neftianoe Delo. Oshibki proshalo i vekhi dlia budushchago.*
62 RGAE, f. 4372, op. 5, d. 34, l. 67.
63 For the role of tsarist-era specialists and liberals in the early Soviet period, see Hirsch, *Empire of Nations*; Peter Holquist, *Making War, Forging Revolution: Russia's Continuum of Crisis 1914–1921* (Cambridge, MA: Harvard University Press, 2002).
64 RGAE, f. 4372, op. 5, d. 34, l. 67ob–68.
65 Ibid., l. 77.
66 Ibid., l. 75–84.
67 See Sargent, "The 'Armeno-Tatar War' in the South Caucasus, 1905–1906," 143–69.
68 RGAE, f. 4372, op. 5, d. 34, l. 75–6.
69 Ibid., l. 76. Flooding was overcome without the aid of foreign concessions, but the use of Western equipment helped.
70 RGAE, f. 4372, op. 5, d. 34, l. 68–9.

71 Ibid. Timothy Mitchell argues that this type of dismantling was at the heart of political power in the second half of the twentieth century, Mitchell, *Carbon Democracy*.
72 For a discussion on the economic-administrative paradigm and the nationality paradigm, see Chapter 2 of Hirsch, *Empire of Nations*, 62–98. For example, the Soviet government expanded refining capabilities and machine-building to increase exports, not benefit Azerbaijan. Igolkin, *Sovetskaia*, 42.
73 RGAE, f. 4372, op. 5, d. 34, l. 2. The Baku-Tblisi-Ceyhan pipeline completed in 2006 does exactly this.
74 Ibid.
75 RGAE, f. 4372, op. 5, d. 34, l. 2ob–3.
76 Ibid., l. 3.
77 Ivan Mikhailovich Gubkin was a well-known petroleum geologist and went on to become the founder of Soviet geology. For a discussion of Gubkin's view against concessions, Farhad Jabbarov, *Bakinskaia neft' v politike sovetskoi Rossii (1917–1922 gg.)* (Baku: Azerbaijan National Academy of Sciences, 2009), 192–5; Serebrovskii against concessions, ARDA, f. 1610, op. 1, d. 364, l. 20–2, also, Serebrovskii, *Rukovodstvo*, 5–10.
78 RGAE, f. 270, op. 1, d. 8, l. 55ob; also in Serebrovskii, *Rukovodstvo*, 10–11.
79 RGAE, f. 270, op. 1, d. 8, l. 55ob.
80 Igolkin, *Sovetskaia*, 114; Sutton, *Western Technology*, 18.
81 Sutton, *Western Technology*, 317.
82 Ibid., 349.
83 Igolkin, *Sovetskaia*, 119; For a refutation of Sutton's thesis in general, see Kostornichenko, *Inostrannyi*, 123–37.
84 A. P. Serebrovskii, "Vospominnaniia o S. M. Kirova," in *Sergei Mironovich Kirov v bor'be za neft'*, ed. L. Beriia, M. D. Bagirov, and R. Akhundov (Baku: Azpartizdat, 1935), 125. This work is a hagiography of Kirov after his assassination. Despite the pervasive cult of personality rhetoric, the factual details, if not the interpretation, are substantiated by the archives.
85 Matt Lenoe, *The Kirov Murder in Soviet History* (New Haven: Yale University Press, 2010), 60.
86 Serebrovskii, "Vospominnaniia," 117, 199. Some of the other reasons are explored in Chapter 5.
87 Serebrovskii, "Vospominnaniia," 124–5.
88 Ibid., 120, 126.
89 There were two agreements, in one Barnsdall agreed to drill in Balakhani and provided the equipment to do so in exchange for oil; in the second agreement, Barnsdall agreed to install 100 deep drills, Igolkin, *Sovetskaia*, 113–14.
90 Igolkin, *Sovetskaia*, 114–15.

91 "Krassin Confers on American Help. Meets Mason Day Regarding Projects for Oil Development in Baku Fields," *New York Times,* May 6, 1922, ProQuest Historical Newspapers.
92 RGASPI, f. 159, op. 2, d. 15, l. 79, 227.
93 RGASPI, f. 159, op. 2, d. 15, l. 32, 74, 127. This was mentioned throughout the documents from the Preparatory Commission.
94 RGASPI, f. 159, op. 2, d. 14, l. 104.
95 RGASPI, f. 159, op. 2, d. 16, l. 54.
96 Ibid., 55.
97 On no directives from the Central Committee, see RGASPI, f. 159, op. 2, d. 16, l. 56, 105–6.
98 Ibid., 17.
99 Serebrovskii, *Evropeiskaia*, 53–7.
100 Nowell, *Mercantile States*, 154–7, 162–3.
101 ARDA, f. 1610, op. 1, d. 287, l. 5, 8–9, 12–13, 23–4, 28ob; Jabbarov, *Bakinskaia*, 201–2; Igolkin, *Sovetskaia*, 117.
102 Nonetheless, at least fifty-five new rotary drills were installed, dramatically altering the situation on the ground. Igolkin, *Sovetskaia*, 117–18.
103 GARF, f. 8350, op. 1, d. 51, l. 123, 139.

4 The Bolsheviks Go into the Oil Business, Kevir-Khurian, Ltd.

1 Gosudarstvennyi Arkhiv Rossiiskoi Federatsii (GARF) f. 8350, op. 1, d. 2525, l. 10–11.
2 David R. Stone, "Soviet Arms Exports in the 1920s," *Journal of Contemporary History,"* 48, 1 (2013): 75–6.
3 GARF, f., 8350, op. 1, d. 2525, l. 7.
4 Not everyone agreed with this approach. Maxim Litvinov, for example, argued that the focus of Soviet foreign policy should be on the West and not bother with the Middle East. Igolkin, *Sovetskaia*, 103, quoting Litvinov.
5 For more examples of how the Soviet Union used oil concessions as an arm of foreign policy, see chapter 4 in Kostornichenko, *Inostrannyi*, 123–81; A. Kocheshkov, "North Iranian Oil in World Politics," *International Affairs* 5 (2008): 119–27. Numerous companies were set up throughout the world to sell Soviet oil. See Igolkin, "Sovetskii," 139–41; Iurii Demin, "Sovetskaia politika v otnoshenii byvshikh tsarskikh kontsessii v Irane (1921–1927 gg.): regional'nyi i mezhdunarodnyi konteksty," t. 20, vyp. 1 (Izv. Sarat. un-ta.

Nov. ser. Ser. Istoriia. Mezhdunarodnye otnosheniia: 2020): 14–21 https://doi.org/10.18500/1819-4907-2020-20-1-14-21; Sokolov, "Sovetskii," 101–31.

6 For background on the convention, see Firuz Kazemzadeh, *Russia and Britain in Persia. Imperial Ambitions in Qajar Persia* (New York: I. B. Tauris, 2013 [first ed: 1968]), 483–500.

7 George Lenczowski, *Russia and the West in Persia, 1918-1948. A Study in Big Power Rivalry* (Ithaca: Cornell University Press, 1949), 76–7.

8 On some of these ties, see Houri Berberian, *Roving Revolutionaries. Armenians and the Connected Revolutions in the Russian, Persian, and Ottoman Worlds* (Oakland: University of California Press, 2019).

9 Genis, *Krasnaia*, 148.

10 GARF, f. 8350, op., 1, d. 2525, l. 27–9. *Zapiski Khoshtariia. Prilozhenie II. Ekonomicheskie Interesy v Persii.*

11 Khostariia's concession had encompassed the northern provinces of (Iranian) Azerbaijan, Gilan, Mazandaran, Astrabad, and Khorasan.

12 GARF f. 8350, op. 1, d. 2525, l. 58–60. *Zapiski Khoshtariia.*

13 Harry Sinclair, the owner of Sinclair Oil, was one of the main investors in the USSR through an oil concession in the Sakhalin Islands and in Baku through the Barnsdall Corporation. Kostornichenko, *Inostrannyi kapital*, 138–65.

14 For background on the Khoshtariia concession, see Fischer, *Oil Imperialism*, 208–36. For a succinct account of the jockeying for the Khoshtariia concession from a different perspective, see George Sweet Gibb and Evelyn H. Knowlton, *History of the Standard Oil Company (New Jersey). The Resurgent Years, 1911-1927* (New York: Arno Press, 1976), 308–17.

15 Rossiiskii Gosudarstvennyi Arkhiv Sotsial'no-politicheskoi Istorii (RGASPI) f. 159, op. 2, d. 51, l. 144, 147.

16 RGASPI, f. 159, op. 2, d. 51, ll.13–21. Report from Rotshtein to Chicherin, January 1921.

17 Ibid.

18 Ibid., 15. According to Michael Zirinskiy, outside of the Foreign Office "Persia was relatively unimportant to Britain. London's financial position was weak; Whitehall did not have enough money to defeat the Soviets, suppress unrest in Iraq, occupy Persia, and subsidize the Tehran government." Michael P. Zirinsky, "Imperial Power and Dictatorship: Britain and the Rise of Reza Shah, 1921–1926," *International Journal of Middle East Studies (IJMES)* 24, 4 (1992): 644.

19 RGASPI, f. 159, op. 2, d. 51, l. 18–19.

20 Ibid., l. 19.

21 Ibid., l. 19–21.

22 GARF, f. 8350, op. 1, d. 2525, l. 15. Letter from Krasin to Lenin outlining his negotiations with Khoshtariia.

23 The concessions committee was copied on correspondence about oil concessions in Iran but claimed no responsibility because they were not on Soviet territory.
24 Correspondence on the concession, Khoshtariia's submission to the Main Concession Committee, a copy of the original concession agreement between the Iranian government and Khoshtariia, as well as other related material, can be found in GARF, f. 8350, op. 1, d. 2525.
25 The Russian Ministry of Foreign Affairs had supported his businesses in Iran. He received concessions for oil extraction and logging as well as for the construction of a rail link between Resht and Enzeli. He also owned a sawmill on the Caspian coast between Enzeli and Astara. Genis, *Krasnaia*, 148.
26 GARF, f. 8350, op. 1, d. 2525, l. 29–30.
27 Ibid., l. 7.
28 Ibid., l. 6–7.
29 Ibid., l. 6–16.
30 Ibid., l. 157.
31 Genis, *Krasnaia*, 148.
32 The Russian Discount Bank was also renounced by the Soviet government in 1919, at the same time the concessions were annulled. Miron Rezun, *The Soviet Union and Iran. Soviet Policy in Iran from the Beginnings of the Pahlavi Dynasty until the Soviet Invasion in 1941* (Geneve: Sijthoff & Noordhoff International Publishers, 1981), 14. For a history of the bank, see Boris Anan'ich, *Rossiiskoe samoderzhavie i vyvoz kapitalov, 1895–1914 (po materialam Uchetno-ssudnogo banka Persii)* (Leningrad: Nauka, 1975).
33 GARF, f. 8350, op. 1, d. 2525, l. 94–5.
34 For example, GARF, f. 8350, op. 1, f. 2525, l. 157. Letter from Main Concession Committee, top secret, to Stalin and Rykov; Genis, *Krasnaia*, 148.
35 GARF, f. 8350, op. 1, d. 2525, l. 9–16.
36 Ibid.
37 Ibid., l. 135–41. Report on Khostariia's presentation to the State Planning Committee. Piatakov held many posts and essentially ran the Supreme Soviet of the Economy (VSNKh) through the mid-1920s. See Andrea Graziosi, "'Building the First System of State Industry in History.' Piatakov's VSNKh and the Crisis of the NEP, 1923–1926," *Cahiers du Monde russe et sovietique* 32, 4 (1991): 539–80.
38 GARF, f. 8350, op. 1, d. 2525, l. 155.
39 Despite Chicherin's repeated insistence that the *semnanskoe delo* not be referred to as a concession, it was still referred to as such in official correspondence. For more on Kevir-Khurian and the Semnan concession, see Kostornichenko, *Inostrannyi kapital*, 167–80.
40 GARF, f. 8350, op. 1, d. 2525, l. 142–5.
41 The decree for Semnan and Demgan was originally given to Mirza Ali Khan Madanchi by Shah Nasr ed Din in 1878. Some documents say 1877. Another decree

to the land was granted in 1880 to Hajji Ali (Amini Maadin), this one with mining rights. After Amini Maadin's death, the decree passed on to his heirs, from whom Khoshtarria purchased it. Who owned the rights to which decree and how they were obtained is unclear. Some sources claim that the Semnan and Demgan fields were included in the 1916 Khoshtariia concession, while others say he did not procure the rights until after the First World War.

42 GARF, f. 8350, op. 1, d. 2525, l. 23-4.
43 Ibid., l. 157-8.
44 Ibid., l. 228.
45 Ibid., l. 160.
46 Ibid., l. 190-1.(emphasis in original).
47 The terms of the secret agreement were, first, in the event that the government of the RSFSR was forced, for political reasons, to terminate the agreement, then all mutual obligations between the RSFSR and Khoshtariia be nullified. Second, in case of such a rupture, all property and enterprises pass to the Russo-Asiatic Joint Stock Company. Third, the agreement would remain in force for two years from the signing of the main agreement and would be considered a part of that agreement. GARF, f. 8350, op. 1, d. 2525, l. 228.
48 On the creation of the National Bloc and its role in Soviet foreign policy, see Iurii Demin, "Sovetskaia diplomatiia i ee rol' v sozdanii i deiatel'nosti natsional'nogo bloka v Irane (1922-1924 gg.)," *Vestnik Volgogradskogo gosudarstvennogo universiteta* 22, 4 (2017): 66-75.
49 Azərbaycan Respublikası Dövlət Arxivi (ARDA) f.1610s, op. 1s, d. 352, l. 1. Letter from Chicherin to Serebrovskii.
50 On the requirement of a loan, see Rubin, "Stumbling," 222; and ARDA, f. 1610s, op. 1s, d. 352, l. 20.
51 This reasoning is laid out by Shumiatskii to Karakhan in a June 1923 letter. ARDA, f. 1610s, op. 1s, d. 352, l. 19-23.
52 ARDA, f.1610s, op. 1s, d. 352, l. 1-2ob. Letter from Chicherin to Serebrovskii. They were also in negotiations for transit fees and a marketing agreement that would have seen Soviet oil on the international market had it gone through, Kostornichenko, *Inostrannyi kapital*, 172.
53 Soviets should support Busheri, ARDA, f. 1610s, op. 1s, d. 352, l. 22-3. That he has mining rights in the Persian Gulf, ARDA, f. 1610s, op. 1s, d. 352, l. 2.
54 ARDA, f. 1610, op. 1, d. 304, l. 7.
55 Demin, "Sovetskaia diplomatiia," 19.
56 ARDA, f. 1610s, op. 1s, d. 352, l. 2-3, 22-23; Letter from Chicherin to Serebrovskii; letter from Shumiatskii to Karakhan at the Narkomindel.
57 Rubin, *Stumbling*, 225.
58 Ibid., 225-8; Gibb and Knowlton, *History of the Standard*, 314.

59 The Bolsheviks also supported his claims against the Iranian government for the return of his confiscated property. In return, the Soviets would also gain the rights to participate in forestry and railroad concessions. Demin, "Sovetskaia politika," 19.
60 M. Abdullahzadeh, "The Kavīr-i Khūriān Oil Concession," *British Institute of Persian Studies* 33 (1995): 162.
61 ARDA, F. 1610s, op. 1s, d. 199, l. 26ob- 27. The Iranian government successfully delayed the ratification. The Soviets responded by limiting Iranian exports and forced them back to the negotiating table and managed to include an agreement on fishing rights in the process, Demin, "Sovetskaia politika," 16.
62 The owners of the four decrees were Abdul Hussein Amini Madan (Ma'adan) and Hadzhi Ali Akbar Khan Tekhrani. They had already sold the mining rights based on the decree to Khadzhi Makhmed Sadyk Banki in 1923 but were able to annul that agreement only in February 1924. ARDA, f. 1610, op. 1s, d. 199, l. 26–53. Other shareholders with less significant amounts are listed as Davar, the Minister of Social Work, former foreign minister Nosrat-ed-Dowleh, Fatemi the Minister of Justice, Emir Monazzam, Shabani, and the editors of various newspapers.
63 GARF, f. 8350, op. 1, d. 3265, l. 393–5.
64 The whole report can be found at GARF, f. 8350, op. 1, d. 166, l. 74–7; Kostornichenko, *Inostranny kapital*, 175–6.
65 ARDA, f. 1610s, op. 1s, d. 199, l. 27. I use Kevir-Khurian, Semnan, and the Semnan concession interchangeably, as it reflects usage in internal correspondence.
66 ARDA, f. 1610s, op. 1s, d. 199, l. 27–28ob. Emir Monazzam was also known as Aga Mir Ramzevi (spelling vary). The Iranian owners who technically registered the company are listed as (1) Hadzhi Mirza Akbar Sutude, (2) Mirza Abdul Hussein Khan Emine Maadan (one of the previous owners of the firman), (3) Mirza Ibrahim Khan Shabani, (4) Aza Mir Gazanavi, and (5) Mirza Abdul Razzag (Ravzag) Hazhi-Zade.
67 The engineer on site reported that the oil in the south was a light-weight variety "with a specific gravity of 0,840 with gasoline content reaching up to 27%, and kerosene up to 10%; at Khurian the specific gravity of the oil is 0,887, gasoline 2.5% and kerosene 30.3%." ARDA, f. 1610s, op. 1s, d. 199, l. 52.
68 Demin, "Sovetskaia politika," 18.
69 ARDA, f. 1610s, op. 1s, d. 199, l. 32–3. History of the origin of the concession and current state of affairs.
70 ARDA, f. 1610s, op. 1s, d. 165, l. 50. Present included Yurenev, Mdivani, Lavrentev, Merts. Konstantin Konstantinovich Yurenev, Soviet diplomat and representative to Iran 1925–7. He replaced Shumiatskii in 1925.
71 On the additional agreement and opposition within the Majlis, see ARDA, f. 1610s, op. 1s, d. 166, l. 19–22; also, f. 1610s, op. 1s, d. 199, l. 36–7.

72 The Soviet Union, contrary to the assumptions of the secondary literature, still entertained the idea that Semnan may produce commercially viable deposits. ARDA, f. 1610s, op. 1s, d 166, l. 16–16ob.
73 ARDA, f. 1610s, op. 1s, d. 166, l. 19–22.
74 GARF, f. 8350, op. 1, d. 166, l. 146–50; Kocheshkov, "North Iranian," 123; For an overview of Franco-Soviet relations during this period and the role of oil, see Gregory P. Nowell, *Mercantile States and the World Oil Cartel, 1900–1939* (Ithaca: Cornell University Press, 1994).
75 GARF, f. 8350, op. 1, d. 166, l. 108–32.
76 Ibid., l. 150.
77 Ibid., l. 147–8 (emphases in original).
78 ARDA, f. 1610, op. 1s, d. 206, l. 94, 96–97ob.
79 ARDA, f. 1610s, op. 1s, d. 206, l. 96.
80 Ibid., l. 96.
81 ARDA, f. 1610s, op. 1s, d. 199, l. 251–251ob.
82 Ibid., l. 251ob. After this source of credit dried up, Lavrentev complained that there was now no way *Kevir-Khurian* could continue to work because they did not have "a single kopek of Persian money." ARDA, f. 1610s, op. 1s, d. d. 206, 96ob.
83 ARDA, f. 1610s, op. 1s, d. 199, l. 252.
84 Ibid., l. 252 (emphases in original).
85 ARDA, f. 1610s, op. 1s, d. 165, l. 49.
86 ARDA, f. 1610s, op. 1s, d. 199, l. 28ob.
87 ARDA, f. 1610s, op. 1s, d. 166, l. 68–70.
88 ARDA, f. 1610s, op. 1s, d. 199, l. 13ob.
89 Ibid., l. 252ob.
90 ARDA, f. 1610, op. 1, d. 168, l. 16ob.
91 Ibid., 17. Additionally, he noted that the Soviet government needed to send an engineer to act as a go-between for Azneft and the workers, and Azneft and the Iranian government. Azneft had already sent a Russian, but Babaev reported that the local workers, of whom he spoke very highly, wanted a Muslim so they could communicate better. He highlighted the difficult working conditions on site, noting that the workers did not have access to clean drinking water or medical assistance, and urged Azneft to take better care of its Iranian workers.
92 Ibid.
93 ARDA, f. 1610s, op. 1s, d. 206, l. 97.
94 ARDA, f. 1610s, op. 1s, d. 199, l. 9ob.
95 Serebrovskii, *Evropeiskaia*, 55; Kostornichenko, *Inostrannyi kapital*, 178.
96 The conditions of the agreement with the French, signed on October 14, 1927, included: (1) the French will participate in exchange for a percentage of stocks; (2) their participation will be proportional, that is, if the value of the stock

increases or the number of stocks increases so too will their share; (3) Kevir-Khurian will have the right to use the territory of the USSR for the transport of its products as well as use Soviet means of transport; and (4) that the French have the same rights as other non-Soviet countries to exploit oil and it products in territories not belonging to the Semnan region. ARDA, f. 1610s, op. 1s, d. 199, l. 13–13ob.

97 Kostornichenko, *Inostranny kapital*, 178. For more on Gulbenkian see chapter 10 of Daniel Yergin, *The Prize. The Epic Quest for Oil, Money & Power* (New York: Free Press, 1991, 2009), 168–89. Khoshtariia proposed opening a Turkish-Persian bank in Constantinople to raise money through cotton production to fund *Kevir-Khurian* but it is unclear whether anything ever came of the suggestion, GARF, f. 8350, op. 1, d. 2525, l. 24–5; For other proposals, Sokolov, "Sovetskii," 124–5.

98 ARDA, f. 1610s, op. 1s, d. 199, l. 252.

99 Iranian merchants boycotted Soviet goods beginning in 1929. Further, Reza Shah's distrust of the Soviet Union grew, and he increasingly pursued closer relations, first with Great Britain, and then with Germany albeit through customs agreements, not capitulations. Mikhail Volodarsky, *The Soviet Union and its Southern Neighbors. Persia and Afghanistan, 1917–1933* (Portland: Frank Cass, 1994), 82–99, 100–20.

100 GARF, f. 8350, op. 1, d. 2553, l. 36–43. Golubiatnikov's geological report.

101 By the end of 1929, Piatakov wrote to the Politburo with an update detailing both the French-Persian talks and a new guarantee from the Iranian government to expand the territory open to exploitation by *Kevir-Khurian* to close to 8,000 square kilometers, a development he considered a huge success. GARF, f. 8350, op. 1, d. 2553, ll. 78–82.

102 Abdullahzade, "The Kavīr-i Khūriān," 163. The potential expansion of *Kevir-Khurian*'s exploitation rights may have also played a role.

103 The Majlis finally liquidated Kevir-Khurian in March 1951. Kocheshkov, "North Iranian," 126.

104 RGASPI, f. 159, op. 2, d. 15, l. 113–14.

5 A Contribution to the History of the Revolution in the Periphery

1 "Tov Narimanova," *Izvestiia*, March 20, 1925, East View; "Pamiati Tov Narimanova," *Izvestiia*, March 22, 1925, East View; "Pokhrony Tov N. N. Narimanova" *Izvestiia*, March 24, 1925, East View; "Pokhorony Tov. Narimanova," *Pravda*, March 24, 1925, East View.

2 Rossiiskii Gosudarstvennyi Arkhiv Sotsial'no-politicheskoi Istorii (RGASPI) f. 588, op. 2, d. 177, l. 33–4.

3 His history was published in Baku in 1990, but the files on the Control Commission investigation weren't opened to researchers until 1997, Baberowski, *Vrag est' vezde*, 283. He was rehabilitated after Khrushchev's speech at the Twentieth Party Congress, but nothing was known of the Control Commission investigation, Alexandre A. Bennigsen and Enders Wimbush, *Muslim National Communism in the Soviet Union: A Revolutionary Strategy for the Colonial World* (Chicago: University of Chicago Press, 1979), 93.
4 In addition to the posts mentioned earlier, he was also the head of the Soviet of Nationalities within the Soviet Parliament and as of April 1923 a candidate member of the Central Committee of the Russian Communist Party.
5 While these were positions of influence within the state, authority was concentrated first and foremost in Communist Party organizations. In Azerbaijan, this was the Caucasian Bureau of the Central Committee of the Russian Communist Party (Caucasus Bureau), which was renamed the Transcaucasian Regional Committee in 1922. These bodies were headed by Sergo Orjonikidze.
6 Narimanov also forwarded copies to Lev Trotsky and Karl Radek, the head of the Communist International, at the Central Committee. A copy of the original history and the Control Commission transcripts can be found in RGASPI, f. 588, op. 2, d. 176, l. 2–49 and 58–86. Further supporting materials can be found in RGASPI, f. 588, op. 2, d. 177, 178, 179. I cite the published version, which includes two addendums written by Narimanov after the investigation as well as other letters. Nariman Narimanov, *K istorii nashei revoliutsii v okrainakh* (Baku: 1990).
7 Officially the Control Commission was independent of the Central Committee and had equal authority. In practice, it was increasingly an enforcer of the Central Committee's positions.
8 There is extensive literature on nationalities policy. For example, Adrienne Lynn Edgar, *Tribal Nation: The Making of Soviet Turkmenistan* (Princeton: Princeton University Press, 2004); Goff, *Nested Nationalism*; Hirsch, *Empire of Nations*; Martin, *The Affirmative Action Empire*.
9 See Smith, "The Georgian Affair," 519–44.
10 As Adeeb Khalid notes, activists developed Muslim national communism independently across the empire. It was not a unified or organized movement. Khalid, *Making Uzbekistan*, 111–12.
11 RGASPI, f. 588, op. 2, d. 176, l. 59.
12 RGASPI, f. 588, op. 2, d. 179, l. 36.
13 RGASPI, f. 588, op. 2, d. 178, l. 49.
14 Ibid., l. 51. Russian: *net li zdes' i v doklade Narimanova kornii Sultangalievshchiny*.
15 RGASPI, f. 588, op. 2, d. 178, l. 54.
16 Ibid., l. 50–1. Narimanov's relationship with Sultan-Galiev remains unclear.

17 Blank, "Bolshevik Organizational Development in Early Soviet Transcaucasia," 305–38.
18 RGASPI, f. 588, op. 2, d. 176, l. 59.
19 RGASPI, f. 588, op. 2, d. 177, l. 8.
20 RGASPI, f. 588, op. 2, d. 178, l. 51.
21 RGASPI, f. 588, op. 2, d. 177, l. 9. It reads, "He was very surprised [*ochen' udevlyen*] that the TsKK [CCC] was discussing his report, which was not designated for the TsKK." See also, RGASPI, f. 588, op. 2, d. 179, l. 36. Meeting minutes. Russian: *Eto ne nashe delo razbirat' ego doklad*.
22 RGASPI, f. 588, op. 2, d. 177, l. 51ob. He continued that the Bolsheviks were making a mockery of reason believing Narimanov to be a statesman. Letter to Stalin, with a copy forwarded to Narimanov.
23 One indication that Narimanov believed that the process was rigged was his refusal to engage his accusers on any real level verbally. Instead, he submitted written reports to be added to the record after the investigations, much as Shliapnikov and Medvedev did, leading up to the "Baku Affair" in 1926. As Barbara Allen notes, this went against standard procedure, which relied on discussion. Barbara Allen, "Transforming Factions into Blocs: Alexander Shliapnikov, Sergei Medvedev, and the CCC investigation of the 'Baku Affair' in 1926," in *A Dream Deferred: New Studies in Russian and Soviet Labour History*, ed. Donald Filtzer, Wendy Z. Goldman, Gijs Kessler, and Simon Pirani (Bern: Peter Lang, 2008), 138; also, RGASPI, f. 588, op. 2, d. 177, l. 192. 89; Ibid., f. 588, op. 2, d. 176, l. 58.
24 RGASPI, f. 588, op. 2, d. 176, l. 62.
25 The full passage reads:

> Today in Baku there was a ceremonial meeting of the Soviet [in connection with the establishment of Soviet power in Armenia] where Narimanov read the declaration of the Azerbaijani government indicating that there would no longer be borders between Soviet Armenia and Soviet Azerbaijan, that from now on Zangezeur and Nakhichivan are an integral part of Soviet Armenia. Armenians in Nagorno Karabakh have the right to self-determination. The wealth of Azerbaijan, oil and kerosene, belong to both republics [*iavliaiutsia sostoianiem obeikh soiuznykh respublik*] … Tomorrow a second group of comrades will be sent [to Armenia] and will take with them kerosene, manufactured goods etc. Make sure that's in the newspapers.

A. V. Kvashonkin, O. V. Khlevniuk, L. P. Koshelev, L. A. Pogovaia., eds. *Bol'shevistskoe rukovodstvo. Perepiska. 1912–1927* (Moscow: ROSSPEN, 1996), 168–9.
26 Narimanov, *K istoriia*, 62.
27 Ibid., 65–6.

28 Ibid.
29 RGASPI, f. 588, op. 2, d. 176, l. 28–9.
30 This type of relationship would also have been present in such places as the Donbas, Ukraine SRR, and where the Coal Trust Donugl also had All-Union status or in Turkestan with cotton. For more on Serebrovskii, Azneft, and Baku, see Crawford, *Spatial Revolution*, 15–118.
31 For more on the origins of the oil fund and Narimanov's attempts to secure oil products for Baku, see Jabbarov, *Bakinskaia*, 139–49.
32 Azərbaycan Respublikası Dövlət Arxivi (ARDA) f. 411, op. 1, d. 98, l. 12. The agreement was frequently amended and updated.
33 ARDA, f. 28s, op. 1s, d. 46, l. 57.
34 A. Andreev, "Azneft i Baksovet," *Krasnyi Baku. Organ Bakinskogo Soveta*, 8 (1924): 23.
35 On July 20, 1923, at the same time that Narimanov was defending his accusations against Serebrovskii before the Control Commission, the Soviet of Labor and Defense sided with Baku and confirmed that the Azerbaijan SSR had the right to independent allocation [*otchisleniia*] of oil products from the oil fund. ARDA, f. 413, op. 1, d. 16, l. 53; The details for the distribution of Azerbaijan's oil in Armenia and Georgia were worked out, haphazardly, through the new Transcaucasian federal structure. ARDA, f. 413, op. 1, d. 16.
36 Sara Brinegar, "The Oil Deal: Nariman Narimanov and the Sovietization of Azerbaijan," *Slavic Review* 76, 2 (2017): 372–94.
37 RGASPI, f. 588, op. 2, d. 177, l. 273.
38 Others in the left faction included Levon Mirzoyan, (Aleksandr Ivanovich) Egorov, and Beybut Shahtakhtinski (switched sides, former friend of Narimanov). For factions, see Baberowski, *Vrag est' vezde*, 224–34, 272.
39 On centralization, see Blank, "Bolshevik Organizational Development," 307–40.
40 For example, RGASPI, f. 588, op. 2, d. 176, l. 68. Orjonikidze speaking at the Control Commission.
41 Baberowski, *Vrag est' vezde,* 270.
42 Ronald Grigor Suny, *Stalin: Passage to Revolution* (Princeton: Princeton University Press, 2020), 374–403, 428–51.
43 I am arguing that the Stalin-aligned faction took over the party apparatus but by no means does this mean that the party had consolidated control over society in either Azerbaijan or Transcaucasia. Nor were the party factions static; there was constant reconfiguring. For an example of the chaos in Azerbaijan during this period, see Jörg Baberowski, "Stalinismus an der Peripherie: Das Beispiel Azerbajdzan 1920–1941," in *Stalinismus vor dem Zweiten Weltkrieg: Neue Wege der Forschung*, ed. Manfred Hildermeier, 307–36 (Berlin: Oldenbourg Wissenschaftsverlag, 1998).

44 RGASPI, f. 64, op. 1, d. 20, l. 83. Serebrovskii petitioned Moscow to consolidate control of food distribution and rationing under Azneft to prevent both shortages and such requisitions.
45 On food shortage and the social conditions in Baku see, Grigor Suny, *Baku Commune, 1917–1918*, 110–15. These requisitions continued after the fall of the Commune, see *Kaspii*, 25 Aug; 29 Aug 1917.
46 Narimanov, *K istorii*, 30.
47 For the text of his petition, see RGASPI, f. 64, op. 1, d. 90, l. 172.
48 RGASPI, f. 64, op. 1, d. 90, l. 13–17.
49 Ibid., l. 19.
50 Ibid., l. 21.
51 Ibid., l. 24.
52 RGASPI f. 588, op. 2, d. 176, l. 63–4. Orjonikidze also accused Narimanov of lying, saying that in a Central Committee meeting he voted against Mikoyan's transfer even while he was trying to remove him from the South Caucasus. Orjonikidze cited a letter that Narimanov had sent to his former deputy, Beybut Shahtakhtinski, as support, demonstrating Narimanov's true intentions. Given the circumstances, neither Orjonikidze nor Shahtakhtinski should be seen as particularly reliable narrators, but there is no question that Narimanov consistently petitioned Lenin to intervene in party affairs in Baku.
53 Ibid.; Kharmandarian, *Lenin i stanovlenie*, 78. Orjonikidze says he requested the directive, not Narimanov.
54 Kharmandarian, *Lenin i stanovlenie*, 78.
55 Ibid., 76–8.
56 Ibid., 79; RGASPI, f. 588, op. 2, d. 176, l. 64.
57 Kharmandarian, *Lenin i stanovlenie*, 79; Baberowski, *Vrag est' vezde*, 274.
58 Baberowski, *Vrag est' vezde*, 276–7; A. Kh. Khalilov, "Vnutrennie protivorechiia i bor'ba v rukovodstve Azerbaidzhanskoi ChK v 1920–1922 gg," *Voprosy istorii*, 5 (2016): 126–7.
59 RGASPI, f. 588, op. 2, d. 176, l. 3.
60 Narimanov, *K istorii*, 22.
61 RGASPI, f. 588, op. 2, d. 176, l. 71.
62 RGASPI, f. 85, op. 13, d. 12, l. 101; also, Gasanly, *Vneshiaia politika*, 27.
63 RGASPI, f. 159, op. 2, d. 51, l. 157–9.
64 For more on Orjonikidze and the Transcaucasian Federation, see Eitienne Forestier-Peyrat, "Soviet Federalism at Work: Lessons from the History of the Transcaucasian Federation," *Jahrbücher für Geschichte Osteuropas* 65, 4 (2017): 529–59.
65 Huseynov was born in 1894, making him only twenty-six when the Red Army occupied Azerbaijan (Narimanov and Lenin, in contrast, were born in 1870). Akhundov was even younger, born in 1897.

66 Mikoyan echoed the sentiment: "We viewed Narimanov as an old man [*starik*] and knew that he wouldn't be able to lead the masses. But let him do his work. He was necessary for us," RGASPI, f. 588, op. 2, d. 176, l. 69.

There was also a personal element. Narimanov and Orjonikidze met in 1908. At the time, Narimanov had been kicked out of Iran for funneling weapons into the country. Orjonikidze was looking to escape a political crackdown in Russia and Narimanov helped him escape to Iran, where he stayed for two years. It is plausible that Orjonikidze initially backed Narimanov as head of the Azerbaijan Soviet in return for this earlier help. Baberowski, *Vrag est' vzde*, 222.

67 RGASPI, f. 588, op. 2, d. 176, l. 62–5.
68 Ibid., l. 67.
69 For more on how Orjonikidze's personality shaped his style of rule, see Smith, "The Georgian affair," 519–44.
70 Khalilov, "Vnutrennie protivorechiia," 127.
71 RGASPI, f. 588, op. 2, d. 176, l. 61–8.
72 For example, Sheila Fitzpatrick, "The Civil War as a Formative Experience," in *Bolshevik Culture: Experiment and Order in the Russian Revolution*, ed. Abbott Gleason, Peter Kenez, and Richard Stites, 57–76 (Bloomington: Indiana University Press, 1985).
73 For a discussion on this point, largely from Mikoyan's point of view, see Blank, "Bolshevik organizational," 317. For Mikoyan's account of these years, see his memoir, especially chapters two through six: Mikoyan, *Tak bylo* (Moscow: 1999). http://militera.lib.ru/memo/russian/mikoyan/index.html (accessed May 9, 2021).
74 RGASPI, f. 588, op. 2, d. 176, l. 69. Mikoyan was the only surviving commissar from the so-called 26 commissars of the Baku Commune.
75 Tadeusz Swietochowski, "The Himmät Party: Socialism and the National Question in Russian Azerbaijan 1904–1920," *Cahiers du Monde russe et sovietique* XIX, 1–2 (1978): 128–31.
76 Narimanov, *K istorii*, 33; 43–4; Smith, *The Georgian Affair*, 529.
77 Smith, *The Georgian Affair*, 529–30.
78 Baberowski, *Vrag est' vezde*, 248.
79 Ibid., 247.
80 Baberowski, *Vrag est' vezde*, 249–64.
81 *Shakhsei-Vakhsei* is the Russian rendering of "Shah Huseyn, Va Huseyn" or Lord Huseyn, Alas Huseyn, which members of the mourning procession chant. For more on the Bolsheviks and the procession, see Smith, "The Russian Revolution as a National Revolution," 368–70.
82 RGASPI, f. 588, op. 2, d. 176, ll. 33–5. Narimanov's account. RGASPI, f. 588, op. 2, d. 177, l. 25 Report on the Central Control Commission [CCC] favoring a more aggressive approach than Narimanov's. On the impression this created, see

RGASPI, f. 588, op. 2, d. 176, l. 83. Akhundov accused Narimanov of "to a certain extent supporting Shekhsi-Vekhsi," RGASPI, f. 588, op. 2, d. 176, l. 76.
83 For more on the later campaign against Islam in Azerbaijan, see Jörg Baberowski, "Verschleierte Feinde. Stalinismus im Sowjetischen Orient," *Geschichte und Gesellschaft* 30, 1 (2004): 10–36. http://www.jstor.org/stable/40186098 (accessed May 8, 2021).
84 RGASPI, f. 588, op. 2, d. 177, l. 25.
85 Ibid.
86 RGASPI, f. 588, op. 2, d. 177, l. 156–61ob.
87 Shirvani Mustabeyov was the Extraordinary Commissar for the Azerbaijan Revolutionary Committee in Shemakhe, Karabakh, Zangezur, Zakatakala, and Nukha from 1920 to 1921; the Azerbaijan Representative in Soviet Russia (Narimanov's secretary) from 1921 to 1922; from 1922 the secretary of the Central Executive Committee of the USSR, and secretary of the Central Committee of the Communist Party of Tajikistan from 1927 to 1929. https://centrasia.org/person2.php?st=1108415088 (accessed May 8, 2021).
88 RGASPI, f. 588, op. 2, d. 176, l. 71–3.
89 RGASPI, f. 588, op. 2, d. 177, l. 158.
90 Ibid., l. 158–9. Narimanov's friendships with Molla Baba and Alekperov were sharply criticized by those at the Control Commission meeting. See RGASPI, f. 588, op. 2, d. 176, l. 72–3, 76.
91 RGASPI, f. 588, op. 2, d. 177, l. 165–6.
92 Ibid., l. 159.
93 Khalilov, "Vnutrennie protivorechiia," 125–8.
94 RGASPI, f. 588, op. 2, d. 177. Supporting materials included a short history of the *Hummet* Party, a report on the reasons for the collapse of Soviet power in Baku in 1918, a list of individuals and Narimanov's accusations against them, and reports from the AzCheka (the secret police) on Narimanov and his allies.
95 RGASPI, f. 588, op. 2, d. 177, l. 34.
96 Ibid.
97 Baberowski, *Vrag est' vezde*, 297–8.
98 Narimanov, *K istorii*, 100–3.
99 On Orjonikidze's reluctance to leave the Caucasus for an All-Union post, see Oleg V. Khlevniuk, *In Stalin's Shadow. The Career of "Sergo" Ordzhonikidze*, ed. Donald J. Raleigh, trans. David J. Nordlander (New York: M.E. Sharpe, 1995), 21–5.
100 Narimanov, *K istorii*, 103.
101 Ibid., 105–8.
102 Khanbudagov was himself removed from the party in 1924 for national deviation. He called for the full "turkification" of Azerbaijan and the removal of Russians

from Mughan steppe in southern Azerbaijan so that the land could be given to Azeri peasants. Baberowski, *Vrag est' vezde*, 339.

103 Another topic not addressed in his history and given space in a later postscript was the disputed status of Nagorno-Karabakh. Narimanov firmly believed that Nagorno-Karabakh should be a part of Azerbaijan. He played a role in securing the region, as well as Nakhchivan and other disputed territories, for Azerbaijan from Armenia during negotiations with Turkey in 1921. Baberowski, *Vrag est' vezde*, 237-9.

104 Baberowski, *Vrag est' vezde*, 299.

105 On the importance of funerals in early Bolshevik culture, see Svetlana Malysheva, "The Russian Revolution and the Instrumentalization of Death," *Slavic Review* 76, 3 (Fall 2017): 647-54; Smith, "The Russian Revolution," 363-88.

106 Baberowski, *Vrag est' vezde*, 270.

107 Ibid., 302.

108 Orjonikidze was transferred to lead the People's Commissariat of the Workers' and Peasants' Inspection (Rabkin) and Central Control Commission, Kirov was transferred to Leningrad, and Serebrovskii took over the gold mining industry, among other posts.

109 Forestier-Peyrat, "Soviet Federalism," 542; Baberowski, *Vrag est' vezde*, 744-51.

110 For this argument, see Forestier-Peyrat, "Soviet Federalism," 529-59.

111 Forestier-Peyrat, "Soviet Federalism," 540.

Conclusion

1 Narimanov, *Izbrannye proizvedeniia*, 531.

2 A. A. Igolkin, "The High Price of Soviet Oil," *Oil of Russia: Lukoil International Magazine*, 1 (2005).

3 RGAE, f. 5740, op. 1, d. 277, l. 94.

4 Igolkin, "Neftianoi faktor," 88.

5 Otdel Pechati i Informatsii SNK i VES ZSFSR, *K plenumu ZKK VKP (b). Materialy kommissii ZKK VKP (b) po obsledovaniiu neftianoi promyshlennosti ASSR, Vypusk III* (Tiflis: Gosizdat Gruzii, 1930), 66-7.

6 Altstadt, *The Azerbaijani Turks*, 141-50. On the rehabilitation of Akhundov and others, see A. Artizov, Iu. Sigachev, I. Shevchuk, and V. Khlopov. *Reabilitatsiia: Kak eto bylo. Dokumenty Prezidiuma TsK KPSS i drugie materialy Mart 1953-fevral' 1956* (Moscow: ROSSPEN, 2000), 267-70, 276-8, 280-3.

Selected Bibliography

Main Archives

Azərbaycan Respublikası Dövlət Arxivi
[Republic of Azerbaijan State Archive, ARDA]

  f. 1114 Azerbaijan Soviet of Trade Unions
  f. 1610 Azerbaijan Oil Trust
  f. 2548 Azerbaijan Oil Committee

Gosudarstvennyi Arkhiv Rossiiskoi Federatsii
[State Archive of the Russian Federation, GARF]

  f. 8350 Main Concessions Committee

Rossiiskii Gosudarstvennyi Arkhiv Ekonomiki
[Russian State Archive of the Economy, RGAE]

  f. 270 Personal File of A. P. Serebrovskii
  f. 4372 State Planning Commission

Rossiiskii Gosudarstvennyi Arkhiv Sotsial'no-politicheskoi Istorii
[Russian State Archive for Social and Political History, RGASPI]

  f. 64 Caucasus Bureau of the Russian Communist Party (Bolsheviks)
  f. 85 Personal File of Sergo Ordjonikidze
  f. 159 Personal File of Georgii Chicherin
  f. 588 Collection of Selected Historical-Party Documents

Primary Sources

Arskii, R. *Kavkaz i ego znachenie dlia sovetskoi Rossii*. St. Petersburg: Gosudarstvennoe izdatel'stvo, 1921.

Azneft. *Obzor azerbaidzhanskoin neftianoi promyshlennosti: za piat' let natstionalizatsii 1920–1925*. Baku: Gosudarstvennoe Ob"edinenie Neftianoi Promyshlennosti, 1925.

Azneft. *Obzor bakinskoi neftianoi promyshlennosti za dva goda natsionalizatsii 1920–1922.* Baku: Gosudarstvennoe Ob"edinenie Neftianoi Promyshlennosti 1922 (reprint, 1989).

Beria, L, M. D. Bagirov, and R. Akhundov. *Sergei Mironovich Kirov v bor'be za neft'.* Baku: Azpartizdat, 1935.

Fischer, Louis. *Oil Imperialism. The International Struggle for Petroleum.* Westport, CT: Hyperion Press, 1926.

Narimanov, Nariman. *K istorii nashei revoliutsii v okrainakh.* Baku: 1990.

Narimanov, Nariman. *Izbrannye proizvedeniia. Tom 2.* Baku: Azerbaidzhanskoe gosudarstvennoe izdatel'stvo, 1989.

Otdel Pechati i Informatsii SNK i VES ZSFSR. *K plenumu ZKK VKP (b). Materialy kommissii ZKK VKP (b) po obsledovaniiu neftianoi promyshlennosti ASSR. Vypusk III.* Tiflis: Gosizdat Gruzii, 1930.

Serebrovskii, A. P. *Evropeiskaia neftiania torgovlia i neftesindikat SSSR.* Moscow: Promizdat, 1927.

Serebrovskii, A. P. *Rukovodstvo V.I. Lenina vosstanovleniem neftianoi promyshlennosti.* Moscow: Gospolitizdat, 1958.

Smilga, Ivar. *Vosstanovitel'nyi protsess: Piat' let novoi ekonomicheskoi politiki (mart 1921 g.-mart 1926 g.) Stat'i i rechi.* Moscow: Izdatel'stvo "Planovoe khoziaistvoe," 1927.

Selected Secondary Sources

Abdullahzadeh, M. "The Kavīr-i Khūrīān Oil Concession." *British Institute of Persian Studies* 33 (1995): 161–4.

Aliiarov, S. S. *Neftianye monopolii v Azerbaidzhane v period pervoi mirovoi voiny.* Baku: Izdanie AGY, 1974.

Allen, Barbara. "Transforming Factions into Blocs: Alexander Shliapnikov, Sergei Medvedev, and the CCC investigation of the 'Baku Affair' in 1926," in *A Dream Deferred: New Studies in Russian and Soviet Labour History*, edited by Donald Filtzer, Wendy Z. Goldman, Gijs Kessler, and Simon Pirani, 129–52. Bern: Peter Lang, 2008.

Altstadt, Audrey L. *The Azerbaijani Turks: Power and Identity under Russian Rule.* Stanford: Hoover Institution Press, 1992.

Artizov, A., Iu. Sigachev, I. Shevchuk, and V. Khlopov. *Reabilitatsiia: Kak eto bylo. Dokumenty Prezidiuma TsK KPSS i drugie materialy Mart 1953-fevral' 1956.* Moscow: ROSSPEN, 2000.

Baberowski, Jörg. "Stalinismus an der Peripherie: Das Beispiel Azerbajdzan 1920–1941,"in *Stalinismus vor dem Zweiten: Neue Wege der Forschung*, edited by Manfred Hildermeier, 307–36. Berlin: Oldenbourg Wissenschaftsverlag, 1998.

Baberowski, Jörg. "Verschleierte Feinde. Stalinismus im Sowjetischen Orient." *Geschichte und Gesellschaft* 30, 1 (2004): 10–36.

Baberowski, Jörg. *Vrag est' vezde: Stalinizm na Kavkaze*, trans. V. T. Altukhova. Moscow: ROSSPEN, 2010.

Balaev, Aidyn. *Azerbaidzhanskaia natsiia: osnovnye etapy stanovleniia na rubezhe XIX-XX vv.* Moscow: OOO "TiRu," 2012.

Basinev, K. S., ed. *Professor Ivan Nikolaevich Strizhov 1872-1953*. Moscow: Izdatel'stvo "Neft i Gaz" RGU nefti i gaza im. I. M. Gubkina, 2005.

Bast, Oliver. "Duping the British and Outwitting the Russians? Iran's Foreign Policy, the 'Bolshevik Threat', and the Genesis of the Soviet-Iranian Treaty of 1921," in *Iranian-Russian Encounters. Empires and Revolutions since 1800*, edited by Stephanie Cronin, 261-97. New York: Routledge, 2013.

Bennigsen, Alexandre, and Enders Wimbush. *Muslim National Communism in the Soviet Union: A Revolutionary Strategy for the Colonial World*. Chicago: University of Chicago Press, 1979.

Berberian, Houri. *Armenians and the Connected Revolutions in the Russian, Iranian, and Ottoman Worlds*. Oakland: University of California Press, 2019.

Berberian, Houri. *Roving Revolutionaries. Armenians and the Connected Revolutions in the Russian, Persian, and Ottoman Worlds*. Oakland: University of California Press, 2019.

Blank, Stephen. "Bolshevik Organizational Development in Early Soviet Transcaucasia: Autonomy vs. Centralization, 1918-1924," in *Transcaucasia, Nationalism and Social Change: Essays in the History of Armenia, Azerbaijan, and Georgia*, edited by Ronald Suny, 307-40. Ann Arbor: University of Michigan Press, 1983.

Blank, Stephen. "Soviet Politics and the Iranian Revolution of 1919-1921." *Cahiers du monde russe et sovietique* 22, 2 (April-June 1980): 173-94.

Brinegar, Sara. "The Oil Deal: Nariman Narimanov and the Sovietization of Azerbaijan," *Slavic Review* 76, 2 (2017): 372-94.

Carr, E. H. *The Bolshevik Revolution 1917-1923*, volume 3. New York: Macmillan Company, [1953] 1961.

Chaqueri, Cosroe. *The Soviet Socialist Republic of Iran, 1920-1921. Birth of Trauma*. Pittsburgh, PA: University of Pittsburgh Press, 1995.

Crawford, Christina E. *Spatial Revolution. Architecture and Planning in the Early Soviet Union*. Ithaca: Cornell University Press, 2022.

Cronin, Stephanie, ed. *Iranian-Russian Encounters. Empires and Revolutions since 1800*. New York: Routledge, 2013.

Dailami, Pezhmann. "The Bolsheviks and the Jangali Movement, 1915-1920." *Cahiers du Monde russe et sovietique* 31, 1 (January-March, 1990): 43-59.

Dailami, Pezhmann. "The Bolshevik Revolution and the Genesis of Communism in Iran, 1917-1920." *Central Asian Survey* 11, 3 (1992): 51-82.

Dailami, Pezhmann. "The First Congress of the Peoples of the East and the Iranian Soviet Republic of Gilan, 1920-21." In *Reformers and Revolutionaries in Modern*

Iran. New Perspective on the Iranian Left, edited by Stephanie Cronin, 85–117. New York: Routledge, 2004.

Debo, Richard. *Survival and Consolidation. Foreign Policy of Soviet Russia 1918–1921.* Montreal: McGill-Queens University Press, 1992.

Demin, Iurii. "Sovetskaia diplomatiia i ee rol' v sozdanii i deiatel'nosti natsional'nogo bloka v Irane (1922–1924 gg.). *Vestnik Volgogradskogo gosudarstvennogo universiteta* 4 (2017): 66–76 https://doi.org/10.15688/ jvolsu4.2017.4.7.

Demin, Iurii. "Sovetskaia politika v otnoshenii byvshikh tsarskikh kontsessii v Irane (1921–1927 gg.): regional'nyi i mezhdunarodnyi konteksty." Vol 20, No. 1 Izvestiia Saratovskogo universiteta. Novaia seriia. Seriia: Istoriia. Mezhdunarodnyie otnosheniia: 2020: 14–21. https://doi.org/10.18500/1819-4907-2020-20-1-14-21.

Deutschmann, Mortiz. "Cultures of Statehood, Cultures of Revolution: Caucasian Revolutionaries in the Iranian Constitutional Movement, 1906–1911." *Ab Imperio* 2 (2013): 165–90.

Edgar, Adrienne Lynn. *Tribal Nation: The Making of Soviet Turkmenistan.* Princeton: Princeton University Press, 2004.

Fink, Carole. *The Genoa Conference. European Diplomacy, 1921–1922.* Chapel Hill: University of North Carolina Press, 1993.

Finke, Carole, Axel Frohn, and Jurgen Heideking, eds. *Genoa, Rapallo, and European Reconstruction in 1922.* New York: Cambridge University Press, 1991.

Firuz Kazemzadeh, *Russia and Britain in Persia. Imperial Ambitions in Qajar Persia.* New York: I. B. Tauris, [1968] 2013.

Fischer, Louis. *The Soviets in World Affairs. A History of the Relations between the Soviet Union and the Rest of the World. 1917–1929*, volume 1. Princeton: Princeton University Press, 1951.

Fitzpatrick, Sheila. "The Civil War as a Formative Experience." In *Bolshevik Culture*, edited by Peter Kenez, Abbott Gleason, and Richard Stites, 57–76. Bloomington: Indiana University Press, 1985.

Forestier-Peyrat, Etienne. "Soviet Federalism at Work: Lessons from the History of the Transcaucasian Federation." *Jahrbücher für Geschichte Osteuropas* 65, 4 (2017): 529–59.

Frank, Alison Fleig. *Oil Empire: Visions of Prosperity in Austrian Galicia.* Cambridge, MA: Harvard University Press, 2005.

Gasanly, Dzhamil' P. *Vneshiaia politika Azerbaidzhana v gody sovetskoi vlasti (1920–1939)*, volume 2, *Istoriia diplomatii Azerbaidzhanksoi Respubliki: V trekh tomakh*, trans. I. N. Razaeva. Moscow: Flint, 2013.

Genis, Vladimir. "Bol'sheviki v Giliane: provozglashenie persidskoi sovestskoi respubliki." *Voprosy istorii* 1 (1999): 64–81.

Genis, Vladimir. *Krasnaia Persiia: bol'sheviki v Giliane. 1920–1921. Dokumental'naia khronika*. Moscow: Tsentr strategicheskikh i politicheskikh issledovanii; MNPI, 2000.

Gibb, George, and Evelyn K. Knowlton, *The History of the Standard Oil Company (New Jersey): The Resurgent Years, 1911–1927*. New York: Harper and Row, 1956.

Goff, Krista. *Nested Nationalism. Making and Unmaking Nations in the Soviet Caucasus*. Ithaca: Cornell University Press, 2020.

Graziosi, Andrea(s). "'Building the First System of State Industry in History.' Piatakov's VSNKh and the Crisis of the NEP, 1923–1926." *Cahiers du Monde russe et sovietique* 32, 4 (1991): 539–80.

Guliev, D. B., and K. G. Vezirov, ed. *V.I. Lenin ob Azerbaidzhane*. Baku: Azerbaidzhanskoe gosudarstvennoe izdatel'stvo, 1970.

Guseinov, I. A., A. S. Sumbatzade, A. N. Guliev, I. A. Tokarzhevskinin, eds. *Istoriia Azerbaidzhana*, volume 2. Baku: Izdatel'svto Akademii Nauk Azerbaidzhansoi SSR, 1960.

Guseinov, I. A., M. A. Dadashzade, and A. S. Sumbatzade, eds. *Istoriia Azerbaidzhana*, chast' pervaia, volume 3. Baku: Izdatel'svto Akademii Nauk Azerbaidzhansoi SSR, 1963.

Hamm, Michael F, ed. *The City in Late Imperial Russia*. Bloomington: Indiana University Press, 1986.

Hastings, Rebecca. "Oil Capital: Industry and Society in Baku, Azerbaijan, 1870-present." PhD diss., University of Oregon, 2020.

Hirsch, Francine. *Empire of Nations: Ethnography and the Making of the Soviet Union*. Ithaca: Cornell University Press, 2005.

Holquist, Peter. *Making War, Forging Revolution: Russia's Continuum of Crisis 1914–1921*. Cambridge, MA: Harvard University Press, 2002.

Igolkin, A. A. "The High Price of Soviet Oil." *Oil of Russia: Lukoil International Magazine* 1 (2005). www.oilru.com/or/22/359/ (accessed September 5, 2022).

Igolkin, A. A. "Leninskii narkom: u istokov sovetskoi korruptsii." *Novyi istoricheskii vestnik*, 10 (2004).

Igolkin, A. A. *Neftiania politika SSSR v 1928–1940-m godakh*. Moscow: Institut rossiiski istorii, 2005.

Igolkin, A. A. "Neftianoi faktor vo vneshneekonomicheskikh sviaziakh Rossii za poslednie 100 let." *Ekonomicheskaia istoriia* 6, 1 (2008): 87–93.

Igolkin, A. A. *Otechestvennaia neftianaia promyshlennost' v 1917–1920 godakh*. Moscow: Rossiiskii gosudarstvennyi gumanitarnyi universitet, 1999.

Igolkin, A. A. *Sovetskaia neftianaia promyshlennost' v 1921–1928 godakh*. Moscow: Rossiiskii gosudarstvennyi gumanitarnyi universitet, 1999.

Igolkin, A. A. "Sovetskii neftianoi eksport v gody predvoennykh piatiletok." *Neftianoe khoziaistvo* 9 (2006): 139–41.

Igolkin, A. A., and Iu. Gorzhaltsan, eds. *Russkaia neft' o kotoroi my tak malo znaem*. Moscow: "Olimp-Biznes," 2003.

Jabbarov, Farhad. *Bakinskaia neft' v politike sovetskoi Rossii (1917–1922 gg.)*. Baku: Azerbaijan National Academy of Sciences, 2009.

Kaiser, C. *Georgian and Soviet. Entitled Nationhood and the Spector of Stalin in the Caucasus.* Ithaca: Cornell University Press, 2023.

Khalid, Adeeb. *Making Uzbekistan: Nation, Empire, and Revolution in the Early USSR.* Ithaca: Cornell University Press, 2015.

Khalid, Adeeb. *The Politics of Muslim Cultural Reform: Jadidism in Central Asia.* Berkeley: University of California Press, 1998.

Khalilov, A. Kh., "Vnutrennie protivorechiia i bor'ba v rukovodstve Azerbaidzhanskoi ChK v 1920–1922 gg," *Voprosy istorii* 5 (2016): 125–9.

Kharmandarian, S. V. *Lenin i stanovlenie zakavkazskoi federatsii.* Yerevan: Izadatel'stvo "Aiastan," 1969.

Khlevniuk, Oleg. *In Stalin's Shadow: The Career of "Sergo" Ordzhonikidze,* edited with and Introduction by Donald J. Raleigh and Kathy S. Transchel, translated by David J. Nordlander. New York: M. E. Sharpe, 1993.

Kocheshkov, A. "North Iranian Oil in World Politics." *International Affairs* 5 (2008): 119–27.

Kostornichenko, V. N. *Inostrannyi kapital v sovetskoi neftianoi promyshlennosti (1918–1932).* Volgograd: Izdatel'stvo VolGU, 2000.

Kostornichenko, V. N. "K voprosu o natsionalizatsii otechestvennoi neftianoi promyshlennosti v 1918 g." *Ekonomicheskaia istoriia,* 10 (2005): 80–100.

Kvashonkin, A. V., O. V. Khlevniuk, L. P. Koshelev, and L. A. Pogovaia. eds. *Bol'shevistskoe rukovodstvo. Perepiska. 1912–1927.* Moscow: ROSSPEN, 1996.

Lenczowski, George. *Russia and the West in Iran, 1918–1948.* Ithaca: Cornell University Press, 1949.

Lenoe, Matt. *The Kirov Murder in Soviet History.* New Haven: Yale University Press, 2010.

Lund, Nicholas. "At the Center of the Periphery. Oil, Land, and Power in Baku, 1905–1917." PhD diss., Stanford University, 2013.

Malysheva, Svetlana. "The Russian Revolution and the Instrumentalization of Death," *Slavic Review* 76, 3 (Fall 2017): 647–54.

Martin, Terry. *The Affirmative Action Empire: Nations and Nationalism in the Soviet Union, 1923–1939.* Wilder House Series in Politics, History, and Culture. Ithaca: Cornell University Press, 2001.

Menteshashvili, A. M. *Bol'shevistskaia pressa Zakavkaz'ia v bor'be za sozdanie zakavkazskoj federatsii i soiuza SSR (1921–1922 gg.).* Tbilisi: Izdatel'stvo Tbiliskogo Universiteta, 1972.

Mitchell, Timothy. *Carbon Democracy. Political Power in the Age of Oil.* New York: Verso, 2011.

Morrison, Alexander. "Muslims and Modernity in the Russian Empire." *The Slavonic and East European Review* 94, 4 (2016): 715–24.

Mostashari, Firouzeh. "Development of Caspian Oil in Historical Perspective." In *The Caspian Region at a Crossroad. Challenges of a New Frontier of Energy and*

Development, edited by Hooshang Amirahmadi, 89–104. New York: St. Martin's Press, 2000.

Muradalieva, El'mira. *Krov' zemnaia- neft' Azerbaidzhana i istoriia.* Baku: "Mutardzhim," 2005.

Northrop, D. *Veiled Empire: Gender and Power in Stalinist Central Asia.* Ithaca: Cornell University Press, 2004.

Nowell, Gregory P. *Mercantile States and the World Oil Cartel, 1900–1939.* Ithaca: Cornell University Press, 1994.

O'Conner, Timothy. *Diplomacy and Revolution.* Ames: Iowa State University Press, 1988.

O'Conner, Timothy Edward. *The Engineer of Revolution. L.B. Krasin and the Bolsheviks, 1870–1926.* Boulder, CO: Westview Press, 1992.

Pashaev, A. A., and M. I. Naidel, eds. *Dekrety Azrevkoma, 1920–21: Sbornik dokumentov.* Baku: Azerbaidzhanskoe gosudarstvennoe izdatel'stvo, 1988.

Pipes, Richard. *The Formation of the Soviet Union: Communism and Nationalism 1917–1923.* Cambridge, MA: Harvard University Press, 1964.

Reynolds, Michael A. *Shattering Empires: The Clash and Collapse of the Ottoman and Russian Empires 1908–1918.* Cambridge: Cambridge University Press, 2011.

Rezun, Miron. "Reza Shah's Court Minister: Teymourtash." *International Journal of Middle East Studies* 12, 2 (1980): 119–37.

Rezun, Miron. *The Soviet Union and Iran. Soviet Policy in Iran from the Beginnings of the Pahlavi Dynasty until the Soviet Invasion in 1941.* Geneve: Sijthoff & Noordhoff International Publishers, 1981.

Rice, Kelsey. "The Caucasus and Iran." In *Routledge Handbook of the Caucasus*, edited by Galina M. Yemelianova and Laurence Broers, 347–58. New York: Routledge, Taylor & Francis Group, 2020.

Rice, Kelsey. "Forging The Progressive Path: Literary Assemblies and Enlightenment Societies in Azerbaijan, 1850–1928." PhD diss., University of Pennsylvania, 2018.

Rubin, Michael. "Stumbling through the 'Open Door': The U.S. in Persia and the Standard-Sinclair Oil Dispute, 1920–1925." *Iranian Studies* 28, 3/4 (Summer–Autumn 1995): 203–29.

Saparaov, Arsène. "Between the Russian Empire and the USSR. The Independence of Transcaucasia as a Socio-Political Transformation." In *Routledge Handbook of the Caucasus*, edited by Galina M. Yemelianova and Laurence Broers, 121–35. New York: Routledge, Taylor & Francis Group, 2020.

Sargent, Leslie. "The 'Armeno-Tatar War' in the South Caucasus, 1905–1906: Multiple Causes, Interpreted Meanings." *Ab Imperio* 4 (2010): 143–69.

Sicotte, Jonathan H. "Baku: Violence, Identity, and Oil, 1905–1927." PhD diss., Georgetown University, 2017.

Smith, Jeremy. "The Georgian Affair of 1922—Policy Failure, Personality Clash or Power Struggle?" *Europe-Asia Studies* 50, 3 (1998): 519–44.

Smith, Michael G. "Anatomy of a Rumour: Murder Scandal, the Müsavat Party and Narratives of the Russian Revolution in Baku, 1917–1920." *Journal of Contemporary History* 36 (2001): 211–40.

Smith, Michael G. "Power and Violence in the Russian Revolution. The March Events and Baku Commune of 1918." *Russian History* 41 (2014): 197–210.

Smith, Michael G. "The Russian Revolution as a National Revolution: Tragic Deaths and Rituals of Remembrance in Muslim Azerbaijan (1907–1920)." *Jahrbücher für Geschichte Osteuropas* 49, 3 (2001): 363–88.

Smith, Michael G. "Stalin's Martyrs: The Tragic Romance of the Russian Revolution." *Totalitarian Movements and Political Religions* 4, 1 (2003): 95–126.

Sokolov, A. K. "Sovetskii 'Neftesindikat' na vnutrennem i mezhdunarodnykh rynkakh v 1920-e gg." *Ekonomicheskaia istoriia. Obozrenie*, 10 (2005) 101–31.

Sokolov, V. V. "Diplomaticheskaia deiatel'nost' akademika F.A. Rotshteina 20-e gody XX veka." *Novaia noveishaia istoriia* 2 (2007): 156–72.

Stone, David R. "Soviet Arms Exports in the 1920s." *Journal of Contemporary History* 48, 1 (2013): 57–77.

Suny, Ronald Grigor. *Baku Commune, 1917–1918. Class and Nationality in the Russian Revolution*. Princeton: Princeton University Press, 1972.

Suny, Ronald Grigor. *Passage to Revolution*. Princeton: Princeton University Press, 2020.

Suny, Ronald Grigor, Fatma Muge Gocek, and Norman Naimark, eds. *A Question of Genocide: Armenians and Turks at the End of the Ottoman Empire*. New York: Oxford University Press, 2011.

Sutton, Antony C. *Western Technology and Soviet Economic Development 1917 to 1930*. Stanford, CA: Stanford University Press, 1968.

Sweitochowski, Tadeusz. "The Himmät Party: Socialism and the National Question in Russian Azerbaijan 1904–1920." *Cahiers du Monde russe et sovietique* XIX, 1/2 (1978): 119–42.

Sweitochowski, Tadeusz. *Russian Azerbaijan, 1905–1920: The Shaping of National Identity in a Muslim Community*. Cambridge: Cambridge University Press, 1985.

Volodarsky, Mikhail. *The Soviet Union and Its Southern Neighbors. Iran and Afghanistan, 1917–1933*. Portland: Frank Cass, 1994.

Yemelianova, Galina M., and Laurence Broers, eds. *Routledge Handbook of the Caucasus*. Abingdon, Oxon: Routledge Taylor & Francis Group, 2020. https://doi.org/10.4324/9781351055628.

Yergin, Daniel. *The Prize. The Epic Quest for Oil, Money, and Power*. New York: Free Press, [1991] 2009.

Zirinsky, Michael P. "Imperial Power and Dictatorship: Britain and the Rise of Reza Shah, 1921–1926." *International Journal of Middle East Studies* 24, 4 (1992): 639–63.

Index

Adalat 51, 58–62
Afandiyev, Sultan Majid 59, 136, 139
Afghanistan 63–4, 106–7, 141–2
Ahmad Shah Qajar 54, 58, 61, 63, 67, 70, 134
Akhundov, Ruhulla 129, 132, 136–7, 140, 143–6, 148, 155
All-Russian Co-operative Society, Ltd., 106
Allied powers (*see* Entente)
Amtorg Trading Company 106
Azerbaijan Communist Party 144–5, 150–1
Anglo-Persian Agreement 57
Anglo-Persian Oil Company (APOC) 77, 107–11, 114–15, 117–18
Anglo-Soviet Trade Agreement 57, 64–5, 72
Armenia 16–17, 19, 32–3, 35–6, 39–41, 53, 73, 76, 80–1, 132–3, 139, 153–4
Armeno-Tatar War 14, 94
Ashura 145–6
Astrakhan 11, 22, 25, 34, 50, 52, 54, 71, 133, 144
Azadistan 56
Azerbaijan Central Committee 47–1, 60, 136–40, 145–6, 148–50
Azerbaijan Cheka, 146–8
Azerbaijan Communist Party 5, 25, 60, 70, 128–9, 136–40, 144–5, 148, 150, 155
Azerbaijan Soviet of People's Commissars 40, 135, 138
Azerbaijan Democratic Republic (ADR) 16–18, 28, 47, 50–2
Azerbaijan Oil Committee (*see* Azneft)
Azerbaijan Oil Trust (*see* Azneft)
Azerbaijan Revolutionary Committee 23, 36
Azerbaijan SSR (Soviet Azerbaijan) 1, 8, 36, 47, 53–4, 56, 61, 67–8, 70, 95, 132, 134, 139, 141, 144, 149

Azerbaijan's oil 22, 40–1, 133–5, 187 n.35
Commissars 52, 67, 137
oil fund 135, 155, 187 n.35
troops in Iran 48, 57, 61
uprising 35–6, 40
Azizbekov, Meshadi 17, 51
Azneft 6, 25, 31, 42–4, 98–9, 102, 119, 121, 123, 134–6, 155
Azerbaijan Oil Committee 25, 28, 32–4, 42, 44–5, 138

Baghirov, Mir Jafar 148
Baku
  Baku Bolsheviks 2–3, 7, 9, 48, 62–3, 68–74, 90, 98, 139, 143, 149, 171 n.56
  Baku Committee 24, 51, 137, 143, 149
  Baku Commune 8, 17–18, 47–52, 138, 144, 161 n.38
  Baku Oil Commission 28–33
  Baku oil workers (*see* oil workers)
  Baku Soviet of People's Commissars (*see* Baku Soviet) 17, 143
  Bolsheviks, oil policy 2–6, 8–9, 32, 49, 52, 54, 65, 76–7, 84, 95–9, 105, 114, 127–8, 133–4, 153–5
  countryside 47, 53
  invasion 2, 6, 23, 27, 35, 47, 50, 51–3
  oil and security 2, 8, 15, 25, 98, 105, 128
  oil city 1–9
  oil, imperial 4, 11–16
  oil industry 29, 31, 34, 38, 40
  oil industry, nationalization 25, 27, 29, 31, 33, 75–9, 83–4, 86, 89
  population growth 14
Bandar-e Anzali (*see* Enzeli)
Barnsdall 98–100, 102, 177 n.89
Batumi 5–6, 11–12, 17, 24, 26, 34–8, 40–2, 44–5, 81, 105
Black City 1, 13–14, 24, 148
Black Sea 6, 11–12, 26

Bloody Sunday 14
Bolshevik Party 21, 23, 52, 53, 136, 141, 144, 145, 153
  In Baku 1, 5, 51, 52, 146
  South Caucasus 2, 6, 22
Bolshevik policies 52, 62, 73, 136–7, 139
Bolshevik power 6, 48, 130, 141
Buniatzade, Dadash 52, 60, 136
Busheri, Todzhar (Mu'in al-Tujjar) 116–17

Cannes Resolution, 75, 79
Caspian Sea 1–2, 6, 11, 34
Caucasian Bureau of the Central Committee (*see* Caucasus Bureau)
Caucasus Bureau 25, 37–41, 45, 47, 53, 58–61, 73, 81, 130, 140, 153, 185 n.5
Central Control Commission 127–9, 131–3, 143, 147–8, 151, 186 n.23
Centro-Caspian Dictatorship 18
Chicherin, Georgii
  Eastern Policy 53, 57–8, 64, 66, 68, 70–2, 109–11, 116, 140–2
  Genoa 79–84, 90, 100–1
  Transcaucasia 35, 53, 71
coal 12, 15, 19, 22, 26, 32, 86–91, 96–7, 176 n.43
Comintern (Communist International) 55, 62, 67, 83
Commissar of Finance 37, 133, 137, 145
Commissar of Social Welfare 17, 50
Commissariat of Foreign Affairs
  Gilan and Eastern Policy 47, 52, 53, 54, 57–60, 63, 65–7, 69–73, 79–80, 142
  Genoa 83, 102, 106
  Iran 112, 115, 116, 120–1
Commissariat of Foreign Trade 25, 42, 44–5, 65, 73, 111–12
Commissariat of Heavy Industry 156
Commissariat of Nationalities 155
Commissariat of Transportation 24
Commissariat of Ways and Means 25, 43
Concessions (*see* oil concessions)
Congress of the Peoples' of the East 63
Constantinople 11, 42, 44–5
Constituent Assembly 16
Control Commission (*see* Central Control Commission)

Dagestan 13, 35
Dahsnak (Dashnaktsutyun) 17, 36, 49
Davar, Ali-Akbar 114, 117–18
Demgan 113, 118
Denikin, Anton 24, 56, 66
Department of the Muslim Near East 66
diplomatic recognition 4, 75, 79, 101–2, 123
Donbas (Ukraine) 12, 15, 19, 22, 26, 77, 86–8, 90, 97
Dzhaparidze, Prokopius 17

Eastern policy 49, 63, 65–6, 73, 134, 140–1
Ekhsanulla Khan 58, 60–3, 68, 70–1, 148
Elizavetpol (*see* Ganja)
England (*see* Great Britain)
Entente (also Allies) 18, 86, 89, 101
Enzeli 1, 3, 18, 26, 53–60, 68–73, 108, 111

factions 8, 25, 38, 68, 98, 115, 119, 128–9, 131, 133, 136, 138, 145, 150–1, 153
Federative Union of Soviet Socialist Republics of Transcaucasia 81, 175 n.7
First World War 4, 15–18, 24, 27, 42, 55–6, 59, 75, 77, 87, 108–9, 154
food shortages 16, 27, 29–30, 147
food supply 22, 34, 138
foreign concessions (*see also* oil concessions) 7, 36, 65, 90, 153
Foreign Trade 1, 7, 25, 36–40, 42, 44–5, 64–5, 73, 81, 84, 105–6, 111–12
former owners 77–9, 86, 88–90, 100
Fourth Conference of the Central Committee 130–1
France 4, 12, 42, 76–8, 89, 101–2, 119–20, 123–4, 183 n.96
Frunze, Mikhail 21
fuel 12, 15, 18, 22–3, 32–3, 37, 43, 77, 85, 92, 96–7, 99, 135, 154–5

Ganja 17–18, 35–6, 135
Genoa Conference
  Concessions (*see* oil concessions domestic policy)
  Diplomatic recognition, 102
  Oil question 75, 77, 78, 88, 134, 136, 154

Preparatory Commission 79, 82, 89, 93–4
Rapallo 76, 101
prewar Russian debt, 102
Georgia 17, 32–3, 35–7, 39–42, 50, 53, 73, 76, 80–1, 112, 130–2, 139, 145, 153–4
Georgian Affair 38, 130, 145
Georgian Central Committee 38, 145
Germany 12, 17, 75–76, 80, 83, 101, 105
 Brest-Litovsk, 17, 80, 83
 Rapallo 76, 101
Gilan 1, 6–7, 48–9, 53–5, 58, 60–4, 66–73, 116–17, 142, 154
 Gilan Soviet Republic 6, 48–9, 63, 71, 142
Golubiatnikov, Dmitrii Vasil'evich 118, 124
Gosplan 78–9, 84, 90–3, 96–7, 112, 165 n.61
Great Britain
 Baku's oil 11–12, 14, 18, 41, 50, 101–2, 105
 British threat 7, 57, 98
 British troops 42, 53–7, 108
 Coal 15, 96–7
 Iran 57, 58, 60–1, 64–7, 71–3, 105, 107, 110, 112–13, 116–17
 Soviet policy 63–4, 73, 89, 106–9, 111, 114, 121, 125, 141
 Mesopotamia 77–8
Grozny 11, 15, 19, 21–2, 26, 77–8, 89, 91–3, 102, 154
Gubkin, Ivan 98–9
Gulbenkian, Calouste 124

Haidar Khan 62
Hummet 17, 50–2, 59, 136, 137, 144, 168 n.10
Huseynov, Mirza Davud 37, 39, 52, 129, 132–3, 136–8, 140, 143–6, 148, 155

Iaroslavskii, Emelian 131–2, 147
International Barnsdall Corporation (*see* Barnsdall)
international market 4, 11–12, 14, 34, 40–1, 49, 81, 86–7, 154
Iran 1–2, 5, 18, 26–7, 78, 102, 103
 Bolsheviks 2–4, 6–7, 41–2, 48, 51, 53–73, 128, 134, 141–2, 146–9

Bolsheviks, concession 105–15, 117–19, 121–2, 125
Iranian subjects 29, 31, 64, 148
Russian Empire 13–14, 54–5
Iran Communist Party (Iran Bureau) 59–63, 72, 111, 171 nn.56–7

Jangali 55, 58–60, 63, 148
Joint Stock Company (*see* Kevir-Khurian, Ltd.)

Karakhan, Lev 58, 63
Kars 17
Kerosene (*see* oil products)
Kevir-Khurian (also, Kevir-Khurian, Ltd.) 105, 118–25, 182 nn.62, 65
Khalu Kurban 60, 68–70
Khanbudagov, Aiub 140, 148, 150
Khoshtariia, Akakii Mefed'evich 54–5, 105–8, 110–15, 117–18, 120–5, 180 nn.24–5
Kirov, Sergei Mironovich (Kostrikov) 3, 8, 25, 35, 162 n.14
 Factions, Azerbaijan 129, 132, 136–8, 140–1, 145–51
 Oil 98–9
Krasin, Leonid Borisovich
 Baku 1, 3, 5
 Genoa policy 7, 84–91, 93, 98, 99, 100, 102
 Foreign Trade 64
 Iran 105–6, 109–12, 115, 119, 125
Krzhizhanovskii, Gleb 91–2

Lavrentev, Iakov Vasilevich 119, 121
Lenin, Vladimir Ulyanov
 Civil War 21–2
 Death 150
 Iran 53, 56, 64, 65, 70, 72, 112
 Narimanov 3, 47, 49, 52, 53, 66, 127, 128, 129, 133, 136, 139–41, 143, 146, 150
 Oil policy 7, 21, 24, 30, 42, 44, 77, 79, 84, 98–9, 110, 111
 Serebrovskii 23, 24, 33, 44, 45, 98–9
 Transcaucasia 37, 38, 39, 53, 130, 138, 140, 145
Lenkoran 17, 55
Lezhava, Andrei M. 90
Litvinov, Maxim 90, 101–3

Lominadze, Vissarion Vissarionovich "Beso" 59–60, 143

Makharadze, Filipp 130
Main Concession Committee 110–12, 114–15, 123
Main Fuel Administration 43, 92
Main Oil Committee 21, 24, 92, 99
Majlis 108–9, 114–17, 119–20
March Days 17–18, 49, 51, 161 n.40, 168 n.7
Mazandaran 116–17
Mdivani, Polikarp "Budu" 55, 59–62, 69–71, 81–2, 111, 130
   Khoshtariia 55, 111
Mikoyan, Anastas Ivanovich 3, 8, 139, 149, 151
   Baku 50, 62, 136–7, 139, 143–4, 154
   Control Commission, 129, 132, 134, 144, 149
   Iran 59–62, 69–70, 142
Mirza Kuchuk Khan 1, 53, 55–62, 65, 67–73, 148
Mirzoyan, Levon 139–40, 146, 148, 150–1
Molotov, Viachislav 80
Musabekov, Qazanfar 136
Musavat, 17–18, 35–6, 144
Muslim Communists 130, 136–7, 144–5

Nagorno-Karabagh 19, 51, 191 n.103
Nakhchivan 51, 164 n.56
Narimanov, Nariman Karbalayi Najaf oglu
   Azerbaijan SSR 5, 8, 35, 37, 42, 47, 52, 53, 81, 145, 153–4
   Baku Commune 8, 17, 50, 51, 144, 155
   Control Commission, 127–33, 144, 149, 151
   Eastern Policy, 65–6, 140–2
   Factions 129, 136–40, 144–6
   Genoa 140, 146, 81 fig 3.1, 82 fig 3.2
   Hummet 17, 50–2, 136, 137, 144
   Iran 3, 4, 47, 48, 49, 51, 53, 54, 59, 60, 62, 63, 69–73, 142, 146–8
   Lenin 19, 47, 49, 52, 53, 66, 127, 128, 129, 130, 133, 136, 139–41, 143, 146, 150
   National question 129–34, 146, 151
   Oil 2, 6, 40, 41, 44, 45, 47, 48, 52, 128, 133–6, 153

Orjonikidze, 5, 54, 62, 133, 142, 143, 149–51
   Revolution in the Periphery 8, 128–9, 131–2
   Security threat 142, 147, 150
National Bloc 115–17
New Economic Policy (NEP) 28, 33, 36–7, 43, 65, 106, 111
Nobel Brothers 1, 11–12, 15, 40, 78, 86
North Caucasus 19, 21, 24, 35, 40, 92

oil concessions domestic policy (Genoa) 7, 65, 76–7, 83–5, 89, 90, 95–6, 100, 102, 105, 153
oil concessions, general policy 2, 7, 36, 64, 65, 75
oil concessions, objections 76, 90, 91–2, 94, 98–100, 105, 107–8
oil concessions, Iran 55, 105, 110, 107–9, 111, 112–15, 117
oil concessions, pre-revolutionary 64, 112
oil concessions, security 7, 76, 98, 105
oil concessions, technology transfer 77, 99, 102, 154
oil crisis 94–5
oil deposits 77, 150
oil exports 7, 15, 87, 154
oil extraction 11, 33, 108
oil pipeline 21, 116
oil politics 2, 4, 5, 106, 125
oil potential 4, 38, 77–8, 95, 105, 108, 153–4
oil production 11–12, 15, 27–8, 43, 154, 158 n.8, 163 n.18
oil products 11–12, 14, 34, 40, 42–3, 78, 97, 122, 135, 139, 149, 153–4
   domestic market and needs 15, 27–8, 34, 65, 82, 87, 133, 154
   fuel oil 12, 15, 154
   gasoline 119, 123, 154
   kerosene 11–12, 15, 21, 34, 40, 42, 135–6, 154
   petroleum 11, 22, 91, 96–7, 99
oil reserves 19, 21, 66, 78, 108
oil shipments 21, 26, 39, 73
oil workers 13, 15, 27–8, 42, 48, 51, 134, 138
Oil Industry Syndicate 43
Orjonikidze, Grigorii (Grigol) "Sergo"

Azerbaijan 5, 15, 27, 35, 39, 41, 42, 51, 53, 98, 129, 133, 134, 136–43, 145, 146, 188 n.52
Caucasus Bureau 25, 37, 45, 47, 53, 58, 60, 73, 81, 130, 153, 185 n.5
Control Commission 132, 144, 149, 191 n.108
Iran 4, 53–5, 58–63, 66, 67–72
Mikoyan 69–70, 132, 144
Narimanov (*see* Narimanov, Nariman Karbalayi Najaf oglu)
Transcaucasia 3, 35, 36, 37, 39, 41, 53, 81, 96, 130, 142, 145, 151, 153–5
Ottoman Empire 17–18, 48, 51, 63

PersAzneft, 121–3
Petrofina-Fransez 102, 123–4
Piatakov, Iurii 112, 123
Politburo
  Azerbaijan 8, 139, 148–50
  Iran 58–9, 62, 65, 68, 70, 72, 78
  policy, general 103
  Transcaucasia 38, 52, 80, 83–4, 90–1, 99–100, 105, 130–1, 140, 144
Preobrazhenskii, Evgenii 90

Qarayev, Ali Heydar 52, 67, 136–8, 147, 155
Qasimov, Mir Bashir 136

Rabinovich, F. Ia. 45
Railroads 2–3, 6, 12, 15, 17, 21, 25, 35, 37, 39, 43, 55, 81, 86–7, 96, 107–9, 153
  Rail link 5, 11, 21, 124
Ramzin, Leonid 88
Raskolnikov, Fedor 26, 55–9
Red Army 1, 5–6, 21–8, 32–8, 40, 47–9, 52–3, 55, 58, 61, 67–8, 108, 134, 141, 145–6
Resht, 55, 57, 60–1, 63, 67–9, 108, 111
Revolution
  Bolshevik Revolution 1917 16, 55, 73, 76, 92, 93, 107, 114, 130, 134, 136, 137, 153
  February Revolution 15, 24
  Iran 54–5, 58, 59, 60, 63, 67, 70, 72, 73, 141
  Revolution of 1905 4, 12, 14, 24, 51, 54
Revolutionary Committee
  Adalat 59–60
  Azerbaijan 23, 36

Reza Khan Pahlavi 63, 65, 68–9, 73, 109, 117–18, 121, 125
Reza Shah Pahlavi (*see* Reza Khan Pahlavi)
Rothschild 12, 15, 78
Rotshtein, Fedor Aronovich 66–72, 109–10
Royal Dutch Shell 15, 42, 56, 76–9, 86, 89, 92, 98
Russian Central Committee (also see, Caucasus Bureau and Iran Bureau) 8, 25, 32, 37, 45, 53, 55, 90, 101, 128, 130, 132, 140, 141, 142, 149
Russia (*see* Russian Empire and Soviet Russia)
Russian Civil War 7–8, 16, 21, 23–4, 51, 62, 64–5, 76, 79–80, 88, 94, 106, 108, 144
Russian Communist Party 8, 25, 37, 59–60, 70, 128, 130, 140
  Oil industry 9, 12–15, 78
Russian Empire 1, 8, 11–14, 16–17, 21, 24, 29, 34, 39, 45, 48, 50–1, 53, 71, 75, 78, 89, 92, 105, 128, 130
Russian Soviet Federated Socialist Republic (RSFSR, also see: Soviet Russia)
Russo-Persian Treaty of Friendship 63, 65, 67, 107, 112
  Article 13 64, 107, 109, 114
  tsarist-era concession rights, 64, 108

San Remo Agreement 78
Savage Division 17–18
Semnan 113–14, 117–20, 122–4, 180 nn.39, 41
Serebrovskii, Aleksander Pavlovich
  Baku 3, 5–6, 25, 30–3, 36, 38, 43, 92, 134–6, 138, 151, 154–5
  biography, 23–4, 162 n.9
  Concessions 98, 99
  Foreign Trade 36, 38, 42, 44–5, 166 n.9
Shah (*see* Reza Khan Pahlavi and Ahmad Shah Qajar)
Shahtakhtinski, Beybut 37, 132
Shaumian, Stepan 17, 49, 51, 144
Shell *see Royal Dutch Shell*
Shirvani, Ali Heydar 136, 147–8, 190 n.87
shortage (general) 27, 31, 32, 40, 43, 45, 84, 146

food shortage/crisis 15, 16, 27, 29, 31–2, 34, 68, 102, 147
fuel shortage 15, 65
housing shortage 13, 27
Shumiatskii, Boris Zakharovich 115–19
Sinclair Consolidated Oil Corporation (Sinclair), 77, 108, 115–20, 124
Sosifross (Societe Commerciale Industrielle) 42
Soviet Azerbaijan *see Azerbaijan SSR*
Soviet of Labor and Defense 24, 44, 84, 90–1, 119
Soviet of People's Commissars 47, 127, 135, 138, 143
Soviet of People's Commissars of the Azerbaijan Soviet Socialist Republic (see Soviet of People's Commissars)
Soviet Russia 8, 24, 52, 56–7, 151, 153
  Azerbaijan oil 23, 26–7, 39, 41, 47, 48, 64, 133–4, 139
  Genoa and economic policy 75–6, 78–80, 82–3, 87, 91, 97, 100–1
  invasion 28, 53, 64, 84
  Iran 63–4, 67, 70, 72–3, 107, 112, 115
  New Economic Policy 28, 33, 36–7, 43, 65, 106, 111
  Soviet oil 4, 6, 22, 43, 77, 86, 99–100, 102, 106, 113, 154
  War Communism 26–8, 34, 36
Soviet Union 2–5, 25, 41, 45, 71, 75, 124, 127, 129, 144–5, 151
  creation 25, 80, 128, 130–1, 133–4
  oil, hard currency 4, 7, 97, 153
  oil policy 33, 87–8, 102–3, 106, 109, 112, 119–20, 123–4, 154–5
  USSR 75, 105, 119
Stalin, Iosif (Jughashvili)
  Azerbaijan 3, 35, 38, 53, 66, 128, 137, 140–2, 146, 148, 149–51, 155, 187 n.43
  Orjonikidze 25, 53, 66, 138, 141–2, 150
  Stalin's power 3, 8, 124, 128–30, 132, 154–6
  Transcaucasia, patronage 3, 8, 137, 145, 150–1, 154–5
  Transcaucasia, unification 41, 96, 130
Standard Oil 42, 77–9, 86, 89, 91–9, 98, 108, 115–17
Standard Oil of New Jersey (*see* Standard Oil)
Stolypin period 54, 111

Strizhov, Ivan Nikolaevich 92–9
Sultan-Galiev, Mirsaid 130–1
Sultanov, Hamid 35
Sultanzade (Mikaelian), Avetis 61–3, 134
Supreme Allied Council 75
Supreme Soviet of the Economy 25, 43, 92, 118–20

Tbilisi (*see* Tiflis)
Tehran 56–7, 61, 63, 67–8, 108–9, 113–14, 116, 118–19, 121–4, 142, 148
Tenth Party Congress 36–8, 65, 77, 98, 138
Teymourtash, Abdolhossein 118, 120, 123, 125; the Minister of Court, 120, 123
Tiflis 5, 16, 36–8, 41, 44–5, 50, 54, 62, 127–8, 135, 140, 143–5
trade agreements 4, 7, 57, 63–5, 73
Transcaucasian Commissariat 16–17, 38
Transcaucasian Democratic Federative Republic (*see* Transcaucasian Commissariat)
Transcaucasian Federation 6
Transcaucasian Republic 38, 41, 127, 130–2, 134, 137, 140, 143–4, 146, 148, 151, 155, 162 n.4
Transcaucasian republics 18, 37–8
Transcaucasian Soviet Federative Socialist Republic (*see* Transcaucasian Republic) 38
Trotsky, Lev 35, 53, 56, 63, 129
trusts 43, 88–91
Turkestan 21, 42, 62, 67
Turkey 2, 35–6, 40–1, 64–5, 86, 106, 141–2
Twelfth Party Congress 129–31, 134

Ukraine 15, 19, 22, 76, 87, 101
Unified Foreign Trade Commissariat (*also* Unified Commissariat) 44–5
USSR (*see* Soviet Union)

Volga fleet 26, 28, 53, 55
  Volga region, 13, 18, 34, 71
  Volga river 11–13, 25–6, 34, 56
Vosuq ed Dowleh, Hassan 56–7

War Communism 26–8, 34, 36
White City 14

Zangezur 51

www.ingramcontent.com/pod-product-compliance
Lightning Source LLC
Chambersburg PA
CBHW052110300426
44116CB00010B/1613